"Practical. Fast read. Full of ideas that you can put to work immediately to grow your business. That's what I call a formula for business magic."

—Larry Wilson, founder of Pecos River Learning,
and author of *Stop Selling, Start Partnering*

"If you're in business, you need this book. Whether you're a business owner, business professional, marketing executive, sales manager, or salesperson—there are tips, secrets, and just common sense advice that will give you new insights into attracting—and keeping—customers. These pages are jam-packed with solid advice on how to succeed in an increasingly complex marketplace."

—Christen P. Heide, The Dartnell Corporation,
editor, *Marketing Times,* The Official Publication of
Sales and Marketing Executives International

"Better than *abracadabra!* Supercharged strategies and techniques from the experts for marketing any product or service. A storehouse of great ideas."

—David Brandt, PhD, co-author,
Sacred Cows Make the Best Burgers

"In *Marketing Magic,* Rick Crandall has selected first-rate marketing minds and first-class marketing information, then presented it in a highly readable manner. If you're looking for magic in marketing, you'll find it in the pages of this superb book."

—Jay Conrad Levinson, author, *Guerrilla Marketing*

"*Marketing Magic* provides practical information presented in a refreshingly easy-to-read format.

—Keith Bailey & Karen Leland, authors,
Customer Service For Dummies

"It's called *Marketing Magic* but it's really Marketing Common Sense. And good common sense is worth its weight in gold because it always works.

—Jack Trout, president, Trout & Partners, author,
The New Positioning

"One imperative for success is to understand and assimilate the views and strategies of those who have already achieved it. This anthology is an excellent success road map. Read it."
—Jeffrey Gitomer, author, *The Sales Bible*

"*Marketing Magic*" shows the real range of successful marketing, from old-fashioned thank you notes to the Internet. It can help anyone achieve 'Peak performance.'"
—Charles Garfield, PhD,
author, *Peak Performers*, and *Second to None*

"This book represents a great idea—bunching under one cover, insights from many proven marketers to allow the reader to choose the gems that best fit his or her needs."
—Robert Cialdini, PhD, professor of psychology,
Arizona State University,
author, *Influence: The Psychology of Persuasion*

"For all who are hungry for marketing excellence and profit, here it is. This is a superb compendium of tools and insights by fifteen of the nation's great pros. Must reading!"
—Joe Batten, author, *The Master Motivator*

"By adopting the advice of the experts in this book on everything from pricing to SPIN® selling to power networking, the results ...should be nothing short of magic."
—Edmund Lawler, author, *Underdog Marketing*

"The chapter on Online Marketing presents clear guidelines on how to succeed on the Internet. The clean, crisp writing will even make neophytes comfortable with the new paradigms of online marketing."
—Daniel Janal, speaker, consultant, author,
101 Businesses You Can Start on the Internet

"*Marketing Magic* is a terrific example of putting action into the phrase, 'No one of us is as smart as all of us.'"
—D. John Hammond, CEO, American Motivational Association,
past president, National Speakers Association

"Plenty of useful ideas here—and attractively presented too."
—Neil Rackham, author, *SPIN Selling*

Marketing Magic

Magic

PROVEN PATHWAYS TO SUCCESS

Featuring chapters from marketing experts
Bob Bailey ★ Fran Berman ★ Fred Berns ★ Bud Coggins
Larry Cole ★ Rick Crandall ★ Jack Daly ★ Marc Fine
Mary Lou Gutscher ★ John S. Haskell ★ Rick Haberstroh
David Klaybor ★ Jim Pratt ★ Wajed Salam ★ Art Sobczak

EDITED BY RICK CRANDALL

INSTITUTE FOR
EFFECTIVE MARKETING

SELECT PRESS
CORTE MADERA, CA

The Institute for Effective Marketing
The goal of the Institute is to provide information to help companies and individuals more effectively market their products and services by better serving the needs of their customers.

Select Press
PO Box 37
Corte Madera, CA 94976-0037
(415) 924-1612

Marketing Magic: Proven Pathways to Success /
Rick Crandall (editor)

ISBN 0-9644294-0-3   94-76836
                                       CIP

Printed in the United States of America
10 9 8 7 6 5 4 3 2 1

Contents

Preface   vii

Part I: The Starting Points   1

1   Dare To Be Different: Super Positioning
        Fred Berns   3

2   Marketing Success: It's <u>Not</u> Just the Price
        Rick Haberstroh   35

3   Turning Knowledge Into Cash: How To Use
    The Marketing Ideas In This Book
        David Klaybor   67

Part II: Marketing Specifics   71

4   Customer Service: The Real
    Magic of Marketing
        Larry Cole   73

5   Profitable Prospecting: Getting Results
    With Client Newsletters
        Mary Lou Gutscher   101

6   Power Networking: Building Relationships
    for Success
        John S. Haskell   133

7 Using the Phone as a Serious Sales Tool:
   9 Steps to Success
        Art Sobczak   157

8 The New Rules of Selling:
   Building Relationships
        Jack Daly and Jim Pratt   187

9 SPIN® Selling: A Proven Sales Method
        Bud Coggins   225

10 How To Sell Even If You're Not In Sales:
    The 7 Secrets of Heartful Selling
        Marc Fine   247

11 Online Marketing: New Technology
    For New Results
        Rick Crandall   271

12 10 Reasons To Market by Fax
        Bob Bailey   315

Part III: Implementing A Program   339

13 The Power of Personal Notes: 35 Ways To
    Say "Thank You" And Stay In Touch
        Wajed Salam   341

14 Implementing Marketing Programs:
    A Sales Automation Example
        Fran Berman   371

Index   401

(Supplemental marketing material included on attached disk.)

PREFACE

Is There Magic In This Book?

Most of us would like to have someone wave a magic wand and take care of all our marketing for us.

That's not going to happen—in this book, or in life!

Each author in this book is a proven expert on some aspect of marketing. As speakers, consultants, and trainers, they have made magic happen for many clients.

If you define magic as great ideas, then there are magical ideas, stories, and examples in this book. And, as the subtitle suggests, there are many proven methods that can get you more business.

The Magic Is In You

You hold the real magic. By buying this book, you made a commitment to yourself. Each chapter ends with ideas on how to take action on your marketing. And Chapter 3 suggests ways you can get the most out of reading the other chapters. The magic lies in you systematically applying some of the ideas to your situation.

Any chapter in this book can give you the ideas and inspiration. If you will work consistently on your marketing, you can create the magic.

Good luck. And please let any of us in this book know about your success.

Part I: The Starting Points

Dare To Be Different:
Super Positioning
Fred Berns

Marketing Success:
It's *Not* Just the Price
Rick Haberstroh

Turning Knowledge Into Cash:
How To Use The Marketing
Ideas In This Book
David Klaybor

Chapter 1

DARE TO BE DIFFERENT:
Super Positioning

Fred Berns

Fred Berns
is a speaker, consultant and author. His programs for corporations, associations, and other organizations focus on how individuals can sell themselves first so they can do the best job of selling their company's products and services. His "personal sale" presentations point out how professionals can differentiate themselves, communicate with confidence, and make a maximum marketing impact for a minimal investment of time and money.

Berns has appeared before groups as diverse as New York Life Insurance, Microsoft, the National Assn. of Professional Saleswomen, and the Environmental Protection Agency. He has also consulted with sales specialists and business owners from coast to coast.

Berns is the author of numerous audio- and videotape programs and booklets on marketing. His latest book is *Sell Yourself! 501 Self-Promotion Ideas*.

A member of the National Speakers Association, Berns launched his speaking career after working in journalism for 25 years. He founded the Berns Bureau, and helped it become one of Washington DC's largest and longest-established independent news services.

Fred Berns, Power Promotion, 394 Rendezvous Dr., Lafayette, CO 80026; phone (303) 665-6688; fax (303) 665-5599.

DARE TO BE DIFFERENT:
Super Positioning

Fred Berns

You are one of a kind. There never has been, nor will there ever be another exactly like you; you're the only one. Your "only" factor gives you a powerful uniqueness you can use. Your marketing should reflect your differences. These differences—your unique strengths—can help others in unique ways.

THE POWER OF "ONLY"

I discovered the power of "only" months after I set out to establish an independent radio news service in Washington in 1976. My idea was to provide localized news out of the nation's capital for radio stations—news of specific interest to their listeners.

I intended to report on the votes of local Congressmen, cover the testimony at Congressional hearings of visiting local city officials, and produce stories on hometown folks who had relocated in Washington. To personalize my telephone reports, I planned to sign them off with my name and the station's call letters.

Weeks on the road trying to sell radio news directors throughout the Midwest on the idea of my freelance service yielded few results. "Thanks, but no thanks" was the response I received from news directors from St. Louis to St. Paul.

Finally, two stations, KOLT in Scottsbluff, Nebraska, and KFIZ in Fond du Lac, Wisconsin, agreed to try out my service. The deal: $5 for every story of mine that they used on the air.

Advertising Doesn't Work

I was flush with the feeling of self-importance when I returned home to Washington. I was convinced that once I advertised the fact that I was in business, other radio station news directors would come running.

They didn't.

The costly ads I took out in various broadcasting trade publications yielded nothing. The longer I sat in my new office, the quieter it became. The calls didn't come in. My patience was running out. So was my money.

One morning I attended a workshop for new businesses conducted by the Small Business Administration's SCORE staff. The first speaker suggested that we "Look around at your neighbors, because two out of three of them will be out of business within 18 months." It wasn't exactly the motivational boost I was seeking.

The Only One Of Its Kind

During a break I related my concerns about my business to a classmate. His suggestion: "package" the business differently, and refer to it in a press release to *Broadcasting Magazine* as the "only bureau of its kind with clients around the nation."

The Only Bureau Of Its Kind With Clients Around The Nation!

"'Clients around the nation?'" I replied. "You're saying I should promote that, even though I work only occasionally with one small station in Wisconsin and a smaller one in Nebraska?"

"Why not?" he replied. "What do you have to lose?"

A week later I wrote my first press release, a mere paragraph on my brand new letterhead stationery, announcing that I had launched the only independent news service of its kind serving radio stations "around the country." Within a few days after *Broadcasting Magazine* ran the blurb in its radio column, calls came in from news directors seeking more information about this "one of a kind" news service serving radio stations around the country.

Six weeks after the blurb appeared, 35 news directors had signed up to use the only service of its kind for stations "around the country."

Several months later, a radio station called from Toronto to ask for written transcripts for some Congressional hearing. After that, I started promoting my bureau as the only one of its kind serving stations "around the world." Inquiries came in from Australia, New Zealand, England, West Germany, Japan, and South Africa.

By the time I sold the Berns Bureau in April, 1992, it was the only news organization of its kind that over a 16-year period had served more than 5,000 broadcast and print outlets—around the country and around the world.

Basic Marketing: Find A Need

Developing your unique position needs to start with the basics. Your "basics" should begin with a personal message or commercial.

We tend to discuss our "features" ("I am very knowledgeable in the field of personal fitness training"). But our prospects are more interested in the benefits we can provide them ("I will help you improve your endurance and muscle tone").

For others to do as we want them to do—sign a contract, adopt a policy, grant a request for a raise or promotion—they need to perceive a personal benefit.

In the long run, the people you want to do business with don't care a great deal about your state-of-the-art technology, your hardware or your software. Nor are they necessarily persuaded by multimillion dollar advertising campaigns. Rather, they are motivated by what they think they will *get* by doing business with you. I will buy from you what you want to sell me *if* it will help my company make money, save money, or save time.

Your Target Group

As important as it is for us to spell out our unique benefits, it is vital that you target a unique audience. So often I ask sales professionals who their clients are. Far too often I get the response: "Anyone who will buy my products."

I don't know who "anyone" is. I don't know what media "anyone" follows. I don't know what organizations "anyone" belongs to. That's vital information, because getting free publicity in media that clients read, and speaking to organizations that prospects belong to, are among the most effective self-promotion strategies.

Use Varied Marketing Methods

Publicity and public speaking are just two of the dozens of no-cost techniques you can use to promote yourself.

Which of these strategies work for you will depend on whether you own your own business, or work for another. In either case, there are many other moneymaking and moneysaving marketing options available to you. But how you promote

Low-Cost Ways To Promote Yourself

- Distribute evaluation forms that elicit referrals and testimonials.
- Network with "tipster" groups with members from different industries—or start one yourself.
- Create a newsletter for current, prospective, and ex-clients.
- Teach an adult education class.
- Develop an economical personal promotion kit, including a bio sheet, reprints of articles by and about you, testimonials, and lists of products, services, clients and references.
- Barter consultation time for personal photos, brochures, business cards, and other promotional services.
- Donate products or services to a community fundraising event.
- Communicate with prospects, clients and others via audiotaped or videotaped messages.
- "Work the crowd"—but not necessarily a booth—at a trade show.
- Offer and promote a "frequent buyers club."
- Distribute surveys and questionnaires among prospects.
- Conduct seminars for prospects.

yourself is less important than that you promote yourself differently. You will never make a lasting impression if you use the same marketing methods as your competitors.

YOU ARE UNIQUE

We live in a day and age of great diversity and specialization in the workplace. The wonder is that so many people "market" themselves so similarly. Whatever their experience, specialized training, and daily responsibilities, they promote themselves the same way that everyone else does.

It's what others might call "Follow the Leader" marketing, but what I call "Follow the Follower" marketing. Its emphasis is on how most others, rather than just the leaders in the field, sell themselves.

There is no easier way to promote yourself than to play the "Same Game." Players don't try to blow their own horn in a unique way. They don't attempt to discover and describe their unique talents and abilities. They don't attempt to perceive the value in *being* different, nor try to promote their differences.

Same Game participants don't realize that self-promotion is important enough to be everybody's business. And how better to promote yourself than to share the things that are unique about you?

Sell Yourself First

Salespeople must sell themselves before they can sell their products and services. Employees must promote themselves to supervisors if they expect to advance within the company. Entrepreneurs must market themselves before they can market their ideas to investors and, eventually, prospective clients. Executives must convince others of their leadership and management skills.

The fact is, *everyone* is different from everyone else. Yet very few attempt to demonstrate their differences. Few dare to be different in the manner in which they promote themselves.

The Same Old "Stuff" Doesn't Work

If they promote themselves at all, so many professionals in so many industries use the same words to do so. They talk of themselves as "experienced" and "qualified" and "reliable." Chances are they use the same old methods to promote those words: résumés, cold calling, advertising, direct mail—and not much else.

How boring!

The good news is that players of the Same Game can harness all of their "follower" energy, and rechannel it in a more useful direction. They

> "Anybody who is any good is different from anybody else."
> —Supreme Court Justice Felix Frankfurter

can use it to discover their differences, create a truly unique "commercial," and develop unique ways to share it with those they believe should hear and understand it.

At first, this rechanneling doesn't come easily. We're not used to this idea of focusing on our differences. We may be more comfortable following the lead of others.

WHY BE DIFFERENT?

What, you ask, is wrong with your current strategy? Why *not* do as others do? Why *not* follow the lead of others when it comes to promoting ourselves? Surely, it's a lot easier to promote ourselves in the same way others in our field have promoted themselves. Why reinvent the self-marketing "wheel" when so many others before us have used the one already in place?

The problem with copying the marketing methods of others is that too many of those "others" want what we want.

A Crowded Marketplace

Rarely, if ever, is yours the only offer, proposal, recommendation, bid, application, plan, résumé, proposition, deal, or sales pitch. Too many others want to reach who you need to reach.

They target the same decision makers, and they use the same methods to get their attention. When you all use the same methods to reach the same people, no one can stand out as superior. And in a crowded marketplace, that's a recipe for failure.

The marketplace is cluttered with more than your competitors. Sometimes you have to meet and overcome unfavorable impressions of your profession, or deal with the baggage that competitors have left behind. Picture yourself as a sales trainer who is seeking a contract with a corporation that just fired another trainer because he failed to produce positive results. You would have to resell the company on the need and importance of training before attempting to sell the firm on yourself.

> "Positioning is not what you do to a product. Positioning is what you do to the mind of the prospect."
> —Al Ries and Jack Trout, *Positioning: The Battle for Your Mind*

Can You Stand Out?

Another reason for you to promote yourself differently is the perception that many others do what you do.

At the very least, others have the same job title, have worked the same number of years, or are *perceived* to be as qualified. If these "others" haven't surfaced yet, they will. Competitors and challengers can, and do, come along all the time. Your client or customer can be approached by someone tomorrow, and you can be replaced next week.

Meeting *Their* Needs

Competitors want what you want, do what you do and try to reach the same target audience. How can you stand above the crowd? Your prospects, supervisors, and others are all tuned to the same radio station. Its call letters are WII-FM (What's in it for me?).

Oh, to be able to invest in that station! Its ratings must be extraordinary considering that all day, everyday, our clients, prospects and others we need to influence are listening.

It's your responsibility to create a personal commercial for their stations. There are many words you can choose for that commercial, but none packs as much punch as the word "only."

USP

In old sales and marketing training, you were generally told to develop your unique sales proposition, or USP. This is what makes you different and better for the customer. Newer work by Jack Trout and Al Ries has defined a broader concept.

POSITIONING

You want to position yourself in the minds of your prospects in a clear and distinct—different—way. This lets them know exactly how you can meet their needs better than others. It's a more complete way of focusing on your unique advantages.

HARNESS THE POWER OF "ONLY"

"Only." What a word! It is the single word which can distinguish you from all the others who do what you do and want what you want. It puts you in a class by yourself, defining your "differentness" and signaling that you have what others lack.

Identify yourself as the only manufacturer with a public showroom, or the only financial officer with 20 years experience, or the firm's only bilingual attorney. When you set yourself apart, you prosper. Say that you are the *only* account executive in your area who has worked with "Fortune 500" companies, or the *only* scientist who has probed a rare tropical disease, or the *only* sales representative to lead the company six consecutive months. *That's* special.

If *only* I knew, in the early days of my business career, the power of the word "only!"

You, too, should find that power. Do what you must to develop your "only" list. Create a list of what only you can do, and you will be able to do more than simply promote yourself. You will be able to appreciate yourself to a greater degree, and to overcome self-doubts more easily.

Don't Downgrade Yourself

Be advised that the same word that enables you to express your uniqueness can hinder you, as well. "Only" becomes a liability when you use it to mean "merely." "I'm only a government securities analyst," a woman told me following a workshop. "You can't expect *me* to market myself, can you?"

"Don't tell me you're 'only a securities analyst,'" I responded. "Begin the sentence by telling me you're 'the only securities analyst who _____.'"

Be Memorable

A communications specialist once told me that an individual typically remembers only one thing about another person several months after a chance meeting. That is the thing he or she will describe when recounting the meeting.

In other words, if I exchange business cards with a corporate executive at a networking session, the best I can count on is that he or she will remember one thing about me when recalling our meeting months later.

I want that one thing to be that I am "the *only* professional speaker in this area who gives motivational marketing programs that sell people on selling themselves differently." That, after all, is

my commercial, my personal sales pitch that I want others to remember if they remember nothing else about me.

I was in Washington National Airport some time ago when I ran into a computer consultant whom I had met at a local networking function.

"You're the speaker, right?" she said. "The only one who talks about being different." She hadn't recalled the entire 25-word commercial I shared with her weeks before, but she did retain the key: my *only*. My mission had been accomplished.

You, too, should have a 25-word-or-less commercial that incorporates your "only." Sure, it's dandy if you have a four-color, 50-page, state-of-the-art marketing kit; a glossy, award-winning brochure, and a résumé that knocks their socks off. But, if and when someone is to remember you, or judge you, or tell someone else about you, it's that "only" commercial they will think of first.

SURVIVAL TACTICS

Restaurant Examples

Restaurants in this country have resorted to special events to differentiate themselves—and fill their tables. A Denver restaurant puts on dinners designed for cigar smokers, a Chicago establishment conducts olive oil tastings, a New Orleans eatery prepares special dinners for garlic lovers, and a smoke-free New York restaurant arranges special dinners (complete with smoked rabbit dumplings, duck ragout, and related items) to complement certain specialty beers.

Determine your "specialness," and you should be able to hold your own even against larger, more established competitors. For instance, the arrival of Domino's and Pizza Hut in Japan influenced some savvy local pizza outlets to develop and promote such unique varieties as apple or rice on pizza, German sausage and potato pizza with mayonnaise sauce, and shrimp in chili sauce on a sweetened pizza crust. They may not sound great to us, but they worked there.

> ### Answer This Question
>
> "Question No. 1 for the prospective business owner (should be): In 25 words or less, how is my concept (for a plumbing company or software house) notably different from that of others? If you can't succinctly explain how you're special to 'the man or woman on the street,' you're headed for trouble."
>
> —Tom Peters

Do those restaurants appeal to everybody? No. Are they unique? Yes.

"Unique Pancakes"

It was on a bicycle trip that I learned about the power of promoting your uniqueness.

In May of 1986 I set out with seven others to ride along the TransAmerica Bicycle Trail from Yorktown, Virginia, to Astoria, Oregon. I discovered that two central thoughts occupied my mind as I sat on a bike seat for ten hours a day, for 90 days, through ten states, over 4,500 miles: the condition of my rear end and the condition of my stomach.

The farther west we advanced, the more bikers we encountered and the more often the conversation centered on those two simple topics. It was especially important to me that I find the right food stops along the route. I ate at least eight times a day and still managed to lose 23 pounds during the trip.

Word-Of-Mouth Advertising Works

We were cycling through Kentucky when I first encountered an east-bound rider who recommended I visit "Paul and Paula's Pancake Palace" when I reached Western Kansas.

"When you get there, order the 'Biker's Biscuits' and the 'Pedaler's Pancakes,'" he said. "They're famous."

On four other occasions as we advanced through Illinois and Missouri I met bikers who suggested that I experience the biscuits and pancakes at "Paul and Paula's Pancake Palace." What was it about this place, I wondered, that it had cyclists buzzing a few states—and hundreds of miles—later?

The day finally arrived when I rode into that small western Kansas town and spotted the crowd of mostly bicyclists surrounding the cafe with the yellow sign on top that read: "Paul and Paula's Pancake Palace." The waiting line extended out the door and around the block.

Nearly an hour later, when I was finally seated, I had no doubt in my mind when the waitress asked for my order. "For weeks I've been hearing about your Pedaler's Pancakes and Biker's Biscuits," I said. "Better give me an order of each."

When the steaming plate arrived, it was with great anticipation that I dug into a pancake first, and then a biscuit. And it was with great disappointment that I realized that the pancakes tasted like, well, pancakes, and the biscuits had the flavor of biscuits I had tasted many times before.

I was miffed. I asked to meet the manager.

How Can Regular Pancakes Be Unique?

Minutes later, as I sat facing Paul across a cup of hot chocolate, I shared my curiosity. "I've heard so much about your Pedaler's Pancakes and Biker's Biscuits. Yet I found them to be pretty ordinary," I confessed. "How is it they're so famous and this place is so popular?"

"Some folks love 'em, some don't, but bikers come here by the hundreds every season," he said with a friendly smile. "That's because we're unique."

"Unique?"

"We're the only cafe that calls them 'Biker Biscuits' and 'Pedaler's Pancakes,'" he replied. "And we're the only cafe on the TransAm trail promoting itself as the only cafe that sells 'Biker Biscuits' and 'Pedaler's Pancakes.'"

"So?"

"It's a secret of success, friend. You can be successful, but you have to get ready first. And you can't get ready until you get different."

I pulled out of "Paul and Paula's Pancake Place" a few minutes later, doubting I would ever return but newly reminded of an important principal of self-promotion: Good things come to those who "get different."

More Uniqueness: Bed And Breakfasts

Various industries are daring to be different in their marketing in an effort to survive tough economic times. Proprietors of businesses from bed and breakfast inns to fishing tackle stores have tried anything and everything in recent years to stem an economic downturn.

There was an increase in the number of U.S. bed and breakfast establishments from 1,000 to 20,000 in the 10-year period ending in 1993, according to *The Wall Street Journal.* That, coupled with stiff competition from hard-pressed hotels and motels, has made for scarce profits in the B&B industry. To stay afloat, some proprietors began marketing features ranging from bathroom jacuzzis, to barn-yard animals, to two-day courses on Chinese cooking.

"Nowadays, you have to do something different, something outrageous," said Barbara Notarius, a proprietor in Croton on Hudson, New York and the author of the book entitled *Open Your Own Bed and Breakfast.* "B&B owners have never had much marketing savvy, but now they realize they need to do something to stand out."

"Standing out" wasn't easy in her riverside community one hour outside of New York City. Local ordinances forbade her from posting a sign outside her house. To increase its exposure, Notarius hosted silent auctions and other community events, and converted her own room into a $250 per night honeymoon suite.

"We got ourselves written up in a publication called 'The Best Places to Kiss in New York,' and the room was booked every weekend," she said.

Other B&B's promoted sports club privileges, bus tour packages, and more to compete with hotels and motels that slashed rates and offered complimentary breakfasts, concierge service, express check-in, no-smoking rooms, personal computers and day care.

Fishing For Differences

The fishing tackle industry also encountered hard times in the early 1990s, thanks in large part to the aggressive expansion into the marketplace of such discounters as Wal-Mart, Kmart, and sports superstores. That, plus the 11 percent decline in the number of people fishing in the three-year period ending in 1993, forced many independent retailers to close their doors.

But others "dared to be different" to stay in business. They offered new and different services and products that the all-purpose discounters didn't. For the Salmon Stop in Waukegan, Illinois, "different" meant promoting a community program to get children "hooked on fishing, not on drugs," and supplying fishing gear for a local family fishing event that drew dozens of new customers into the shop.

For Quaker Lane Bait & Tackle Ltd. in North Kingstown, Rhode Island, "different" in the early 1990s meant adding a service to repair trolling motors, rods, and reels. By 1993, the company earned profit margins of more than 100 percent on its repair work, and total sales exceeded $1 million.

Other retailers marketed seminars on topics like basic fishing for children and how to hook a big fish.

"The independents that were left after the Wal-Marts moved into the business had to fight back," recalled Bob Vickers, editor of the *The Fishing Tackle Trade News*. "They had to push their knowledge—of where to fish locally, and what lures to use. And they had to make themselves different from the big guys by selling things like soft goods."

Vickers said marketwise, tackle shops lured customers with special discounts on tackle, and then sold them other items such as tee shirts and caps at a considerable mark up.

It Pays To Be Different

Other service providers have used innovative marketing in recent years to overcome stiff competition. Carwashes have promoted such on-site entertainment as rabbit petting zoos, aquariums, sun decks, cable TV and video games. Laundromats have offered inside restaurants, tanning salons, exercise rooms and playgrounds.

Owners of bed and breakfast establishments, fishing tackle shops, carwashes and laundramats may not have much else in common, but in challenging economic times they must embark on a similar mission. They must define what *only* they can do, and what they alone can offer that competitors can't or don't.

You must deliver your "only" message in person or in print. Your "only" belongs on your letterhead, bio sheet, business cards, and brochures, with your secretary and on your voice mail.

Getting Your Price

The importance of your "only" transcends a verbal commercial, a voicemail message or a tagline on stationery. How you communicate your "only" can determine the fees you charge and the amount of money you earn.

You can maintain your price if you can distinguish yourself from others who charge less. You can distinguish your company by your "only" statement. Are you the only firm that guarantees its work? The only one offering free delivery, or free replacement parts or "frequent buyer" privileges? The only one that has been in business for 15 years, or has been honored for its service?

Decide what sets you apart, and you shouldn't have to play with your prices. You should be able to steer clear of the no-price-is-too-low reputation that organizations get when they constantly slash their fees. You should be able to rise above the undercutting game that so many play, and no one wins.

By being unique, you can maintain fee integrity even in the toughest of times. But you need to communicate that you are different from all of the others, and that you offer benefits that others can't. (Also see Chapter 2 on holding your price.)

Interior Designers Fight Price Wars

Interior designers in Omaha have confronted severe price competition for years. They are quick to blame the Nebraska Furniture Mart. The Mart has showroom space exceeding that of several football fields. It is the largest privately-owned facility of its kind in the United States. It sells everything from futons to fabrics

at prices well below those that local designers would charge if they bought the items wholesale and sold them to customers.

Some prospects even seek advice from local designers, only to purchase the items on their own from the Mart and save on the designers' commissions. Similarly, some consumers have taken the free advice and ordered the products through a discount catalog.

They Can't Win On Price

Local designers have complained about the difficulty of getting a fair price for their services and about the pressure to cut their fees to hang on to customers. The designers spent considerable time and energy grousing about—but participating in—a price war. Fee cutting became, for many, the rule rather than the exception.

When I began working with Nebraska designers, I discovered that they were experts on the local price wars. They knew more about price undercutting than about self-promotion. Few could explain what made them different. Few could list services or benefits that they alone could offer. Few could explain why prospects should work with them rather than shopping through the Mart or discount catalogues.

I devoted an entire workshop to persuading those designers to rechannel their "seige mentality" and price war energy into self-promotion. I urged them to write marketing messages defining their differences, and spelling out benefits that they offered exclusively. I recommended that they promote the value of their expertise.

"You may get lower prices elsewhere, but you won't get me" was the approach I recommended they use with their prospects. Substantiate that claim, I told them, and you will be able to maintain the integrity of your fees.

Marketing Unique Baseball

Skilled self-promoters understand the value of promoting their unique message *uniquely*.

Take the case of Lindsey Nelson, the radio announcer for the New York Mets in 1962, their first and worst season. The team was to lose a total of 120 games that year, prompting manager Casey Stengel at one point to inquire: "Can't anybody here play this game?"

Nelson sought a way to attract attention to the pathetic team—and network attention to himself. He began to show up at games in psychedelic sports coats, hardly standard wearing apparel for broadcasters of the day. The gawdy jackets—of which Nelson eventually owned 700—became legendary, and so did Lindsey Nelson, even though he was the voice of one of baseball's worst teams in history.

More recently, professional baseball has witnessed another example of unique marketing.

Hoping to boost attendance and merchandise sales, minor league baseball teams in recent years have adopted a new approach to promotion and marketing. Several teams decided to drop the names of their parent clubs and adopt unusual substitutes.

> "I don't care what you do," campaign strategist James Carville once advised presidential candidate Bill Clinton. "But just make damn sure it's big and different."

"Teams with the same name as their parent clubs have nothing to sell," Al Mangum, the general manager of the Durham, N.C. Bulls, explained. "All they have is a duplicate of their logo."

Prior to the 1993 season, the minor league team in Cedar Rapids, Iowa changed its name from "Reds" to "Kernels." Accompanying the change: a stylish new logo of a baseball sprouting from a corn husk. Within three months, the team sold more than $20,000 in souvenirs, about half the total of the entire previous year.

As soon as the Carolina Mudcats moved from Columbus, Georgia and changed their name from the Astros, their cap and other merchandise sales soared. The team, now based in Zebulon, N.C., adopted a logo featuring a whiskered catfish poking its head through the letter "C". The result: 1992 souvenir sales of nearly $500,000, more than double the 1989 total. That, despite the team's dismal 1992 record of 52-92.

Clearly, the teams discovered the wisdom of thinking big—and differently.

Uniqueness In Love

In 1954, Robert Brachman, a 30-year-old sales representative in Milwaukee, knew he had to do something different if he was to win back his 24-year-old former girlfriend.

"We had a disagreement, and she told me I was an immature, spendthrift playboy," Brachman recalls. "She told me never to call her again. I was heartsick."

Robert had done some creative wooing. He

had shown up at her doorstep with a used car he bought for her, only to be told that her father wouldn't allow her to accept it. He hid a pecan pie—her favorite—in a downtown locker and mailed her the key, along with a variety of scavenger hunt clues to help her find it. She told him his crazy "frivolous antics" were wasting his time—and hers.

"When she refused to talk to me any more, I knew I had to get her attention," Brachman says. "So I kept thinking of even more imaginative things that would make her think of me as more interesting than others."

The most imaginative of his efforts involved renting space for $20 per week on the billboard near the downtown department store where she worked as a sportswear buyer. For seven weeks, until he ran out of money, Brachman ran poetic billboard appeals to his lost Arlene. One, incorporating expressions that she once used, read:

> "Swellsy, Dandy, Peachy Keen
> Why, Oh Why, Are You So Mean?"

Uniqueness Attracts Publicity

The billboard courtship immediately caught the interest of *The Milwaukee Journal*, which carried a front page story on it. The nation's wire services quickly caught on, and hundreds of newspapers worldwide ran stories with headlines like: "She Wouldn't Listen: He Rents Billboard;" "Jilted, He Woos Arlene

by Billboard;" and "Mean Arlene Lets Swain Foot Bills."

Letters poured in from across the country. The billboard company, initially skeptical of the legality of his plan, called to encourage him to rent more space and post more messages. A national bus company offered to transport the couple anywhere in the United States, if Arlene agreed to marry him. A Canadian railroad offered a honeymoon trip.

The unique courtship which captured the nation's attention finally caught Arlene's too. After turning down 12 proposals, she finally agreed to marry him. They have been happily married and living in the Milwaukee area ever since, glad to this day that he persisted and "dared to be different" in his pursuit.

BE FLEXIBLE

Thinking differently requires something of a "midcourse correction." Chances are you didn't learn in childhood to concentrate on your "differentness." You didn't take courses on being different, and may have learned instead to conform to be accepted by others.

Try to recall an instance when, as a youngster, you sought a special privilege. Perhaps it was an extra helping of milk and cookies, or permission to be first in line or the opportunity to stay out longer during recess. How often would the teacher respond by saying: "Just who do you think you are? What makes *you* so special?"

The better you become at defining and refining your answers to those questions, the more focused you will become. That focus will increase your chances of fulfilling your goals and reaching the level of success that you envision.

That midcourse correction in your thinking will send you on your way to the top. Be wary of others, however, who may try to block your progress en route.

Risk Leads To Rewards

By taking the risk of promoting yourself uniquely, you will win the greatest rewards. That's because you'll "win" even if you fail to accomplish your immediate goal. Sell yourself differently from others and you may at least impress someone in a way that will help you "connect" the next time an opportunity arises.

Fail to differentiate yourself, and you make no impression. *That* could be the biggest risk of all.

IT'S SAFER TO BE DIFFERENT

Strive to promote yourself differently, and you will improve your chances for a safe and secure future. Strive, instead, for "safety," and financial security may elude you.

You may think that you're playing it safe by choosing not to promote yourself, or by playing the

How Earl Nightingale Became One Of The Most Successful Radio Commentators In History

 Shortly after getting his first announcing job at KTAR Radio in Phoenix, Earl Nightingale tried to elevate himself to bigger and better things. His fellow broadcasters teased him about his attempts to promote himself to the network level.

Nightingale later recalled how he gave "so much pizzazz to the local commercials—whether for the local mortuary or sporting goods store— that my announcer friends soon dubbed me 'network' and kidded me and found my efforts ludicrous." When Nightingale announced his plans in 1949 to buy a one-way ticket to Chicago to seek employment with network radio, the other announcers responded with "unbelieving stares and vociferous arguments" why his efforts would fail.

But his self-promotion efforts paid off. In Chicago, CBS-affiliate WBBM offered him a network contract that, he said, gave him "more money that I had dreamed of earning."

Nightingale took what others considered a risk by moving to Chicago and promoting himself as a network-caliber announcer. By daring to be different, he pursued what turned out to be a much more secure career course than if he had stayed in Phoenix. He became one of the most successful announcers and commentators in network radio history.

"Same Game" of self-promotion. In fact, by doing so you lose your sense of purpose. Reliquish control of your career to fate, and your future will be determined by chance, not choice.

Self-promotion is an exercise in self-growth. It requires you to identify your positives, differentiate yourself from others, and package yourself accordingly. Practice pays off. The more experience you get in pinpointing your special abilities, the more adept you will become at demonstrating how and why you stand out.

There is a far more substantial risk in *not* marketing yourself. In the words of hockey star Wayne Gretzky: "You miss 100 percent of the shots you never take."

Those who attempt to promote themselves differently take responsibility for their lives. Those who don't, shirk that responsibility.

THE "YOU" THAT YOU'RE SELLING

Who *are* you, anyway, and why should others care? What makes *you* so special?

Appreciate Yourself

Knowing you're special isn't enough. You have to give yourself credit for it, as well.

It is so easy to take ourselves for granted, and fail to give credit where credit is due. You may know people who can drone on for hours about their shortcomings, faults and failures. It's as if they have become experts on the topic of their inadequacies. Funny how those same "experts" can contribute so little information about their attributes and personal successes. Perhaps they don't have time to ponder the subject, preoccupied as they are with negative thoughts about themselves.

There is special joy in savoring the flavor of your daily accomplishments. Only by learning to experience that joy can you graduate from the ranks of the "striver" to become an "arriver." You can't excel at self-promotion until you make that transformation.

Project Your "Specialness"

Arrivers give the impression that they *already* have won. Their attitudes, mannerisms, and words communicate that they have reached the top of their professions. They exude confidence and serenity. Arrivers are leaders who look, act, and talk the part of those who are successful, and are proud of it.

Play the part of the arriver, and you will stand out from the multitudes. You will establish yourself as someone who is different and special.

Self-appreciation is the foundation of self-promotion. Not until you fully understand your unique qualities and special talents are you ready to dare to be different in the way you promote yourself.

VISIBILITY AND CREDIBILITY

Setting yourself apart from your competitors will increase your visibility and credibility. It will give you a competitive edge. It will bolster your self-confidence, and help you understand and appreciate your own uniqueness. It will get you the recogni-

Take Inventory

Sit down in a quiet place some day soon, and compile a list of your:

- Attributes
- Capabilities
- Most admired traits
- Skills
- Qualifications
- Areas of expertise
- Most recent personal and professional accomplishments
- Greatest personal and professional accomplishments
- Awards and honors
- Success stories
- Record of overcoming obstacles
- Record of mastering challenges
- Contributions to your organization and profession
- Career milestones

Review your list carefully, and periodically add to it. Where appropriate, insert superlatives that indicate how you stand out. Indicate, for example, if you are the *most* experienced or the *highest* ranking or the recipient of the *most* honors. Your list should convince you, if you are not convinced already, that you really *are* special.

tion and rewards that you deserve.

Whoever you are, whatever you do, you're too good to be your own best secret. You have worked too hard for too long to go unrecognized.

Not only do you have so much to gain by promoting your uniqueness, but you have virtually nothing to lose.

- You won't lose money, since some of the most effective self-promotion strategies—like free publicity—cost the least.
- You won't lose time, because a period spent differentiating and distinguishing yourself is time well spent.

Perhaps all you *will* lose is your anonymity. That loss can only result in an understanding and respect from others for who you are and what you do.

ACTION AGENDA
The Dare-to-Be-Different Challenge

Accepting the challenge to promote yourself in a unique way assures that you will take responsibility and control over your career. It frees you from the "follow the follower" restraints of the "Same Game." It also prevents you from blaming your shortcomings on the economy, clients, competitors, age, or just plain bad luck.

Accepting the challenge to be different enables you to look into the mirror each day and *believe* yourself when you say: "What is to be is up to me." Accepting the challenge means that you dare to share your differentness.

Consider yourself challenged.

- **I dare you** to be different in the words you choose to use about yourself and your company or organization.
- **I dare you** to be different in selecting your target audience, and deciding who it is that you need to influence.

The Dare-To-Be-Different Checklist

Work toward promoting yourself differently, and you will discover new and different rewards. Begin by following these guidelines:

- SAY DIFFERENT THINGS ABOUT YOURSELF. Emphasize your "onlys."
- THINK DIFFERENTLY. Focus on today, rather than yesterday or tomorrow.
- ACT DIFFERENTLY. Give the impression that you already are successful.
- SOUND DIFFERENTLY. Talk the talk of an "arriver," rather than a "striver."
- LOOK DIFFERENT. Take on an appearance that distinguishes you from others.
- SELL YOUR SERVICES DIFFERENTLY. Spell out their unique benefits.
- OFFER SOMETHING DIFFERENT. Make available options that others don't.
- GUARANTEE SOMETHING DIFFERENT. Back up your services in a way that others don't.
- TARGET DIFFERENTLY. Pursue a different niche in the market.
- COMMUNICATE DIFFERENTLY. Get your message across in a unique way.
- FOLLOW UP DIFFERENTLY. Stay in touch in ways to which clients are unaccustomed. (Also see Chapter 13 on thank you notes.)

Do all that, and you will discover how being different makes a difference.

- **I dare you** to be different in the methods you use to communicate your message.

It Works

Accept these dares, and you will discover the most important secret of self-promotion: your differences are your diamonds. Believe in that secret, and you will discover the magic of reaching a higher level of personal achievement, income and success than you ever thought possible.

Chapter 2

MARKETING SUCCESS:
It's <u>Not</u> Just the Price

Rick Haberstroh

Rick Haberstroh has been in the sales business since the age of 19. Haberstroh jokes that he has never had a salaried job. He has always been on commission. As a matter of fact, most of the jobs that Haberstroh has had, he created himself. In addition to being a top salesperson, he has been a consultant to businesses as diverse as 3M, Montgomery Ward, ConGel, and the National Shoe Travelers Association. In 1992, Haberstroh took the position as Director of the Insurance Marketing Institute at Purdue University. The Institute was 35 years old and was fading fast. With Haberstroh's innovations and fund raising ability, he was able to turn the Institute around and it is now thriving and on a sound financial basis. In addition to selling and consulting, Haberstroh does over 50 speaking engagements per year. Haberstroh is a member of the Court of the Table, an elite group of Million Dollar Round Table members who triple qualify for the Round Table.

Rick Haberstroh, Richard D. Haberstroh CLU, Inc., 1023 Executive Parkway, Suite 2, St. Louis, MO 63141; phone (314) 275-2100; fax (314) 275-2108.

MARKETING SUCCESS:
It's <u>Not</u> Just the Price

Rick Haberstroh

Most small business people try to out-Wal-Mart Wal-Mart! Whether they are hairdressers, chimney sweeps, accountants, or car dealers, they feel that the only competitive edge they have is price. But they're not Wal-Mart, or Costco, with bare-bones overhead and huge economies of scale.

Competing on price is competing from a position of total weakness. Most small businesses shouldn't make price their unique position in the marketplace. Instead they should use their strengths to determine a unique, sustainable position.

Two Rules About Prices And Profits

There are two aspects of pricing that can determine success in your business. First, the upscale market is willing to pay for good service. And it is often more profitable business for you. Second, understand your true costs, including overhead. Most businesses that try to compete on price endanger their own survival.

SEGMENTING THE MARKET

Several years ago, I was flying home from the East Coast. I was fortunate enough to sit next to a luggage buyer for a major department store. After exchanging niceties, we began talking about the luggage business.

I had lived in St. Louis all of my life, yet the luggage buyer told me something about my city that I found fascinating. His department stores had luggage departments in three different stores in the St. Louis suburbs. He said that even though they were all in St. Louis, they might as well be in different cities.

The Carriage Trade

The upscale market is still called "the carriage trade" because originally the wealthy patrons of a restaurant, theater, etc. were distinguished by the fact that they could afford the comfort and luxury of arriving in a carriage.

Each Area Is Different

The customers, from one store to the other, had few common characteristics. He told me that their store in North St. Louis County had to stock lower grade merchandise with competitive prices.

Their store in West St. Louis County, some ten miles away, had to stock the very latest and best luggage, with pricing of little concern to their customers.

In South St. Louis County, an area of upper blue-collar people of German descent, he had to offer both quality and competitive prices. He didn't know of any other city in the United States that had such product and price diversity.

WHERE'S THE UPSCALE MARKET?

The analysis of luggage sales started me thinking. As a small business person myself, and as a consultant to many small businesses, I wondered how many of us were operating in the neighborhoods where buyers wanted high quality and didn't care about price.

Many of these small business people are trying to give medium quality and low prices. Conversely, many business people in the North St. Louis location are trying to give quality merchandise at low prices.

They do not understand their markets. The only way they know to get and retain business is to out-Wal-Mart Wal-Mart.

Of course, the affluent market isn't just determined by neighborhoods. For instance, the corporate market is full of big buyers. My point throughout this chapter is to understand your market—whatever it is—and aim high.

DON'T LEAD WITH YOUR PRICE

There is an old saying that unsuccessful boxers lead with their chins. It seems to me that unsuccessful businesses lead with their price! Why are most small business people more concerned about offering the lowest price in town, rather than emphasizing service and quality?

I believe that most people going into business make a basic assumption. To paraphrase Ralph Waldo Emerson, the assumption is "build a cheaper mousetrap, and the world will beat a path to your door."

Technicians Believe In Low Prices

Michael Gerber, in his book *The E Myth,* states that most small businesspeople are primarily technicians. They are not entrepreneurs in the truest sense of the word. They are not managers in the truest sense of the word.

They are technicians.

They're good barbers, good heating and air con- ditioning people, and good hairdressers. They are good accountants and bakers, and they decide to open their own businesses. Maybe because of their "workmen's" mentality, they feel that everybody is looking for a cheaper price.

You Can't Win On Low Price

It is very difficult to distinguish your business as being the cheapest. The Wal-Marts and the Kmarts and the Ventures of the world can buy merchandise by the truckload. The Denny's of the world can advertise a $1.99 breakfast on national TV.

There is little hope for the small business-person who competes on price. To be successful, your niche must be a narrowly defined market of people who are willing to pay for extra attention and value added. If you try to beat the discounters in the discount business, you will surely lose.

THE BANJO AND BUS STORY

Here is an example of a business that found a market and delivered a great "product." Yet they never realized that they weren't competing on price.

Bill and Marie and Dick and Helen had been friends for years. The two couples were inseparable. They were with each other nearly every weekend. They formed a group called "The Old Time Vaudeville." They entertained at church socials, bar mitzvahs, and in nursing homes.

Dick and Bill both retired at age 62. Neither one of them had much of a pension. They got to talking and they came up with an idea. Why not take other senior citizens on bus trips?

Not only would they take them to vacation spots, but they would entertain them along the way. Marie could play the banjo, Bill could do standup comedy, and Helen could sing the blues. Dick could just be Dick and take care of the business part of the business.

Successfully Targeting Their Market

How would they get business with little or no money? They decided that they would contact senior citizens' clubs. In return for 15 or 20 minutes of entertainment, they asked to hand out brochures and give a presentation on their travel business, which was aptly named "Banjo and Bus."

A Winning Niche

Banjo and Bus was a success from the beginning. Seniors who had gone on bus trips with other tour groups were used to being dropped at their motel at 5:00 at night. The tour guide was typically a college student and when 5:00 p.m. came, his or her shift was over.

But, Dick and Helen, and Bill and Marie were tour guides like no others. If you wanted to go to your motel at 5:00 p.m. and watch TV and rest that was certainly your business. But if you didn't, there was a bingo game down the hall or there was a sing-along. Or they might even take the bus downtown to Otto's tavern to drink a few beers and sing some more. Forty people on a bus trip felt like they were on a family vacation.

Banjo and Bus began receiving thank you notes. People told of how they had been depressed and that the trip with Banjo and Bus had changed their lives. Typically, Banjo and Bus would go on twenty trips per year. The new year schedule was sent out around Thanksgiving. By the first of the year, most of the trips were sold out.

Family, Not Price

One of Banjo and Bus's non-bus trips was a Caribbean cruise. I attended the cruise party. Five hundred of Banjo and Bus's customers attended. One-half of the ship was sold out in one evening.

An official with the ship lines said he had been in the cruise business all of his life and had never, ever, witnessed anything like that before. I talked to a few of their customers. They told me that Dick and Helen and Marie and Bill were the greatest thing that ever happened to them.

One person told me that he had been on every trip they had ever taken. They felt that they had an extension of their family with Banjo and Bus. They were offering people friendship, care, and love, something that transcends price.

The two couples made more money in retirement than either one of them made while they were working.

> "Upscale buyers like to be entertained. They appreciate humor and wit in the sale."
> —*International Journal of Bank Marketing*

A Priceless Service

In talking with them about the success of their business, Helen said to me, "The reason we were successful is because we were cheap." After having run a successful business for twelve years, she missed the whole point!

People did not go on Banjo and Bus trips because they were cheap. They went on Banjo and Bus trips because the trips changed their lives! They felt as if Banjo and Bus were family. They were traveling with friends.

How many small businesses, even after twelve years in the business, misunderstand the value added that their businesses give? If Banjo and Bus had charged $25 more per trip, they would not have lost a customer. Twelve years times 20 trips times $25 is a $240,000 shortfall.

THE CHIMNEY SWEEP

About four years ago, I was asked to give a presentation to the National Association of Chimney Sweeps on how to increase their business. As usual, I met with one or two of the members before the engagement and interviewed them regarding their business.

For me, this was a very informative session. I was about to address three hundred people and I did not have a clue what they did for a living.

I asked for the name of the most successful chimney sweep in St. Louis. I went to breakfast with Victor Imgarten, a very energetic, bright individual. At the time, he was president of the National Chimney Sweeps Association. Victor was proud of his business, and well he should have been.

He had built it from a small, one-man, one-truck business to an organization of eight employees and five trucks. He explained to me that chimney sweeping was only a small part of their job. There were chimney repairs, guards to be placed in the chimneys, and different types of flues to be installed. There was much more to the business than I had originally thought.

Upscale Vs. Downscale Business

I said, "Victor, I assume a large percentage of your business comes from the more affluent parts of our town. After all, in the affluent parts of our town, most every home has a chimney. In the smaller homes, maybe one in five homes has a chimney. The market is certainly broader. And once you have a commitment to clean the chimney on an annual basis, it would seem pretty much automatic."

Victor responded, "Rick, I really do not relate to people in the better neighborhoods. I do business with the people in neighborhoods like the one that I was raised in."

I said, "Victor, we've got to talk."

Ken Wylie, marketing guru, once told me that when you do business in an upscale market, "no" means the same as it does in a downscale market.

If someone refuses your product or service, this results in no sale. No sale, whether it's to someone very affluent or the poorest man on earth, is still no sale.

What's a Yes Worth?

When marketing to the affluent, a "yes" can mean much more than a "yes" from a less affluent prospect!

I said, "Victor, many people who live in the better areas of town where you do not want to work are professionals and executives with dual incomes. They are very security conscious. They are very concerned about fires in their homes. However, the last thing they want to do is climb up on their roof and try to clean their own chimneys. It is worth a lot of money to them to have someone who they know is knowledgeable and competent do that for them."

The Upscale Want Service

You will find that the upscale market does not have time to concern themselves about cleaning

---

THE AFFLUENT CHOOSE DIFFERENTLY
"Affluent consumers use different criteria than the non-affluent in selecting services. They place more emphasis on knowledgeable, experienced people who can offer a variety of services. And they value personalized relationships."
—*Journal of Services Marketing*

their own chimneys or, in fact, getting several bids to have their chimneys cleaned. Once they find a company that does a good job and keeps in touch with them throughout the year, the number of repeat customers is extremely high.

In other words, instead of reselling your service every year and concerning yourself with the price, a yes in the affluent market would mean that you would clean and care for a customer's chimney for as long as they owned the house. It's like a built-in annuity.

A repeat customer does not require the money that it takes to get a new customer: phone solicitations, direct mail, advertising, and all the methods that Victor had to use to get new business.

Repeat Business And Referrals

Once you're working in a good neighborhood, people will refer you to their friends.

Few people clean chimneys. Clearly, the value of upscale customers applies in many other areas even more. Sometimes to test this market, you need to stretch beyond the market you "grew up with." After all, don't you deserve the best customers, just as upscale clients want the best service?

> "The affluent respondents whom I have interviewed report that interpersonal endorsements (word-of-mouth) were the most influential in their decisions to patronize a variety of product and service providers."
> —Thomas J. Stanley, *Networking With the Affluent*

TIRED OF CLERKS

There are many upscale customers in your market who are willing to pay for better service. They want to be treated as special people, like I do.

For instance, my wife and I were recently at dinner with my sister-in-law, Karen, and her husband, Tom. After dinner, we began talking about the stock market. Tom told me some of the stocks that he had bought and sold. I told him similar stories. He asked me with whom I did my brokerage business. I told him the name of a local broker with a local brokerage house.

Tom asked, "What is the commission you pay on a one hundred share transaction?" I said, "I don't know, Tom, I think it's about $79."

"Oh," he said, "did you know that you could go to a discount house and they would buy or sell your shares for $39 for one hundred?"

I Am Special

I said, "Tom, I'm just not interested."

He gave me a look of puzzlement.

I said, "Tom, in my daily business, with my traveling, I am forced to do business with clerks. They get paid $6 per hour, whether I do business with their company or not. They receive their $6 an hour, whether I'm their biggest customer or their smallest. These clerks get $6 an hour, whether I remain a client for lifetime or whether I walk out and never come back.

"Whenever I can, I do business with someone who treats me as special, with someone who gives me extra service, with someone with whom, frankly, I have some clout. I look for that type of relationship."

For instance, with the new securities settlement rules, all accounts must be settled within three days. Many times I place an order from out of town. My broker, on his way to his office or on his way home, will stop by my office and pick up a check.

On a rare occasion, I have to call my broker at his home. Because I do not do it very often, and because he is receiving commissions, I feel no compunction about the inconvenience. As a matter of fact, he is glad to hear from me.

Everyone Wants To Be Special

There are millions of people who do business everyday with clerks and have no control over it. They are not necessarily looking for the lowest price.

I make about ten transactions a year. The difference between the discount house and my full service broker is about $40 a transaction. That means about $400 extra per year. Frankly, that $400 is not going to make a big difference on my return on my stock portfolio.

I read recently that, in 1995, for the first time, no load mutual funds failed to get the increase in market share they've been enjoying for the last several years. The conclusion of an article in *USA Today* was that as more mutual funds come into the market, people feel a little bit confused and are willing to pay an extra fee for the services of a professional who knows his or her business.

This is true in industry after industry. Small businesses have great opportunities to fill the gap, to provide the service, to give the value added. Yet, small businesses are still trying to out-Wal-Mart Wal-Mart.

"People like to be recognized because they see themselves as important and worthwhile; a business that acknowledges this importance is a business that maintains customer esteem."
—B. Schneider and D.E. Bowen, *Winning the Service Game*

How Important Is Price?

I don't mean to imply that business and salespeople can gouge and get whatever the market will bear for their products and services. However, businesses must know what services they provide, and the value of those services.

Corporate Seminars Reach the Affluent

"If you want an affluent client base, you should go to the corporate and executive market. Seminar selling continues to be one of the best strategies to penetrate this market....Our research has shown that the phone is the most successful approach for marketing seminars to the corporate market."

—Paul Karasic,
Managers magazine

The Customer Who Knows Your Business Better Than You Do

Several years ago I met two entrepreneurs who owned a net and twine company. They are an example of a cusotmer who takes advantage of businesses that don't know their real costs.

They sold netting to state biology departments, universities, and bait shops. They had about twenty employees who would get orders for a particular type of netting. The employees would cut the netting off of a large bolt, pack it, and ship it to the customer. It was a simple, low-budget operation.

The largest cost that this business had was the printing of their annual catalog. They knew how much it cost to print a catalog better than most printers. Year after year they would bid out their catalog. Some small printer eager for additional business would bid the catalog, unknowingly, for less than his cost.

I can see the jubilation in the small printer when he received the order. It was probably the largest order he had ever received. He probably took his wife and family out to dinner and celebrated. By the time the order was delivered, the printer discovered that he, in fact, had taken the order at a loss.

The net and twine company owners would brag, "What's the number, have we bankrupted six or seven printers?"

Develop A Niche

A "niche" is a place in the ecology where a species has developed an advantage over competitors. A niche is a protected environment where you can dominate. What you want is an "unfair advantage!"

The small business person must know his product, must know his niche, must know how to price his product, so that he can make a fair return.

Remember the old joke: When you are buying watermelons for a dollar apiece, and you are selling them for ninety cents, you can't make up the difference in volume!

Don't Undercut Yourself

Tom Reilly is a friend of mine. Tom is the guru of value-added selling. Tom says that price cutting is a self-inflicted wound by business and sales people. Ninety percent of all salespeople questioned said that they will negotiate price.

Yet fewer than one in six shoppers say that price is their primary consideration in purchasing a product or a service. A business person must know what a service costs and keep the service sufficiently narrow so that there are economies of scale. By becoming proficient in a given area, you can do it better and more profitably than your competition.

You need to narrow your focus so that you are the undisputed expert in a specific area. Tom Reilly says that most businesses' services are a mile wide and an inch deep! The goal of a successful business should be to have services an inch wide and a mile deep.

As business people we must overcome the urge to do it all.

Don't Chase Lizards!

A story I like to tell is the lizard shoe story. Let's suppose that you were affluent and decided that you wanted a custom pair of lizard shoes. You could go to any one of ten shoe chains and tell them that you would be willing to pay almost anything for a pair of custom-made lizard shoes.

The manager of the chain store would politely say to you, "Sir, let me tell you how we operate. We manufacture millions of pairs of shoes, mostly in Southeast Asia, for an average of four to five dollars a pair. We import to the United States and sell them in our stores for fifty to seventy dollars a pair. We do this millions of times a year. That's how we do it, that's our niche. We are not interested in filling your order for custom-made lizard shoes."

By contrast, let us imagine the small business person whose services are a mile wide and an inch deep. The customer would walk in, ask for custom-made lizard shoes, and say that he was willing to pay almost anything for those shoes. The businessman would take the order, close the store, call his wife and say, "honey pack up your things, we're going out hunting for a lizard."

PAY THAN DO

A well known expression is, "I don't do windows." Many people, like myself, have many jobs they are willing to pay a lot to have done.

About four years ago, I was making a call on a business client. I noticed a meticulous van and a well-groomed woman in a uniform. She was washing the windows of the business I was calling on.

I said to her, "Is this your business?"

She said, "Yes it is."

I said, "Do you do residential?" She said, "Yes I do."

My two-story home overlooks the Missouri River. There are windows along the entire backside of our home. Cleaning the windows is a very onerous task. I've tried a time or two myself. It was difficult taking the windows apart to clean them, I was very satisfied with the job I had done until that evening. Then the lights shone through the windows and showed my many streaks.

Do the Dirty Jobs

I asked this woman for her card; and I asked her how she got into the business. She said that she had looked for something that she could do that people did not want to do for themselves.

Notice that she did not mention price. I contacted her to do my windows without an estimate.

I was so happy to find somebody who looked as if she knew what she was doing,

WHY DO THEY BUY?

In every marketing transaction, there is an "exchange that satisfies the needs of both parties." One way to achieve this is to do something that people would rather not do themselves. They will be more willing to pay for it!

who took pride in what she was doing, and was willing to do this task for me.

"Windows by Patty" has now washed my windows for the third year in a row. The charge is $600. I might be able to shop around and get the job done for less. But why?

I know Patty, I know her work, I'm happy with her work, and I don't have to concern myself with letting strangers into my home. As long as I own the house, Windows by Patty has my work. I wasn't concerned about price, but rather who could do the work and do it well.

Remember, you too are selling more than your product or service. For many buyers you are selling peace of mind.

GREAT DANE DILEMMA

About four years ago, my daughter "allowed" us to baby-sit her Great Dane. That was a life-changing experience.

First of all, I got the job of walking, or should I say being pulled by, this animal every night! Although I complained about it bitterly, my wife felt that it was a great opportunity for me to get some exercise.

All I had to do was mention the word walk, and the dog was pulling open the drawer where his leash was kept. This was the easiest part of keeping the dog. The unpleasant part was when I got a look at my backyard. We had a small schnauzer. Cleaning up our backyard was a minor, five-minute task. I now saw the results of a 125-pound dog doing its business in my yard.

I Predict A New Service

It looked as if I were keeping a camel! I told my wife that someone needed to start a business in the better neighborhoods of St. Louis cleaning backyards for the owners of large pets. She laughed at me and called me the consummate delegator.

Not too long ago, the *St. Louis Business Journal* ran an article about a new business called "Yucko's." Yucko's now has three trucks that cover St. Louis County cleaning up backyards for people who have large dogs.

Since my baby-sitting tenure with the Great Dane has ended, I am not in need of their service. But believe me, if the Great Dane returns, I will immediately call Yucko's. And you can bet I will not argue about the price!

FORD OR MERCEDES?

From my home in St. Louis County to downtown St. Louis, is about a twenty-minute drive. Frankly, I could get there in the same amount of time whether I drove a Ford Aspire or a Mercedes.

The last time I checked, a Ford Aspire could be purchased for about $6,000 and a minimum Mercedes was about $50,000. Wouldn't it make sense for everybody to drive a Ford Aspire?

If they both get you to work in the same amount of time, why pay $50,000 for an automobile?

Obviously, there's a lot more to consider in buying a car than price. There is safety, there's comfort, and there's status. There are probably fifty real and perceived reasons to drive a Mercedes over a Ford Aspire.

"You may have to live in a crowd, but you do not have to live like it."
—Henry Van Dyke

Many Will Pay More

As a business person, the next time you want to out-Wal-Mart Wal-Mart, look around the highway. Are all the cars passing you Ford Aspires?

No. There are Cadillacs and Mercedes and Lincolns and BMWs. Chances are, those are the type of people to whom you should offer your services or products. Many of the reasons that they are not driving a Ford Aspire are the same reasons that they want to do business with businesses like yours that can deliver quality and great service.

THE ABUNDANCE MENTALITY
"The abundance mentality...results in a sharing of prestige, of recognition, of profits, of decision making. It opens possibilities, options, alternatives, and creativity."
—Stephen Covey

MORE CONSEQUENCES OF UNDERPRICING: THE TED BELL STORY

I know a fellow named Ted Bell. Upon graduation from college he went to work for a large corporation. He had a meteoric rise.

Ted was conscientious, hardworking, and friendly. He was promoted and was held in high esteem in his company. A few years into his career he was given the job of evaluating and purchasing new technology for the entire company.

The vendor mislead Ted. As a consequence, his company ended up buying a new system that was inadequate, a white elephant. Ted was told, tacitly, that he still would have a job with the corporation, but that he probably would not be promoted. The mistake would be on his record forever.

A New Career

After about three months of sitting in his office and reading *The Wall Street Journal,* Ted decided that was no way to live his life. He bought an established consulting practice. Again, the energetic, conscientious Ted Bell went to work. Immediately, people were impressed with the quality of work that Ted did. I referred several clients to Ted because I knew of his diligence.

People do not change consulting firms capriciously—unless their present consultants get sloppy, make mistakes, and miss deadlines. The clients would decide that they didn't feel real comfortable, so they'd look for another consultant. Ninety-five percent of the time the clients would be unhappy.

What Do Clients Want?

Very seldom did clients change because of the price of their service. When I would refer a new client to Ted, I would tell him of the problems that they were currently having with their present consultant.

Ted, would invariably ask me, "What are they paying?" I would say, "Ted, they are not having problems with the price, they are having problems with the service. Charge them a fair rate." Well, Ted insisted on asking them what they were paying.

What Do Customers Want?

The American Society for Quality Control (ASQC) asked 1,005 adult consumers what quality factors they consider important when purchasing a product or service. For manufactured items they ranked: performance, durability, ease of repair, service availability, warranty, and ease of use. Price was ranked seventh out of nine factors!

The same survey defined good quality service as courteous, prompt, responding to one's basic needs, and being provided by someone with a good attitude.

Not only would he promise and deliver more service than they were currently getting, but he would do it for less than they were currently paying.

Obviously, none of his new customers complained. More service, less cost. Who wouldn't take the deal?

After about six or seven years of seven-day weeks and fourteen-hour days, Ted Bell was nearly exhausted and certainly not wealthy. He did some deep soul searching, and eliminated those clients who were not profitable to his firm. He re-priced his services and concentrated on those areas in which he was particularly adept. He was able to turn around his consulting firm.

> To every man there openeth
> A High Way and a Low
> And every man decideth
> The way his soul shall go
> —John Oxenham

Ted was one of the fortunate ones. He was able to come out of the "ether," regroup, and survive. Most businesses never make the transition. I think after his experience, Ted will finally say, "It's *not* just the price!"

CONCLUSION

My point in this chapter is simple. You have a number of choices in positioning your service or product.

Some businesses try to be all things to all people. I recommend that, instead, you specialize and be the best thing for *some* people. Some businesses think they have to be the low price leader. Competing on price like the Wal-Marts of the world is not what I recommend.

I believe that the upscale market will serve you well. Try to find people who appreciate what you do and are willing to pay a good price for it.

Even if you don't go after the upscale market, be sure you know your real costs so you can make a fair profit.

If the market doesn't respond, you may have to reposition what you offer. You do not have to be the most expensive in your markets. But you should be the "most" something.

Perhaps you're the best value. Or the most reliable. Or the fastest. Or the best referred. Be the best at something, find your market, and you'll enjoy success.

Go to it!

ACTION AGENDA

- Do an analysis of your real overhead and costs. Make sure you're not underpricing.

- Analyze each client, type of customer, and product line for profitability. Drop areas where you can't make money, unless they bring you other profitable business.

- Identify the upscale customers among your current clients.

- Decide what you can do now to take extra good care of them. Start by dropping them each a brief personal note. (See Chapter 13 on thank you notes for ideas.) You could even send a very brief survey asking them what else you could do for them.

- Create a plan to offer more services to your existing clients. What are their unmet needs?

- What else can you do to make these people feel special?

- List who your best clients' friends and trusted advisors are. What groups are they in? What charities do they support? How else can you get to know them?

- Create a plan to find more customers like your best ones. Hint: they have many of the same types of friends and advisors as your current best clients.

- Start developing a list of the resources you can offer upscale clients. Can you bring them business? Advice? Contacts? Information? Entertainment? Can you make them heros with their spouses? With their children? With their clients?

Chapter 3

TURNING KNOWLEDGE INTO CASH:
How To Use The Marketing Ideas In This Book

David Klaybor

David Klaybor provides companies and entrepreneurs with marketing advice and tips that immediately increase sales. Klaybor researches both corporate and home-based businesses, analyzes their problems, and provides innovative solutions.

Klaybor has gained his experience as an airline captain, broker, business owner, radio talk show co-host, and personal development instructor. He is a member of the National Speakers Association, the International Network Association, and the Educational Committee for the Natural Foods Association.

Klabor's teaching technologies have earned him feature and cover story articles in major magazines. He has given thousands of wealth building seminars worldwide to his direct sales and network marketing clients: Fuller Brush, Rexall, Avon, Amway, Shaklee, Enrich, Quorum, Alliance, LifePlus, FreeLife, and hundreds more. Klabor is the author of *Books Don't Work Unless You Do*. He has a Time Management Business Planner and several audiotapes, and has published his own magazine.

David Klaybor, 1223 Marquette Avenue, South Milwaukee, WI 53172; voicemail (714) 450-3123, (714) 433-2128, or (801) 288-2434.

Chapter 3

TURNING KNOWLEDGE INTO CASH: How To Use The Marketing Ideas In This Book

David Klaybor

IS KNOWLEDGE POWER?

"It is the organization of knowledge, that is further put into action, that gives us the 'power' we wish to possess."

—Napoleon Hill, *Think and Grow Rich*

You bought this book to improve your marketing skills. This chapter will give you a specific strategy to help you use this new marketing knowledge right now.

Is knowledge power? When I ask this question in my seminars, 60–80 percent of the attendees say "yes"—but I suggest that we reflect on the above words from Napoleon Hill. You probably know many intelligent people with impressive résumés who have very little money in their bank accounts. Knowledge alone does not give us the power we crave.

I'm going to introduce you to some simple and easy-to-perform success strategies that will enable you to get more from the authors in this book than you ever thought possible. I will help you "install" the information from this book, and weave it into your life.

These success technologies work IF you apply them. I challenge you to try them out while you read this book and then write to us with your testimonial success story.

FIRST STEP: GET THE PROPER EQUIPMENT

You didn't know you needed special tools to read effectively, did you? You will need four to eight different colored highlighter pens and a "sticky note" pad. Plan on using lots of colored markers and writing all over the margins on each page. The pages should look like they're covered with gang graffiti on a subway wall!

As you read this book, use the assorted colors to identify different information you find to be significant and important in accomplishing one of your goals. It's foolish to read a book and not highlight the great tips you discover.

It is equally unproductive to mark all the important data with one color (usually yellow). Then the whole book is inundated with slashing yellow highlights, none distinguishing one particular type of data from another.

Color Code Your Information

Use a red or pink highlighter to identify each time the author pinpoints some "warning." This makes sense: red = warning. Use the color green when you discover a money-

> You are never taught how to get the most out of a book. You'll learn much better if you use a different approach.
> —Phil Zimbardo, Stanford University

Book Readers' Success Tools

making tip. Blue might make sense for inspirational points. How about brown for environmental or grounded issues?

You get the idea. Make up your own formula. But never read a book without at least four different colored marker pens.

After you've finished reading a book and you've used all these different colored pens, the rainbow effect will differentiate one important set of data from another.

You will have immediate *access* to the information you need. It is this access to information that will set you apart from your peers and vault you to the fore! You'll market better, raise more money for your nonprofit organization, or increase your sales if you use this strategy.

SECOND STEP: "BE PREPARED"

The old boy/girl scout motto suggests that you should always plan ahead. In the case of book reading, know what you're looking for before you start reading.

What Do You Need?

Why did you spend the money to buy this book? Know from the start what you want to gain. This will focus your reading but won't cut you off from unexpected ideas.

Let me give you some suggestions on how to identify the information you want to install into your life from this book. You might look for specific data referring to specific sales phraseology used in:

- answering objections
- trial closing or closing lines
- good questions to ask the prospect
- phonics or body language
- follow-up techniques or checklists
- how to get referrals, etc.

If you were a salesperson, this book would be of great value to you because it would enable you to earn greater income and make bank deposits within days or hours of reading. How?—by taking action on the strategies disclosed by the authors.

"X" Marks The Spot For Treasure

Even if you locate and identify key phrases in the book you're reading, you'll probably forget the phrases minutes after you finish the book. You couldn't find those key phrases that are buried in the manuscript if you tried. Why? Because you didn't put a "stake in the ground" as you discovered these nuggets of wisdom. You didn't highlight *anything*—or you highlighted *everything*.

Think of a series of "code

Code Word: Book

Every time I get to a place in a book where the author recommends another publication I should purchase, I write the word "book" in the margin. Then, when I go to the bookstore or library to do my homework, it's a snap to find all the publications I need. It's amazing how impressed people are when I do this. They think I'm Mr. Organization, when all I did was write a simple code word in the margin so I could retrieve the information when I needed it.

symbols" or "code words" to use every time you discover one of these bits of wisdom. Write these codes in the margins at the top, bottom or side areas where there is some white space. It will then be easy for you to retrieve the information. This is not rocket science here. But like the simplicity of a napkin, if you don't have one when you need it, you've got egg on your face!

THIRD STEP: DO YOUR HOMEWORK

In this book, every author gives the reader a brief "action agenda" at the end of the chapter.

It is very important that once you've high-lighted information in different colors, and written codes in the margins, etc., that you take action on the tips and ideas the authors give you. Most readers fail to carry this strategy out. This is a huge mistake because you might make more money, communicate more effectively with your spouse, save more whales, or learn how to do something you enjoy better.

Once you've identified the information that will help you accomplish your goals, go all the way and finish the task. For instance, go to the book store and buy that book the author has recommended. This is easy because you have coded this information in the side margins of this book.

USE BOOKS

When was the last time you were inside your local bookstore or library? Do not waste this powerful asset. Using the Internet is your only excuse not to visit your local library several times a month.

FOURTH STEP: INSTALL THE INFORMATION

If I say, "Winston tastes good, _____" (like a cigarette should), or "Plop, plop, fizz, fizz _____," I'm willing to bet you just filled in the blanks with the rest of the jingle ("oh, what a relief it is").

If you didn't, you were either out of the USA for decades, or you are very young.

The point I have just made is that these TV commercials, and thou-

Eat 5 servings of fruits and vegetables today!

Place 5-10 Stickies Everywhere You Look Throughout The Day

sands of others like them, have been permanently *installed* into our subconscious mind. It is important to understand how they got installed. Alka Seltzer paid an advertising agency to come up with a catchy phrase. But the story doesn't end there. The next step is vital to the sales process. It's the very step most book readers fail to take in acquiring the knowledge contained in the books they buy and read.

Once the Alka Seltzer commercial was created, the ad had to be *delivered*. They used TV, radio, news publications, and word-of-mouth advertisement. And slowly, painlessly, and almost subliminally, hundreds of millions of us were *conditioned* via the relentless repetition of the ad campaign.

Repetition Is The "Mother Of Skill"

Repetition is also the way other people condition our belief systems or install information in our minds. This strategy is being used on us every day. Many of us, knowingly or unknowingly, use this formula to get what we want from others.

Every advertiser in the world is attempting to

REPETITION WORKS

Extreme repetition of novel material can cause initial boredom. But in delayed tests, people later liked the familiar items better.
—University of Michigan study

Creatively Condition Yourself

Put your sticky notes:

- on the bathroom mirror
- on the ceiling above your bed
- inside your clothes closet
- in the automobile glove box
- inside the refrigerator
- under the toilet seat
- on the sun-visor in the car

Be creative!

persuade you, condition you, and install their information inside your mind.

Let me share a simple system that will allow you to "recondition" yourself. I call it, "Re-Programming Your Habits for Success." You will find the following strategy either fun or embarrassing...but this technology flat-out works!

You need to find a "vehicle" to act as the "delivery mechanism." I suggest a large sticky note pad. Place 5–10 stickies everywhere you look throughout the day. The concept is to surprise yourself so you notice and read and re-read the sticky notes over and over and over.

Post Your Messages

On a sticky note, write a message that you choose from this book. Repeated readings of the message you write will bombard your mind. Eventually the idea or information you wrote down (and read and re-read) will become a part of you. The information has now been "installed." It's yours to use anytime to accomplish your goals.

Make A Commitment Now

Posting notes may seem like a lot of work (it isn't), and it may seem silly as your family members ask you why these notes are posted all over your living environment. But if you make the decision with me right now to commit to doing it,

I guarantee that this new-found information will be added to your store of knowledge. You life will surely change.

But change isn't change until it's changed. You must *do* something different in order to get a different and better performance. Therefore, if you are looking for results, if you are truly interested in taking actions that will alter the course of your life and make the reading of this book significant and memorable, then put the silly notes up all around your house, work, and car.

Use the ideas from this book to get what you want from life! Whatever you write on the notes will be installed within 5–21 days. The exact time depends on where you place them, how many you place, how complicated the information is, and your willingness to receive and install the information.

> **DON'T BE INSANE**
> "The definition of insanity is doing the same thing over and over and expecting a *new* result."
> —Albert Einstein

FIFTH STEP: USE THE KNOWLEDGE

Let's say you are a salesperson and you placed sales phrases throughout your living environment via the sticky notes. You'll be surprised when, one day, out of your mouth springs one of the phrases from the notes—the very information you highlighted—the data you wanted to learn and make part of who you are.

Because you installed and then *used* that phrase, your prospect bought an item you were selling. That's usually when I get a letter from someone who was skeptical about this strategy, but used it anyway, and made $800 extra in commissions within 30 days (or saved an 11,000 acre rainforest).

Other readers have improved their relationships with their co-workers or family members due to new ideas they have installed into their minds. The potential is unlimited.

You can read this book and not remember any of the ideas. Or you can install the information contained in this book and make millions. The choice is yours.

SIXTH STEP: DOCUMENT THE SUCCESS

A life worth living is a life worth documenting. Every time you accomplish anything, write it down in a diary. Put newspaper articles, company publication materials, certificates, awards, thank-you cards, promotion letters, photographs, etc. in a scrap book or presentation book.

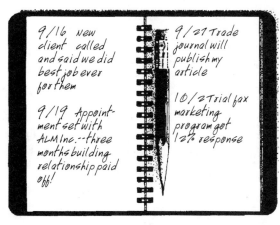

Documenting your successes helps encourage you to do more. It can make you feel better. And it can remind you of ideas you can use later.

SEVENTH STEP: TEACH SOMEONE ELSE

You haven't learned a thing until you can teach it to others. Research shows that teaching others helps you learn.

Once you've shared this success strategy with another human being, you'll have given them a tool to accomplish all the things they want in life. And, as a bonus, you'll never forget how to perform this strategy.

EIGHTH STEP: SHARE YOUR SUCCESS WITH US

We want to hear from you. Write to us and brag about your success as a result of one of our contributing authors. Maybe we'll share your story in one of our future books.

NINTH STEP: SET ANOTHER GOAL

Now that you know how to get anything you want, what do you want to accomplish next? Set yourself another goal to achieve. Set your sights higher and do this installation formula all over again.

Marketing can help you in many areas. You can get whatever you want out of life. Don't waste it.

Good luck and God bless.

Part II: Marketing Specifics

Customer Service: The Real
Magic of Marketing
Larry Cole

Profitable Prospecting: Getting Results
WithClient Newsletters
Mary Lou Gutscher

Power Networking:
Building Relationships for Success
John S. Haskell

Using the Phone as a Serious Sales Tool:
9 Steps to Success
Art Sobczak

The New Rules of Selling: Building Relationships
Jack Daly and Jim Pratt

SPIN® Selling: A Proven Sales Method
Bud Coggins

How To Sell Even If You're Not In Sales:
The 7 Secrets of Heartful Selling
Marc Fine

Online Marketing: New Technology For New Result
Rick Crandall

10 Reasons To Market by Fax
Bob Bailey

Chapter 4

CUSTOMER SERVICE:
The Real Magic of Marketing

Larry Cole

Larry Cole, PhD, is a consultant, author, and professional speaker who assists organizations to improve their internal and external customer service culture.

Cole is founder of Cole Training Consultants. His corporate mission statement is *"To assist individuals to accept the challenge to change."* In doing so, he knows the importance of structuring the change process in order to get change to work. Without it you have chaos.

Cole's recently published book, *Frustration Is Your Organization's Best Friend: Measuring Corporate Culture Change* focuses on continuously improving internal customer service. This book emerged from his work with organizations to implement quality improvement processes and external customer service.

Larry Cole, Cole Training Consultants, 100 S. University, Suite 401, Little Rock, AR 72205; phone (800), 800-880-1728, (501) 666-4131; fax (501) 664-8886.

CUSTOMER SERVICE:
The Real Magic of Marketing

Larry Cole

C ompanies waste billions of dollars to convince their public they put "Customers First." Most companies mouth the words, "We are customer service driven," but relatively few companies follow their words with action.

CHEAP WORDS, EXPENSIVE ACTION

Billboard slogans and other advertisements can be cute, catchy, and clever. But what do you remember about your interaction with a company? I would dare to say it's not their billboard. It's how you were treated by representatives of that company—the level of customer service you received.

Which criteria are used to decide whether to continue doing business with the company? Again, I dare to say it's not what's written on the billboard. It's the service level.

Bad customer service acts like a memory magnet—we remember it for infinity.

Bugs In Restaurant Service

About five years ago I had lunch in a restaurant associated with a well-known hotel chain. I stood by the "Please wait to be seated" sign for at least five minutes while several uniformed hotel employees walked by me without acknowledging my presence. I was getting ready to seat myself, when, from the back of the room, a lady got up from a table to seat me. Needless to say, I was not impressed.

The sandwich was excellent. Then while I was at the counter to pay, a huge cockroach walked aimlessly across it. I looked at the young cashier and jokingly said, "Now I know why my sandwich was so good!" I guess she didn't hear the joke—she didn't utter a word about the bug.

I haven't revisited that particular restaurant. But I think about this poor service episode every time I visit a restaurant associated with that hotel chain.

Banking Inconvenience

It's well known in the financial industry that convenience is the primary reason consumers select a financial institution. This is exactly the reason I selected one located about 200 feet from my office building.

During the last two years of our banking relationship, I watched customer service dwindle to the point that a couple of tellers struggled to look at me

"Have an adequate day."

during the transaction. (Am I ugly? Yes! That ugly? I hope not.) Plus, the counter was filled with money and paperwork. I wondered about lost transactions in the mess. As much as I hate to reconcile bank statements, I reconciled my statements from this bank to make certain my deposits didn't get lost in the mess.

Once again, the level of customer service determines consumer's behavior. I decided that I had had enough and told the young man who waited on me that I wanted to close the account. He looked at me as though I had insulted him.

He left for about five minutes to complete the necessary paperwork and returned to give me a cashier's check. Did he say, "Thank you for banking with us?" Did he ask me to return with a simple, "I'm sorry we're losing your business, what can we do to get another opportunity to be of service to you?" No. He did, however, tell me good-bye.

This particular bank spends considerable money trying to convince us about its wonderful customer service. Wasted dollars!

When will people learn? It's not the dollars spent on advertising customer service that counts...it's the customer service that counts.

Customer Loyalty

I purchase clothes at Norman's, a privately-owned business. He has my sizes emblazoned in his memory. I receive notes about sales opportunities and about new styles that he thinks I would like. I receive thank you notes after purchasing items. He doesn't spend big bucks telling the world

"The names of the marketing game in the 1990s and beyond are *relationships* and *service*...it takes time to nurture the customer relationships and render the superlative service."

—Jay Conrad Levinson, author of the *Guerrilla Marketing* books how good he is. He shows the world through his actions.

My wife has asked me about buying clothes during those big name department store sales to save money. I won't even look at their clothes, because I purchase from Norman's.

Customer loyalty through quality customer service is the best marketing tool a business can have. How many folks do you think have heard about my business relationship with Norman's in Russellville, Arkan-

"Notice how the $1,111 matches the pin stripes?"

sas? The next time you visit this beautiful community, visit Norman's and see for yourself. Now that's marketing!

OCCASIONAL TRAINING DOESN'T DO IT

Many individuals in responsible customer service positions believe that training is the key to unlock great customer service. So an employee is designated to organize a customer service program. An expensive video package is purchased for in-house training or employees are sent to a seminar.

It's foolish to think that either will produce lasting behavioral changes. In all fairness, though, such training opportunities can be excellent sources for ideas.

The problem is, that after attending such training, the employee returns to a work environment that does not support implementation of the ideas. Or, the ideas are tried and no one is held accountable to implement the changes. Or, there are no ongoing practice or refresher sessions. The training manual and video package are placed in the bookshelf and after a few weeks begin to collect dust. Eventually, they get lost. (I've gone into organizations and found books and training programs that employees never knew existed!)

About three years ago I met with ABC company to discuss creating a customer service culture. I outlined the process such as you are about to read in the following sections. The CEO, instead, elected to spend hundreds of thousands of dollars (not counting staff time) to present a series of seminars throughout their multiple locations. The results? These are some of the videos and manuals collecting dust.

There is no logical reason I can think of to waste such money. It's time to find a better way. Now let's read about that better way.

KEYS TO CUSTOMER SERVICE EXCELLENCE

A comprehensive approach to utilize customer service as a marketing tool will be presented in the following sections. The components of this approach are:

1. Create a customer service mission statement.
2. Decide how to measure great service.
3. Design and implement a program.
   - Manage the customer service moments-of-truth.
   - Ensure employees have adequate product knowledge.
   - Make decisions closer to the customer.
   - Show customers you care. (Create the WoW! factor.)
   - Practice out-of-the-box customer service thinking.
4. Hold customer service meetings.
5. Provide accountability.
6. Measure, measure, measure, and measure some more.

YOU MUST KNOW WHERE YOU WANT TO GO IN ORDER TO GET THERE

There is a very important prerequisite for change that is often forgotten. Many companies implement customer service training without taking the time to define what they want customer service to mean. Instead, they approach the subject much like eating at a buffet—"I guess I'll try a little bit of that, that, and that."

A Customer Service Mission Statement is a brief statement expressing the overall direction for customer service. For example, "Providing service beyond your expectations" or "Meeting the challenge to put customers first."

The next step is to give the statement additional meaning by defining value statements. These statements provide more specific detail as to what must be done to ensure that the Mission Statement is alive and well in the organization. Think in terms of creating a customer service personality for your organization.

Involve Employees

A good procedure includes using employees to develop the Mission Statement and associated value statements. This encourages ownership. This is in contrast to the typical procedure where senior managers create a statement and then send a memorandum throughout the organization announcing the change.

Let's work with an example created by the employees of ABC financial institution (see box on opposite page).

The Bank's Commitment

To create its customer service personality, this financial institution is committed to asking customers to define their expectations. Then the bank will strive to exceed these, and measure the level of customer satisfaction. That means designing and implementing an aggressive market research campaign. That means a willingness to spend time and money.

Mission Statement
ABC Financial Institution

"Big enough to service you, and small enough to care."

The Underlying Values:

1. Eager to exceed the customer's expectations.

2. Use market research to define the customer's expectations and the degree these are being met.

3. Go the extra mile by defining and implementing procedures to show customers we really care.

4. Create inconveniences for ourselves, when necessary, to create conveniences for the customer.

5. Implement innovative customer service delivery systems.

6. Employees need to be trained and empowered.

7. The organization will work as a team to create the desired customer service environment.

8. The management structure is to remain focused and hold people accountable for implementation.

Note the commitment to show customers that the bank really cares, even if that creates inconveniences for employees.

The fifth value statement speaks to creating an innovative environment. Most organizations discourage new ideas.

New Ideas Needed

The rules have changed. The reason ideas were killed yesterday is the very reason ideas should be carefully considered today. Even if an idea did not work in the past, it may work today.

The employees are to be trained and empowered to deliver customer services. Employees are now going to be the valuable asset that is often discussed, but seldom realized.

Last, but not least, the employees decided to work as a team to deliver these services and to be held accountable to create their defined customer service environment.

Now you see the major transformation impact the Customer Service Mission Statement and value statements can have on the organization.

HOW DO YOU MEASURE GREAT SERVICE?

There is another prerequisite to get where you want to go. You must know your point of origin.

I often ask seminar participants, "How would you get to work tomorrow morning if you woke up and did not know where you were?" Obviously you wouldn't.

You need to quantify your point of origin. That can easily be done by using the value statements to generate a questionnaire to be completed by employees and/or customers.

Necessary Feedback

The value of quantifying the customer service mission statement is to serve as a baseline from which to measure improvements. Then you will want to collect these data every 12 to 18 months to measure progress.

Remember, to know where we are (with anything we do), information is a crucial feedback system. My fingers' nerve endings provide feedback that I'm touching the keyboard as I type this chapter. The same is true when you use customer service as your major marketing tool. Only by receiving feedback do you know where you are.

> Remember, most dissatisfied customers won't tell you...they just leave.

MAKING CUSTOMER SERVICE WORK

Customer Service Moments Of Truth

This concept was introduced by Jan Carlson in his book, *Moments of Truth.* Carlson implemented this concept to complete a financial

Bank Ignores Message of Litter

Returning from lunch with a bank's senior vice president, I noticed a child's shoe laying by the entrance, and jokingly commented about the bank's tough treatment of its customers. The VP looked at me and said, "That has been laying there for two days!"

Was this bank employee managing the moments of truth? Allowing the shoe to continue laying there, the bank communicated a lack of concern about details. Is that the bank you want taking care of your money?

turnaround of Scandinavian Airways.

A customer service moment of truth is *any interaction with the customer.*

This includes both personal and non-personal contact. A non-personal contact includes the physical appearance of the building, parking lot, stationery, or any other interactions which do not include eye-to-eye contact with an employee.

McDonald's offers a great example of a non-personal customer service contact. Many travelers use McDonald's as their designated rest stops, because of their clean restrooms.

Answering The Phone

The telephone greeting is often the first window through which a customer sees an organization. The typical employee greets callers with, "This is ABC Company, how may I direct your call?"

Opportunities to improve the traditional greeting include the following. Which one would you use?

- "Thank you for calling ABC Company, how may I help you?"
- "Thank you for calling ABC Company, this is _____, what may I do to help you?"

Many front-line receptionists resist introducing themselves on the telephone with the excuse, "I'm too busy." It's as if using one's name requires an inordinate amount of time. In fact, it personalizes the interaction and encourages customers to further the relationship by giving their names.

In contrast to most phone greeters, a receptionist in a North Arkansas bank slowly and clearly welcomes you, and introduces herself. She gives you the pleasant impression that you're her only customer. And, unless you think about it, you feel like the only customer. Now that's putting the customer in a positive frame of mind.

Use Your Moments Of Truth

Moments of truth must be defined to be managed. Literally walk a customer through the department and identify every interaction. Once these are identified, each interaction must be placed under the magnifying glass and the question asked, "How can this interaction be improved?"

Examine these moments of truth. How can you ensure each is as customer friendly as you can possibly make it?

It's disappointing to hear a manager say, "I don't think we can improve upon..." Obviously, a manager demonstrating this mentality to their staff will cre-

What Keeps Customers?

Consider research done by the Forum Corp. Fifteen percent of those who switched to a competitor did so because they "found a better product...Another 15 percent changed because they found a "cheaper product"...Twenty percent high-tailed it because of the "lack of contact and individual attention"...and 49% left because "contact from the old supplier's personnel was poor in quality." It seems fair to combine the last two categories, after which we could say 70 percent defected because they didn't like the human side of doing business with the previous product or service provider.

—Tom Peters

ate a non-thinking department. That is the kiss of death to a customer-service improvement process. I mention this to illustrate the important phenomenon that "fish rot from the head down." A rotting manager yields a rotting department. We cannot afford rot in today's rapidly changing, competitive environment.

Identifying, improving, and managing customer service moments of truth is the foundation for peak customer service performance. Create opportunities to ask your customers about improving these interactions. You may be surprised at the quality of their ideas when they are given the opportunity to share them.

Product Knowledge

It's easy to *assume* that employees know all about their organization's products and services. But there's an old saying about the embarrassing situation "assume" creates.

Speaking of embarrassment, our research shows that bank employees typically have a working knowledge of about 50 percent of the features associated with the banks' checking accounts.

Even new account representatives have only about a 60 percent level of knowledge of these features. Would you consider 50–60 percent an adequate knowledge level?

After calling in a pizza order to our local Pizza Hut, my wife wondered why two large pizzas were less than two mediums. So I asked that question of the person who waited on me. That person did not know. While I was talking to her, another employee came to her rescue, yet she didn't know.

> When you assume things about others you can make an ass of U and me.
>
> (ass • u • me)

These two employees asked a third who read the menu and said, "Yep, that's right." I gave the employee at the cash register money for the purchase. While she was working with it, the register quit working to which she promptly yelled, "Does anyone know how to work this thing?" Talk about the importance of product knowledge!

What Customers Expect

What message is sent when employees are asked about some aspect of their company and the answer is "I'm not sure who handles that, let's try ABC department." Even worse is "I don't know because that's not my department/responsibility."

Our focus group research shows that hotel customers expect front desk personnel to know the community as part of their "product knowledge." That means the location of shopping centers, restaurants and, in some instances, major events occurring in the community. These customers do not want to hear, "I don't know."

For instance, I recently visited an Olive Garden restaurant and watched a waiter explain how every entrée was cooked to four senior citizens who peppered him with questions. That was impressive!

The "I Don't Know" Options—Let Your Actions Do The Talking

What typically happens in organizations? Employees say "I don't know." Or, the Olive Garden waiter would run to the kitchen for the answers to these questions. Or some companies would send the patrons to another department.

"If you're looking up at me (the boss), you've got your ass pointed at the customer."
—Jack Welch, GE

We're impressed by company representatives who can answer our questions and solve our problems—and seem to enjoy doing so. That's why we continue as loyal customers, not because of fancy advertisement slogans.

The ironic fact is that those responsible for advertising dollars know that it's customer contact that develops loyal customers. Yet they continue to spend dollars to tell consumers they're customer service driven, rather than let their actions do the talking.

I've asked CEOs why they give lip service to customer service without backing it up. Are you ready for the answer? "Our competition is doing it so we must show our customers we're matching the competition." Such CEOs demonstrate a follower's mentality while wearing leader's clothing!

Decisions Made Closer To The Customer

It is just good common sense for every employee to be armed with the knowledge and authority to work with their customers. It's extremely annoying to be discussing a concern with an employee who makes the statement, "I have to check with my supervisor."

Then you wait while the employee searches for the supervisor. Once found, you repeat the same information you provided to the first employee.

Don't Take the Monkey

William Oncken, Jr. pointed out that employees will delegate TO their bosses by asking questions about how to solve problems. Don't take the monkey on your back. Make them come to you with suggested solutions too. (From Managing Management Time)

You fervently hope this person has the necessary authority to resolve your questions and concerns.

Interacting with some organizations is even worse than the simple transaction described above. Most companies will agree that this scenario is not good customer service. But nothing is done about it. Yet, they want a loyal customer base. Does this make sense?

Customer service is an integral component of any marketing campaign. Decision making must be as close as possible to the customer. Any question taken to a supervisor should be a red flag, a signal for change. Ask "Who should answer this question?" The answer, "The employee closest to the customer."

Use Questions

Here's the process to reengineer your customer service:

1. Identify every question that is presented to the up-line supervisor.
2. Once identified, decide who will provide future answers to that question.
3. Provide employees with the knowledge and authority to make the decisions.
4. Monitor the success of this procedure.
5. Constantly empower employees to take more and more responsibility to please customers.

Creating The "WoW" Factor

Scott Gross popularized the concept of the "WoW Factor" in his book *Positively Outrageous Customer Service*. He suggests doing the unexpected for customers. For example, one of my clients had to reschedule an appointment two days before the planned visit. This was an inconvenience to me, as the date had been scheduled for several weeks. On the day I would have been at the client's office, a beautifully wrapped package of Corky's Barbecue arrived in the office. That was a "WoW from the client to me!"

Here are more WoWs! A bank learned that one of its customers was ill but needed to transact business. The president of the bank made a house call to take care of it.

While enjoying a hamburger that my wife and I had taken out from Brangus Steakhouse, an employee called to check on the quality of the food. Have you ever been contacted by a fast food service regarding the quality of the food? Neither had we.

Have you ever had a bank teller order your lunch? Yes, the customer made a deposit at the drive through and asked the teller to order a hamburger at the local fast food restaurant! Obviously, this would not be appropriate for every bank branch office, but it worked for this one.

Customer Recovery WoW

It's even more important to WoW customers when you've made a mistake. But what usually happens? We get an "I'm sorry for the inconvenience." And hopefully the problem is fixed.

But not always. During a Christmas shopping trip, an acquaintance and her daughter shopped a well-known department store. After they had left and were putting packages into their car, a store employee ran up to them and asked them to return. The security buzzer had sounded the alarm when they left the store.

Nothing was purchased in that store, so the mother was dumbfounded, but followed the persistent employee back to the store. She then had to unwrap the several packages. It turned out that the security device had not been removed from an

> "In whatever you do...make sure there is a 'wow factor,' something that will grab people's attention and make them notice that you've sweated the details."
> —Carl Sewell
> *Customers for Life*

article of clothing purchased in another store.

After locating the problem, did the store offer to rewrap the Christmas packages? No.

Was anything offered to compensate for the inconvenience and embarrassment? No.

Did that store lose a customer? Yes. Upon returning home, she immediately cut up the store's credit card.

Has she told others about this incident? You bet she has.

What Could They Have Done?

At the minimum, the store should have rewrapped the packages. The store employee *could* have been authorized to provide a coupon or gift certificate to demonstrate compassionate caring, and to ensure she returns to spend future dollars. If they had, perhaps the customer would be advertising a "WoW" today.

Another example is the bank customer who parked in a metered parking spot while conducting bank business. As luck would have it, time expired and a friendly policeman issued him a ticket. The customer promptly took it into the bank and asked a bank employee to compensate him for the ticket.

The employee did not have the authority to do that. This irritated the customer who promptly withdrew his money, which was reported to be a seven-digit number. Ouch!

Setting Up A Great Service System

There are only four procedures that a company must implement to provide extra value customer service.

1. Give employees the authority to ask the customer what can be done to compensate him or her the first time the inconvenience occurs or the authority to do something to elicit a "WoW!" This is the only way to prepare for the unexpected.

2. Create a record of each problem. Flag it for steps three and four.

Recovery Essential For Legendary Service
by Ken Blanchard

Legendary Service describes service so good your customers want to brag about it. When I developed a program on this with Rick Tate and Gary Heil, we felt that the most important part of creating legendary service is story generation. If your customers are telling positive stories about you and your service, you could not ask for—or buy—better publicity.

One of the best sources for service stories is all-out recovery. Recovery means if you make a mistake with a customer, you do *whatever* is needed to fix the problem and create, or win back, a devoted customer.

Customer Recovery In Advance!

Let me give you an example of the power of customer service recovery. A hotel in Southern California had a history of poor guest comment ratings. A foreign owner took over the hotel. The new owner felt the poor guest comments were the result of a worn-out and battered physical plant. They put millions of dollars into refurbishing the hotel. The general manager brought all the hotel workers together and told them, "It's going to be tough sledding around here the next nine to twelve months. The noise and inconvenience may not be popular with our guests. Do whatever it takes to recover from any inconvenience caused by our refurbishing. If you want to send someone a bottle of wine, do so. If you want to hire a baby sitter for them, do it. Do whatever it takes to recover from this bad situation."

Empowered Workers

The hotel entered their remodeling phase. Management was amazed that guest comment ratings were now the highest ever in the history of the hotel. Guests' memories of their experience with the hotel were formed by the customer-oriented staff that was willing to admit when things went wrong and recover as well as they could.

Don't Penalize Your Good Customers

Most businesses believe that fewer than 10–15% of the people are out to take advantage of them, while the majority—85–90% of their customers—are basically honest and loyal. Yet many businesses set all their policies, procedures, and practices to try to catch the 10–15% and miss out in servicing the 85–90%.

3. Define a new standard operating procedure to correct the problem.
4. Define what can be done to walk the extra mile to show the customer you really care. For instance, a local bank offers customers $10 for any error that occurs during a bank transaction.

If there is any doubt about what can be done to walk the extra mile, then ask your customers. I'm sure they will be willing to tell you in a focus or discussion group, or via a written survey. What do you have to lose? Money—if you do not show customers you care!

An inconvenience should never happen a second time without a plan to go the extra mile to WoW the customer.

Out-Of-The-Box Customer Services

Ask most executives why their company spends so much money advertising their customer service. A typical response is, "Other companies are doing it." That attitude says, "We've got to keep up with the Joneses."

Instead, why not be the Joneses? What about setting the pace for other companies in your industry to follow?

If you follow the crowd, you'll go where the crowd goes. Is that where you want to go?

Old vs. New Approaches

I'm sure I couldn't come close to guessing what AT&T, MCI, and Sprint spend on advertising and telemarketing to convince us they should be our long distance carrier.

Here's how a brand new phone company, Excel, attacked these powerful players. They were recently included as number 72 in *Inc.* magazine's annual rating of the top 500 privately held companies. They are now the sixth largest long distance carrier.

Here's how they did it. The owners made a conscious effort to market differently, to "get out of the box." Excel doesn't spend millions of dollars splashing its name all over the news media. Instead, it markets its service through networking. Individual consumers build a business by asking others to switch their long distance carrier and helping others to establish their businesses. This is one-to-one marketing in a normal mass market.

More Creative Marketing

There is a computer manufacturing company that is also enjoying out-of-the-box thinking. Gateway sells directly to the consumer. They use catalogs, ads, and telemarketing.

A bank in Missouri also decided on a non-traditional course. The president gave each teller a desk! Imagine not walking up to a teller window. Consumers like this idea.

More subtle out-of-the-box thinking is the bank that decided to allow new account representatives to take deposits at their desks. This procedure saved time and allowed the bank representative to remain with the new customer during the entire transaction.

Customers are important. You don't leave important people during a transaction.

How To Up Your "Creativity Quotient"

What are the requirements to be an out-of-the-box leader? The answer: creative thinking. Here are some techniques to create this level of thinking:

1. **Hold brainstorming sessions.** The department manager schedules such sessions to generate ideas for non-traditional

service delivery and stimulate thinking.

2. **Visit competitors.** Study your competition and build on their ideas. Shop your competitors when possible.

Brainstorming Rules
1. Free associate
2. Bounce off other ideas
3. No criticism
4. No discussion
5. No questions
6. The wackier the better

3. **Read.** Search trade journals and books for additional ideas. Ask the staff to participate in this reading. Have them report what your department can do to use what was read.

4. **Follow other industries.** What are other companies doing that your department may be able to incorporate?

There is nothing magical or mystical about creative thinking. It simply needs an environment that encourages such thinking and a corporate culture ready to try new ideas.

Leaders enjoy being creative.

Do you want to be a follower or a leader? You can't be a leader with a follower mentality.

CUSTOMER SERVICE MEETINGS

Pulling It All Together

I've got a challenge for you. Record the amount of time employees in your department or organization spend each month deciding how to improve customer service.

Be careful—your heart may be in for a shock. Based on my research, most companies have zero meetings to discuss improvements in their customer service delivery system!

Invest The Time

How can you improve if you don't spend time planning for improvements? It isn't going to happen by itself.

I'm always amused when I ask personnel in service industries to identify the amount of time they could devote to improving the customer service delivery system. The most frequent response is, "perhaps an hour a month." When asked, "Why only one hour a month?" the typical answer is, "We are meeting to death as it is."

Think about what is being said. You may be able to find 12 hours in a 2,080-hour work year to devote to improving customer service! Does that make any sense?

The real problem is not the number of meetings your organization holds, it's the inefficiency. The meetings usually begin at least ten minutes later than scheduled. Participants chew up valuable time by straying from the topic. There is no agenda, thus members are ill-prepared. Attendees are called out of the meeting for "important" telephone calls. Finally, there is a lot of discussion with no decisions. Consequently meetings run overtime, and people leave the meetings frustrated.

Meetings That Focus on Customer Service

Meetings are perceived as "lumps of coal" instead of the "diamonds" they are intended to be. Consequently, you probably are not going to like my suggestion of weekly customer service meetings.

The intent of this chapter is not how to conduct efficient meetings. But you can make excellent progress by avoiding the pitfalls listed in the previous paragraph.

Agenda-driven customer service meetings focus on the following topics:

- Identification of, and improvement on, customer service moments-of-truth.
- Training and testing on product knowledge.
- Listening to other departments present their priorities.
- Improving coordination between departments to better serve customers.
- Identification of decisions that need to be made closer to the customer, with implementation of procedures to do so, and evaluation of the impact on customer satisfaction.
- Identification of inconveniences your department creates for the customer, and the

Creative Meeting Tips

- Schedule meetings before or after work, 7:30 am or 5:00 pm. This saves valuable nine-to-five hours and encourages people to keep meetings short.
- When it's time for the meeting to begin, put all extra chairs against the walls. Latecomers will have to sit outside the circle.
- If you want to get even tougher with latecomers, lock the door. The latecomer will have to make an obvious and embarrassing entrance.
- Don't use chairs. Stand-up meetings are shorter.
- Keep the number of participants to a minimum. As the size of the meeting increases, decision-making effectiveness decreases.

development of solutions to prevent a reoccurrence.

- Deciding what can be done to cause your customers to exclaim "WoW!"
- Defining, implementing, and evaluating nontraditional customer-service delivery systems.
- Setting up a reward system for great customer service.
- Collection and analysis of customer satisfaction data, with changes based on the results.
- Review of journal articles, books, videos, and visits the staff has made to mystery shop or benchmark competitors.

These are plenty of agenda items for a weekly meeting. And once employees know you are serious, they'll come up with more. Any manager who thinks otherwise is certainly not customer service driven.

Accountability

There is no question about the importance of accountability to keep your customer service focus. Where is the accountability in many organizations? There is none!

Accountability does not have to be a complicated process, as can be seen in the accountability table on the next page. It summarizes accountability for each phase of the customer service process.

Creating A Customer Service Culture

Let's look at accountability from the CEO's perspective, and then cascade it throughout the organization.

> "Be like the company that keeps one chair empty at all management meetings. The chair is for the customer who should have a say in all policy decisions."
>
> —John Schuster, *Hum-Drum to Hot-Diggity*

Accountability Chart	
Phase	*How you know it's completed*
Customer service mission statement	Completed statement and values
How to measure	Collect data and changes made based on this data
Moments of truth	Identified and defined; Progress reports on improvements
Product knowledge	Tests and completed training
Decisions made closer to the customer	Track and count the decisions
Creating the WoW	Customer feedback
Out-of-the-box thinking	Count suggestions

First, the CEO needs r*egularly scheduled* reports based on the information presented in the preceding table. These reports are completed as scheduled. All lower-level managers complete their respective responsibilities according to a defined time schedule so the CEO receives their report.

Your organization may also consider a procedure whereby every department manager is expected to implement improvements to the customer service delivery system on an ongoing basis. Some of you will reject this idea based on the premise that such scheduled and forced procedures encourage the flow of junk ideas. If that's the case, then there is a manager who is not doing his or her job.

The accountability procedure does not need to be cumbersome, complicated, or time-consuming. Keep it simple. But hold people accountable for implementing improvements.

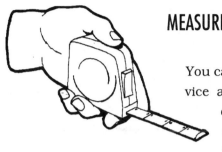

MEASURE, MEASURE, AND MEASURE SOME MORE

You can measure your customer service at many levels. Earlier in the chapter, I discussed the importance of quantifying the Customer Service Mission Statement, and the importance of remeasuring at 12–18 month intervals to monitor progress.

Scheduling ongoing discussion groups with consumers can provide extremely valuable data. The two major topics for discussion will be:

- to further identify areas for continued improvement, and
- to examine the satisfaction levels of implemented changes.

Customer Comment Cards

Customer comment cards are another valuable tool. For example, we have designed comment cards for use by outside sales staff. These are given to prospects and cus-

How Are We Doing?

Recalling the last time you called our office, was the person who answered the phone:
___ Friendly
___ Impolite
___ Neutral

Was the first person you spoke with able to answer your question or concern?
___ Yes   ___ No

If your answer to the question above was "no," were you promptly steered to the appropriate person?
___ Yes   ___ No

tomers to measure their satisfaction with the company and sales staff.

A specific, brief comment card can be used to measure a variety of changes. The procedure does not have to be a complicated one.

The important point is—collect information!

ACTION AGENDA

Customer service is the heart of successful marketing. Customer service is the heart of any business. To deliver great customer service, you must have a plan and a process.

- Create your mission and values statements.
- Define your contact "moments of truth" with customers.
- Designate a time to collect customer satisfaction data.
- Create a regular meeting time to discuss customer service issues.
- Involve employees by offering incentives for new service ideas.
- Test employees on product knowledge.
- Keep a record of new customer problems.
- Decide how you can WoW customers.
- Shop your competitors.
- Listen to how your staff answers the phone, and then determine how you want the phone to be answered.
- Empower employees to do anything to recover from a customer problem.

Chapter 5

PROFITABLE PROSPECTING
Getting Results With Client Newsletters

Mary Lou Gutscher

Mary Lou Gutscher is a professional speaker, author, and program development specialist. She heads a team of coaches and consultants specializing in helping clients market themselves more effectively.

Gutscher is president of M L Communications, Inc., publishers of client newsletter services and other professional communication tools for the life insurance and financial planning industry. Gutscher and her associates counsel clients on how to use marketing tools in their overall sales strategies. Through a proven training and coaching process, clients achieve increased revenues, improved appointment ratios, better retention of clients, and more quality referrals—referrals which produce a shorter selling cycle and a higher average sale than most other prospects.

When this Results System™ approach is applied to exclusive programs developed for commissioned sales-driven companies, the added benefit to the company is an improvement in the relationship with the field force.

Mary Lou Gutscher, M L Communications, Inc., 100 Sheldon Drive, Unit 28, Cambridge, Ontario N1R 7S7, Canada; phone (800) 387-6058, (519) 622-7100; fax (519) 622-7102; e-mail 102767,2645@compuserve.com

PROFITABLE PROSPECTING
Getting Results With Client Newsletters

Mary Lou Gutscher

Welcome to a new world of results.

Over the last decade, I've worked with more than 5,000 sales professionals, helping them to market themselves more effectively. Many of these clients get outstanding results using a client newsletter.

Here are a few examples of what I mean:

> *"I wrote my first million dollar case as a result of my newsletter!" —Glen P.*

> *"Each time I send out my newsletter, my sales jump by 25 to 35%." —Russ W.*

> *"I get an average of 50 referrals and 25 new clients through my newsletter every year!" —Victor C.*

> *"10 new clients in my first six months!" —Marianne P.*

> *"My client retention rate has gone from 90 to 95% since using newsletters." —Denis L.*

"From time to time, I'd sense some resistance when trying to arrange an appointment with a client I hadn't seen for some time. This resistance has disappeared since I've been sending newsletters to them on a regular basis. My newsletter also fits well with my philosophy of building long-term, solid relationships with my clients." —Gwen H.

Most of these comments came from sales professionals whose results are in the top three percent in their industry. Their newsletters helped get them there. And newsletters help them stay there, year after year.

GET RID OF NEWSLETTER MISCONCEPTIONS

Let's start with some common misconceptions about what a client newsletter is. You need to understand what it can and can't do for you.

Newsletters Won't Do Your Selling For You

With existing contacts, newsletters help you provide quality service to your clients. And they make it easier to ask for and get a continuous stream of high quality referrals.

> "Forget information overload. All people crave information and, even more, being 'in the loop.'"
>
> —Tom Peters

With new contacts, newsletters make it easier to get the first appointment with a prospect. And they make it easier to close a prospect in one appointment instead of two.

Newsletters make your job easier.

You are the sales professional. Your newsletter is one tool that you can use to get better results. The secret is to use this marketing tool creatively and effectively.

Oh, once in a while, you'll get lucky. You'll have an article in your newsletter that hits a client's or prospect's desk at just the right time, and you'll get a call that leads to a nice big sale. That's why the content of your newsletter is important, and why frequent and consistent contact is critical.

But if you rely solely on your newsletter to generate those easy sales for you, you'll have trouble meeting your mortgage payments!

Just Because It's Called A Client Newsletter, Doesn't Mean It's Only For Clients

A good client newsletter is the single most versatile prospecting tool for attracting prospects that you can find. I've used newsletters myself, in associations, retail operations, and in direct sales.

I've seen firsthand how much more profitable prospecting can be when you use a client newsletter as a marketing tool.

Our research shows that almost everyone starts by sending their newsletter just to clients. Even after several years, sales professionals in our test group are still sending 70-95% of their newsletters to clients.

That's OK, because clients deserve that extra service as a thank you for their business.

Even more important, it's a good idea to send your newsletter to your clients because your clients are your best prospects!

But they're not your only prospects.

To make your newsletter a profitable prospecting tool, you must include all of your other prospects in your newsletter marketing plan.

FOCUS ON THE THREE Rs FOR RESULTS

The key to success with your client newsletter is a system that gets results in these three areas:

Revenues, from new clients
and from existing clients

Retention of clients

Referrals, your second-best prospects, next to your clients themselves

You already work to market yourself, sell, and maintain good relationships with your clients. To enhance your results, you'll need to develop and integrate a system for using your newsletters effectively.

THE RESULTS SYSTEM

The system that we teach our clients is called The Results System, and consists of these four proven steps:

One Client's Story

"I worked with one very prosperous client for almost 11 years, and tried everything to get him to give me referrals, but to no avail. He just said that he never gave referrals. Then I tried what Mary Lou suggested and offered to send a newsletter to his associates. He laughed and said, "Is this another attempt to get referrals from me?" I admitted that it was, but a good way for him to acknowledge his associates as well. He was impressed. And he gave me three referrals!"

> **Marketing Plan**
>
> - Generate 30 referrals this month.
> - Send newsletters to 100 top prospects in target industry.
> - Follow up with phone call one week later.
> - Develop new brochure.

1 **Identify your goals and write them down.** Make them time-specific and measurable, for example: I will generate 30 referrals a month, or I will increase my average size order by 10% in the next six months.

2 **Identify your market and write it down.** This is a market where you can best use your unique ability to produce outstanding service for your clients. (And you can obtain an outstanding income and sense of satisfaction for yourself.) Look at your existing client base to see where your best market already is. Then focus 80% of your attention on developing that market. (See the computer disk for a planning worksheet.)

3 **Develop a plan of action and write it down.** This includes mapping out a schedule of mailings and follow up calls. Write and use special cover letters for specific circumstances. Prepare and practice scripts (the words that work the best to make you and your prospects comfortable). And prepare the back-up support to handle all the extra business you'll generate once you get started!

4 **Start now.** As the Chinese say, "A journey of 1000 miles begins with the first step." Take the first easy step and start talking about your newsletter with your clients. With the right approach, you'll find you can get appointments to write new business, and start generating referrals before you do your first newsletter.

NEWSLETTERS WARM UP PROSPECTS

Market research in the financial services industry shows that when you send your newsletter to a prospect five times before calling, the prospect thinks he knows you when you call. Karl proves this with his prospecting method.

Karl sends his newsletter to business people with whom he'd like to do business. This is part of his system of "warehousing" prospects. He religiously adds ten names to his warehousing list every week. Karl chooses the list to use, and his assistant handles the details as part of her weekly routine.

Prospects Are Ready

After the fifth newsletter, Karl shows up at the prospect's office. When he shakes hands with the prospect, he may say something like this, "Hi, I'm Karl. I'm the one who's been sending you my newsletter every two months, and I'm here to apply for the job—the job as your financial advisor."

Karl's closing ratio on appointments and on acquiring new clients is exactly the opposite of industry statistics. It is generally held that for every ten qualified prospects you call, you'll get three appointments, and close one sale. This is a ratio of 10-3-1.

---

4 Marketing Levels

Newsletters function at four different marketing levels to help you RISE above the competition.

R ecognition. Your prospects need to know who you are, where to find you, and what you do before they do business with you.

I mage. You create an image for yourself in print.

S pecifics. Tell readers exactly what you can do for them.

E nactment. Show and tell readers what you want them to do (like contact you).

—Elaine Floyd,
Marketing With Newsletters

Out of ten qualified prospects, the average salesperson gets three appointments and closes one sale.

Using newsletters to warm up prospects, one salesperson gets nine out of ten appointments, and closes seven in the first year, two more in the second year.

In Karl's case, he gets the appointment with 9 out of 10 people. He closes 7 of them in the first year. The other two, he closes in the following year, for a total prospect to client ratio of 90% over two years: 10-9-9.

Even One Newsletter Helps

Susan had a booth at a trade show aimed at the retirement market. She gave away a free newsletter subscription in a drawing to attract people. This brought her quite a few names of prospects to call after the show.

Unfortunately, when she followed up to arrange appointments to help them with their financial affairs, there was a lot of resistance. This is a natural tendency for those around retirement age. After all, they've worked hard all their lives to save what they have. Why should they risk it all by trusting a stranger?

She was not satisfied with her results with the first group of names she called. So instead of giving just one newsletter subscription to the drawing winner, Susan sent out a copy to each person on her list. Then she followed up and tried again to get appointments. This time her results were more than 25% better, with just one newsletter in between.

NEWSLETTERS STRENGTHEN RELATIONSHIPS

We conducted an informal study of a group of prospects who we hadn't spoken to since a trade show a year before. In the meantime, I had sent them six newsletters with my name and photo on them, one every two months.

When we met again, after greeting the prospect, I casually said, "When was it that we spoke last?" The answers were consistent—everyone thought it was within the last two or three months!

Keep In Touch

This tells me that, once you've established a relationship with a prospect or client, your newsletter makes the time between visits seem shorter—much shorter.

Why is this important? After all, a salesperson's job is to follow up all leads as quickly as possible, isn't it?

That's the theory. But, in fact, not all prospects are equal. At any point in time, you should have more prospects than you can effectively follow up in person. This is especially true if you attend trade shows and gather business cards, as we do in our business. Your newsletter can keep these prospects warm. With a good marketing strategy, it will help qualify which of these prospects to call first.

Better Client Contact

When you first signed up a client, you intended to make follow-up calls at least several times every year, didn't you?

When your client base reaches a certain size, it becomes impossible to maintain that frequency of calls to every client. And some clients deserve more.

Research in the life insurance industry shows that top producers make contact with their most valuable clients at least eight to ten times a year. Your newsletter allows you to maintain this momentum, by

Follow up with clients

taking care of four to six of those contacts, and adding value to your client relationships at the same time.

YOUR NEWSLETTER: AN EXPENSE OR AN INVESTMENT?

Those who use their newsletters only as a method for keeping in touch usually have no objective way of measuring their results. A casual comment from a client may be the only feedback they get. Or, they may see the newsletter on the desk or table of a client when they meet. As Alex C. says, "Whenever I see my newsletter on a client's desk, I know we're going to write business before the meeting's over."

But cost control is a fact of life in every business. Somewhere down the line, you'll have to ask yourself, "Is this newsletter really working for me"?

At the very least, you must arrange to deliver your newsletters. That's an expense. And whether you produce it yourself or purchase an outside service, you must still pay for the newsletter itself. That's another expense.

NEWSLETTER MISTAKES

If your focus is on controlling expenses, you might be tempted to break one of these rules.

1 **Never make your clients pay for their newsletter subscriptions.** Here's how this can look from your clients' perspective: "Okay,

when did you get into the newsletter publishing and direct mail business? I thought you were selling XYZ, and XYZ is what I need!" You can also leave the impression that you want to nickel and dime your clients for every cent you can get. Not a good image!

2 Don't write a letter and say "This newsletter costs me money, so I'll continue it only if you check this box."

From your clients' perspective: "Thanks a lot. Is that all my business is worth to you?"

Besides, busy people may not notice your note, or get around to responding. Then they'd lose a service that they do appreciate.

3 Don't reduce your mailing list to reduce costs. From your clients' perspective: "I wonder what happened to George. He's not sending a newsletter anymore. Maybe he's fallen on hard times."

How long can your sales operation sustain that kind of image?

You get the picture. When you cut people off, you create a negative image, not a positive one. You throw the money already spent down the drain.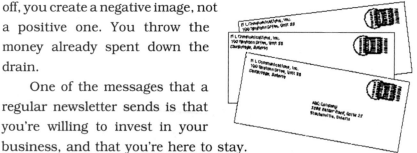

One of the messages that a regular newsletter sends is that you're willing to invest in your business, and that you're here to stay. Newsletters require a commitment on your part. So don't make the decision lightly. Don't say, "I'll try it for a few months, and if it doesn't work, I'll drop it." Only make the commitment as part of the way you want to do business from now on.

GET A GOOD RETURN ON YOUR INVESTMENT

You can meet your long term newsletter commitment more easily by making sure you get a consistently good return on your investment. You owe this to yourself and to your clients.

When you save or invest money in CDs, bonds, stocks, or investment funds, what sort of steady return do you expect to get? 6%? 10%? 12%? 15%? Perhaps even as much as 20%?

If you don't like the return you're getting, you can move your savings into better performing investments.

You have the same flexibility with your newsletter. If the first thing you try doesn't work as well as you thought, you can change your strategy and try something else. But one thing's for certain. You will get a significant return on your investment if you put some thought and effort into it.

HOW ABOUT A 1000% RETURN ON INVESTMENT?

It's quite normal for our clients to achieve a 1000% return on their newsletter investment in the first year! And after that, the return builds on itself through referrals and extra business. Here are a few examples:

Example # 1: New Reps Get A Fast Start

Company A has a field development program for new representatives, which, among other things, teaches new sales agents to get two referrals during each face-to-face appointment with a prospect or client. The reps are required to track the details of their first 30 appointments, and list the referrals they get. Although the importance of referrals is stressed in the training program, the average for referrals for new reps is only five or six total referrals from the first 30 interviews.

Manager Recommends Newsletters

Mike was himself a top-producing representative and sales manager earlier in his career. He was impressed with the results he'd gotten from his own newsletter, and wanted to improve the productivity of his new agents. He brought in one of our specialists to conduct a workshop on how to use newsletters with two new reps. When the reps offered complimentary newsletters, they found it easier to get the referrals.

Both of these sales reps went on to achieve the two referrals per appointment average. One of them, Tim, actually generated 62 referrals in his first two weeks.

Improvement over previous methods—1,000%!

Even Generic Newsletters Work

These referrals were generated before these new reps had their own personalized newsletters. Their initial newsletters were provided by their manager. Mike's investment in those first 90 newsletters each (30 for the prospects, and 60 for the referrals), was

How Do Increased Referrals Translate Into Dollars?

New reps will normally close about half of their referrals within six to nine months. The average commission from a new client is $300. Tim's extra 56 referrals (62 minus the normal average of 6), will produce this extra revenue for him:

(56/2) = 28 new clients X $300 commission = $8400

The cost of this newsletter service for the first year was $756. (All figures quoted include postage, envelopes, reply cards, and clerical wages to mail them.)

That's a return on investment of 1,011%! Not bad for a beginner.

only about $72. The real return on investment could be calculated on just that initial investment, which is what did the trick to get them started. If we include an average fee of $250 per rep to attend a workshop, then Mike's investment is $322 to achieve an improvement of $8400.

That's a return on investment of 2,508%!

Example #2: Big Sale To Kick Off Continuing Returns

Russ's clients appreciated the work he had done for them in taking care of their basic insurance and financial planning needs. But most of them were not aware that he could also help

them with more sophisticated estate preservation and business planning situations, because he hadn't approached them about these issues before. Russ's first newsletter issue contained several articles which dealt with more complex estate planning issues, and raised his clients' awareness of Russ's capabilities in these areas.

Russ tells us, "Within the first two months of using the newsletter, I wrote a case that generated enough commissions to pay for the newsletter for a full year. So it is working! I just placed another $9,500 case with that same client."

Because commissions are paid on a graduated scale over the life of the policies, a conservative estimate of the value of these cases to Russ is about $10,000, given his good record of client retention.

Russ's total newsletter investment in his first year—$900.

Russ's return on investment— over 1,000%!

If we look only at Russ's investment for his first newsletter issue, which is when these results were achieved, then his return on investment is an astounding 4,900%!

Example #3: Steady Returns for a Sales Veteran

Victor was a creative sales professional. He enjoyed his work. He enjoyed his clients. He liked to have fun with them and had a very light-hearted approach to his life and his business. He worked hard, very hard, and studied hard, but he absolutely loved what he did for a living.

He told me the story of a client, a farmer, whose newsletter got slightly chewed at the edges by a mouse in the night. After that, Victor would brag to his clients that his newsletter was so good, even mice liked it! Perhaps they knew someone who might like to try it?

Every year, when Victor sent back the survey that we request from our clients, he'd tell us that he got at least another 50 referrals and 25 new clients through his newsletters.

At an average first-year commission for each client, that meant about $25,000 in extra income for Victor. He sent newsletters to more people than average because he enjoyed providing this extra service to those who helped him in his business. His average newsletter cost per year was about $2150.

Victor's return on investment—1,063%, year after year.

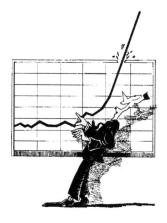

Example #4: Client Retention

After sending several issues of his newsletter to his top clients, here's what Andy told us:

"Just this week, I learned that an agent tried to replace one of my Universal Life policies. My client ended the conversation by saying, "My agent sends me a newsletter every two months. He cares and he keeps me informed." What impressed me was that this client put such weight on the newsletter!

Andy's newsletter saved his client from possibly making a bad decision, and saved Andy from a commission charge-back—not to mention the value of the continuing relationship with his client.

Andy's long-term relationship with this client could easily be worth $14,000 to $15,000 in commissions, not to mention the value of referrals.

His first year's investment in his newsletters was about $1,200.

The return on investment—1,066%.

DON'T PLAY A NUMBERS GAME

Activity-based selling has been the focus of sales training for many years. Years ago, I heard Zig Ziglar speak at a Sales Achievement conference. He told the story of two sales people, each with a different script, knocking on doors on either side of a street. The first one used an approach that had proven very effective over time. The second one simply said, "You don't want any insurance today, do you?" The test was to prove that Persistence Pays. No matter how inexperienced you are, if you just keep knocking on enough doors, you'll eventually get a sale.

Even A Bad Approach Can Work

As I remember it, the first salesman was invited in after the fourth or fifth attempt. And the second salesman kept knocking on doors—"You don't want any insurance today, do you?" "You don't want any insurance today, do you?" And sure enough, after the 62nd door, someone said, "As a matter of fact, I do! Come on in!"

Why Not Use A Good Approach?

Although the story made its point, there is a downside to it—that salespeople are still being taught to approach people cold, with a canned pitch. They're told that it's just a numbers game. No wonder the sales profession still has an image problem. Yet it's really one of the most important roles played in any economy.

In the life insurance industry, many successful sales people are still using this activity-driven approach—not knocking on doors, but sending out 50 letters a week, followed by a phone call to try to get the appointment. Result? Two or three appointments a week from these efforts. Oh, some prospects do come through later, after developing a relationship with them, but this is a 94-96% rejection rate on the first pass!

> Newsletters are the single most versatile tool you can buy to market yourself more effectively. And they're easy to use.

RELATIONSHIPS + PRO-ACTIVITY = RESULTS

Newsletters help build relationships, but it's you who must use your newsletter proactively. When you do, your newsletters bring much better results.

Newsletters give you a legitimate reason to call and a starting point for your conversations. They make an excellent complimentary gift to introduce yourself to your clients' friends and associates. A newsletter reminds people of what a professional you really are. It tells people that you're there to serve them, that you're in business to stay, that you understand their needs, and that you care enough to make an investment in your relationship with them.

RELATIONSHIP SELLING AT ITS BEST

Don agrees. He literally "changed his mind" after being in the sales business for a few years. He decided to become "The Newsletter Man," using his newsletter as a communication bridge wherever possible. All it took was a shift in thinking. Don's good work habits did the rest.

Don retired early from a life-long career in public education. In the mid-1980s, he started a second career as an insurance and financial advisor.

GET PUBLICITY TOO

Your newsletter can also be used to build relationships with the media. Put the trade press and local papers on your mailing list. When you call them, they'll know you. They may even call you.

"The media is your customer. In today's environment with more competition, more products and more media, the press can be an ally."

—Tom Peters

A Consulting Approach

He earned his income on commissions from the products he sold, and took a consultative planning approach with his clients.

After four years, Don had run out of his natural market. He had sold to everyone he knew and needed to expand his market. The most effective way for him to do that was to become "referable." Even though he had used a newsletter all those years, it had not achieved near its potential for him, because he was simply using it to "keep in touch."

Good Results Get Better

Don heard me speak at a Million Dollar Round Table annual meeting, and joined our newsletter program in August 1989. He broke all personal records that year. The last 12 cases he wrote were all referrals from his newsletter.

In the past few years, Don's decided to slow down a bit, take more vacation, and cut back his hours to about 20 a week.

In spite of less time on the job, last year Don's income was triple what it was in 1989. And he attributes all the new income he's earned in that time to the use of his newsletter. As Don says, "I literally could not get referrals, no matter how many times I asked, until I started using Mary Lou's approach. Since then, virtually all of my business has come either from existing clients or referrals. I'd say that my newsletter has helped me create at least half of my income over the last six years." Here's how Don does it:

PERSONALIZE YOUR NEWSLETTER

Don sends his newsletter to all of his best clients and to those who have the most influence over others. In his circles, they are school superintendents, principals, and those who are on the executive committeesof various organizations, including the golf and country club.

Every issue, six times a year, he takes the time to "visit" with

ADD PERSONAL NOTES

Many of the successful people I know are constantly sending out short notes...It takes only a moment. It's all a matter of personal recognition and courtesy.

—Harvey Mackay, *How to Swim With the Sharks Without Getting Eaten Alive*

his clients by writing personal notes to them along with their newsletters. Sometimes it's a note in the margin—"Bill: I thought you'd enjoy this article." Sometimes it's a separate note attached, and sometimes a word-processed letter that draws attention to a particular article.

Follow Up For Sales

Don follows up with a phone call, setting aside a few days every other month to do that. He uses the topics in his newsletter to open the discussion and zero in on the services his clients and prospects need right now. He also offers to provide copies of the newsletter to anyone who his clients refer to him.

Says Don, "I know my clients are happy in our relationship, and glad to see me when it's time to talk business."

Once a year, in advance of the deadline for tax-deferred retirement savings, he mails his newsletter to all of his clients. This year, Don sent a pen with each newsletter. With some, he jotted a note, "Mark me on your

Newsletters Get Speaking Engagements

Don also provides copies of his newsletter for the teachers' lounges at various schools. Soon after starting this program, Don was invited to speak to a group of teachers and principals. What a great way to position yourself as the expert! Don has since done several seminars a year, and it was at one such seminar that his manager recruited one of Don's clients into the insurance business.

calendar," or, "Here's a pen you can use to write your check this year." The response was super. Most clients simply picked up the phone and called Don to thank him, and to set a time to take care of their retirement savings needs.

Some came to his office, gift pen in hand, and wrote him a check with it! As Don says, "These were not just $2,000 or $3,000 checks. Most of them were making the maximum allowable contribution to their plans!"

And now, Don's sons are getting started in the same industry. He has advised them to use newsletters right off the bat. And to follow in Dad's successful footsteps, he's recommending that they work with a publisher to provide their newsletter for them, so they can focus on building relationships.

NEWSLETTERS DO MORE

Newsletters can do more than set up sales to customers.

Example #5: Manager's Recruiting Results Improved

Another manager started using newsletters for recruiting in May. In February of the following year he brought five new producers into the business, more than doubled his previous years' results. And he attributed the improvement to the use of his newsletter.

Here's how he did it.

First, we designed a personalized imprint for his newsletter that positioned him as the one to see for a career in sales.

The manager sent two copies of his newsletter to his producers at home, and suggested that they keep one, and pass one on to someone who might be interested in meeting him and talking about a career with the company. He told us that after each mailing, the phone rang off the hook.

Don't Forget Referral Sources

He also sent copies of his newsletter to community leaders who were in a position to refer people to him, and whose recommendations are highly respected. This could include bankers, lawyers, human resources specialists, and other business leaders.

He included a cover letter offering his services as a coach to those who wanted the freedom of operating their own businesses, but with the support of an experienced management team. He included a reply card and reply envelope to make it easy to respond, and to provide confidentiality for the person responding.

At seminars and speaking engagements, he made his newsletters available at a literature table. This allowed him to make known, in a very professional and low-key manner, that there were career opportunities available, even though it was not the topic of discussion in the presentation.

What was his return on investment?

In many companies, a new, productive sales agent can bring between $7,500 and $15,000 in management overrides in the first year—more in subsequent years as the sales volume increases.

Let's take an average of $7,500 each. With three extra new producers, that's a total of $22,500 in extra management revenues the first year.

Art's investment in his newsletter for the first year was $1,766.

His first year return on investment was 1,174%!

WRITING A GOOD NEWSLETTER

There are many ways to write an interesting newsletter. Yours should contain articles that are informative and address issues of importance to your clients and prospects.

Many professionals believe that their newsletters should be quite technical. They want to prove that they have in-depth knowledge of the subject, and want to appeal to the most sophisticated and knowledgeable of their clients. There may be instances where this is important. But they are usually confined to newsletters provided by consultants, and sold as part of the services they offer.

What Goes In Your Newsletter

If you're in a position to produce your own newsletter, the more personal the better. Be sure to include:

- Stories about your clients—how they solved a problem using your product or service. Include photos when possible.
- Explanations of new products or services.
- Quizzes and self-analysis sheets that score your readers on dimensions of interest.
- Short tips.
- Free items to call or send for.
- Stories about your employees. These stories will both develop a relationship between customers/prospects and your staff, and acknowledge employees.

This chapter is not about subscription newsletters, where the reader pays for the information and is predisposed to read it as a result.

Remember Your Goal

Your client newsletter is a marketing tool. Your ability to communicate simply and effectively is of far more value to your clients than whether you are an expert on clause C, paragraph B of Section 2 of your technical manual. It's a foregone conclusion that if you can produce an easy-to-read interpretation of some of these points, then you must know the book inside-out.

I stress that your newsletter should be reader-friendly.

As our client Ross says, "I target the business market. It's important that my newsletter be easy-to-read. They don't have a lot of time to read. When they want more information, they call me!"

Compare Your Readability

EASY READING
The combination of content, layout, and design must make it easy for the reader to scan and quickly grasp the points you are making. This gives readers value, even if they don't have time to read your newsletter from beginning to end.

Here's a good way to judge your own newsletter on the reader-friendly scale. Ask your clients if they are behind on their reading. (The answer will be yes!) Then ask what magazines and newsletters they buy that they read regularly. Then, check it out for yourself. Buy a few copies and use them as a guideline for assessing your own newsletter.

Best of all, make it a point to ask for client feedback frequently. We send a survey to our clients every year. And we frequently ask for feedback and suggestions in conversations with them. In fact, we've created a Client Advisory Board. Each of our clients is entitled to membership, simply by making suggestions on how to improve our service.

Personalization Is Critical

I mentioned earlier that your newsletter should make people feel you are right there with them. If you write the way you talk, in a conversational, down-to-earth way, readers will "hear" you speaking to them.

Your photo and name can also help create that effect on them. So don't shy away from using your photo, even if you think you don't look like a movie star. Your clients want to see you, not Tom

Cruise or Kim Basinger. You're the one who is the specialist in your field, and the one they trust to help them when they need you.

THREE WAYS TO HAVE A NEWSLETTER

This chapter is not intended to make you an expert at the technical side of writing, designing, and producing a newsletter. I believe it's important for each of us to delegate to others in their areas of unique ability, and to focus our own energies on our unique abilities.

But it is important to at least know enough about producing a good newsletter to choose a good provider of these services.

There are three major options for producing your newsletter: *do it yourself, obtain one from a sponsoring company*, or *use a newsletter published by an outside publisher*, and personalized with your own name and photo.

1 **Do It Yourself.** If you chose to produce it yourself, on your personal computer for example, you'll have the ultimate in personalization. (You can also have the ultimate in headaches!) You can talk directly to your readers, and communicate your personal philosophy about the business. But you have to do the work, and live with a whole new set of deadlines every issue.

You'll have to gather information, write articles, produce graphics, and make sure the newsletter comes together on time every issue. Although people don't always appreciate the things you do for them, they do notice if your newsletter isn't arriving.

And then there's the opportunity cost from diverting your attention from income-generating activities to newsletter production.

You could, and likely will, end up working harder for the same or lesser result. That's the opposite of why you want to do a newsletter: to achieve greater results for less work.

Cost Vs. Return

You can hire the writer and designer, and coordinate the printing and other details—in effect, become the publisher. But the same caution applies. I have seen instances where this works very well. If you have your own marketing department, with someone who has the skills, and who understands your business well, this can be effective.

It is important, however, for you to give guidance and feedback to whoever does your newsletter for you. So set up a file where you can put clippings, notes, and ideas for your newsletter. Be clear about the purpose to be served and the audience you're addressing. All of this will help your writer or editor to do a good job for you.

Legal Disclaimers

In the life insurance and securities field, especially in the U.S. and England, the rules for compliance are very stringent. To get each issue approved may add as much as six weeks to your production schedule. And without this approval from the NASD and/or your sponsoring company,

A TIP ON CREATING MATERIAL
Try carrying a tape recorder with you to record ideas, or even phrases, you'd like used in your newsletter to make it "yours." This captures your thoughts all month long, and gives your writer or editor material to work with.

you are playing with fire.

One precaution to take, in any industry which gives professional advice, such as law or accounting, is to have a good disclaimer on your newsletter. This disclaimer would recommend that readers seek professional advice for their particular situation, and not apply the ideas in the articles without checking with their advisors. As part of the setup of your newsletter content and design, have this disclaimer reviewed by a company or professional association lawyer, to make sure you're covered. (See the computer disk with this book for a sample disclaimer.)

2 **Use Company-Sponsored Newsletters.** Many large companies make a newsletter service available to their sales agents. If you choose to use your sponsoring company's newsletter, you'll know that they have more resources available to hire pro-fessional writers and designers. But, the content is often product-biased, and your readers will notice. Ask yourself, "Is this the image I want to project?"

We've seen many in-house publications. Without exception, they do have this weakness of wanting to promote the company and its products. That may be all right for you. But most of our clients prefer to be seen as

Choose Carefully

Choose your editor or publisher carefully. It's your image on the line.

- Ask for samples of previous work, and the editorial guidelines that will be used.
- Evaluate samples to determine the appropriateness of the content to your target group.
- Find out if you can participate in determining future content.
- Find out what guarantees there are if it turns out that the newsletter is not what you expected.
- Evaluate available support.
- Determine costs.

independent advice-givers, who can broker the appropriate products to suit their clients' needs.

3 **Buy a General Newsletter.** Finally, you may choose to buy an outside newsletter service, one that can be personalized with your name and photo. That way you share the cost of professional writers, designers, and printers with other users. You're delegating the overall publishing responsibility.

Make it a point to work with your publisher, offering suggestions to improve the service. That way, you can also influence the content of the newsletter to suit your clients. And, as a bonus, you can tell your clients you're an advisor to the publisher.

A WORD TO COMPANIES SPONSORING CLIENT NEWSLETTERS FOR THEIR SALES PEOPLE

My experience has been almost exclusively in the life insurance and mutual fund business, but these insights may be of value to you, whatever line of business you are in.

Most companies providing client newsletters for their sales agents to use, will attempt to serve corporate clients through their agents. That means that the newsletters will primarily be filled with company and product promotion

On the other hand, in this age of relationship selling, many sales professionals position themselves as advisors to their clients. They see the clients as belonging to them. They want and need to appear independent and unbiased in their recommendations. They must be seen as professionals first, and representatives of your products and services second.

Balancing Your Interests

This creates a conflict which leads to lower newsletter usage than the company would like. This means the newsletter is a less effective sales tool for the sponsor. This can lead to cutting off the service entirely because it can't be made cost-effective.

There's nothing wrong with a company newsletter. It makes sense to keep in touch with people who buy and use your products. But keep the two concepts separate in your mind, and in your administration of programs.

When you are dependent upon your sales people to build and maintain relationships with your clients, your relationship with your sales force is paramount. They can bring you business, and they can take it away to a competitor.

Your ability to retain good salespeople depends on your ability to listen and act in their best interests. These will be completely compatible with your company's best interests if you've set an ethical standard for doing business, and have a good sales force selection program.

Don't Neglect Your Newsletter

Typically, the management of a client newsletter service is delegated to a person who has little or no field experience, and who is likely to be moved from department to department, leaving the administration of the newsletter program up for grabs.

Since the newsletter is a marketing support service to your sales force, your program must be championed by senior managers. These executives at a high level can make certain that there is continuity of support, even through downsizing, mergers and corporate reorganizations.

Then, to make sure that cost-cutting won't affect the continuity of service, make your program so valuable to your sales force that they will be willing to pay for their own subscriptions, in large enough numbers to make it self-financing.

And good luck with your program. Client newsletters in your agents' hands will definitely improve your ability to generate revenue, retain clients and sales people, and build respect for your service with your sales force.

ACTION AGENDA

Here are some ideas for getting started on a newsletter:

- Start today by creating a file of possible topics to cover in your newsletter. Clip relevant articles you see and throw them in.
- Even before you have your first newsletter ready to go, you can use the

"newsletter" as a sales tool. Contact your best clients. Tell them you're putting together a newsletter and would appreciate their ideas about important topics to cover. Use their answers as a clue to what challenges may be on their minds right now.

- This new reason to talk to them can lead to helping them solve immediate problems before the newsletter comes out. Book the appointment, and ask for the order. Then ask them who else they know who might appreciate a copy of your newsletter.
- Even if you end up using a newsletter created by someone else, you can add supplements to it that you write.
- Shop around for sources of "prefab" newsletters in your industry, or from your suppliers. Ask your peers what they use.
- Look on line for sources of information you can use. You may also want to post "newsletter" material on line if you have a Web site. But check the copyright provisions first.
- Create a list of other possible sources of regular information such as: your clients, trade magazines, books, libraries and your local college.
- Go to a local library. Ask the reference librarian for ideas. Browse the magazines and journals available.
- Create a draft editorial calendar with topics you might want to cover over the next six months or year.
- Keep going with ideas that come up as you do your homework. You're on a roll. Don't stop now. And let me know how it went, will you?

Chapter 6

POWER NETWORKING:
Building Relationships for Success

John S. Haskell, "Dr. Revenue"

John S. Haskell, "Dr. Revenue," is a marketing and sales consultant, professional speaker, author, and teacher of business planning at the University of Southern California's Business Expansion Network. His programs "Power Networking", "Dr. Revenue's Marketing and Sales Check Up," and "Give Your Sales A Kick!" are designed for entrepreneurial audiences of business executives and professionals. A recent *Inc.* magazine conference "High Return Marketing Strategies" featured Dr. Revenue doing a full-day seminar, "Creating and Launching Your Marketing Plan" followed by "Do It Yourself Marketing" and "Power Networking." He is currently Chairperson for the National Speakers Association PR/Marketing Task Force and a member of the Board of Advisors of Professionals Network Group.

John S. Haskell; 1700 Mandeville Canyon Road, Los Angeles, CA 90049; phone (310) 476-3355; fax (310) 471-7721; e-mail DrRevenue@AOL.COM.

POWER NETWORKING:
Building Relationships for Success
John S. Haskell, "Dr. Revenue"

Networking has taken on new meaning and new importance in this age of entrepreneurship and downsizing. Whether you've been in business for years or are starting now, you need to bring in new business.

Networking provides the answer. Networking creates relationships. And relationships create business.

PROFESSIONALS NEED TO NETWORK

Lawyers, CPAs, and other professionals call it "rainmaking."

Until recently, in the professions, there were only a few rainmakers in each firm. Many lawyers looked down their noses at the hail-fellow-well-met type of "guy." (It was almost always a guy because very few women achieved partnerships, and if they did get to the holy grail, they were expected to keep their noses to the technical grindstone.)

Many of the established, prestigious firms just assumed that the work would always be there, "after all we are _____" (you fill in the blank with the name of the most prestigious law, accounting, engineering, architecture, etc., firm in your market)

It is now the later half of the 1990s and "We are _____." just is not enough. Every week we see established firms dying because a client that supplied 50 percent or more of the gross income of the firm was sold, folded, or just went somewhere else.

A few years ago, KPMG Peat Marwick, the big six CPA firm, let 400 partners go in one day (it used to be "Big 8," remember?). After that happened, an irreverent speaker like me could ask the question:

> *"Do you think that any of the 400 were rainmakers?"*

This statement is coupled with a corollary question to professionals,

> *"Do you generate enough business each year to cover the cost to the firm of you and any support that you require—forget space and other occupancy expenses—just you and related personnel?"*

At a luncheon presentation these twin questions usually get the partners of CPA, law, and other professional firms uncomfortable enough that they listen carefully to a brief, well-focused presentation.

RETAILERS NEED TO NETWORK

Building human connections works in any business. People like to do business in stores where clerks recognize them, or they know the owner. It's nicer to do business where relationships exist. It even makes it safer for you in case of a problem because, if they're smart, they want to maintain the relationship with you.

I often refer to professionals when I discuss power networking. The need for networking among business people selling hard and soft goods is no less. Networking with "power" is valuable in any business. Here is an example.

I have a friend who sells specialty papers. He is a great salesperson. He is an even better networker. He knows that if he can get in to see the boss, not the production manager, at any reprographics house in the country, he has a better than even chance of selling something from his company, at least on a trial basis.

Building A Network

How does my friend build and cultivate his network?

The first thing he does is get to know the targets very well. He not only knows the individual himself (again it's a man's world), but he knows his wife, kids, vacation home, and almost everything else about him.

He is a great guy and loves to have good food and wine, so whenever possible he gets the person out with him to dinner, lunch, skiing, or any other activity that the customer or prospect likes. This great networker is stretching his tentacles (just think of an octopus) into the network that his new friend has.

The better he gets to know someone, the more effective his networking becomes. The better he knows his "friend," the easier it is for that friend to want to do something for him. What can he do that will be really valuable? He can introduce him to someone just like himself in another part of the country who can use my friend's products. Ironically, his best customers are competitors who have introduced him to each other. They like him so much they sell for him.

"Gentlemen, I think you've taken networking a little too far."

His network keeps growing. As he comes to understand the power of his network better and better, he develops more and more power within his company. He controls the customers.

The company may produce the product, but he can take his network with him wherever he works. And don't doubt that this thought occurred to him very recently when the company was sold. He is biding his time, but the options are open because his network has hard wiring in it...the connections are direct and measurable.

POWER NETWORKING

Why Power? What does "power" mean?

Power is appropriate because networking without power is useless. The true definition of "power" in the networking context:

> *Power refers to contacts that have potential for producing new activity either directly or indirectly.*

A Power Network is one that produces targeted revenue amounts on a consistent basis.

As a consultant and speaker, I have little else to rely on other than networking. Broadcast advertising, print advertising, direct mail, and all other forms of exposure can work at times. But generally cost becomes a barrier.

Today with the World Wide Web on the Internet, there are new opportunities to gain exposure (see Chapter 11). But day in and day out, the strength of my contacts is the source of my continuing flow of business opportunities.

A TYPICAL DAY'S LEADS

So far today, a routine Tuesday, the phone has rung twice with very specific network-related opportunities.

The first, a former client (and friend now), was discussing business with a cousin from Seattle during the holidays and the guy told him about a new trade show that he is developing for salespeople. They need speakers. My friend, David, suggested that we talk. He has seen my Power Networking talk and thought that some version of this might be appropriate for this two-day show.

Even better, this show is being proposed as the first of twenty-plus events for salespeople around the country. What is the potential? I don't know and will not, perhaps, until after I do the first speech, if they want me at all, and if I decide to be involved.

The fact is that without my networking efforts with David, the opportunity would never have come to my desk.

Manage Your Rolodex

"You're only as good as your network. Is your list of contacts in and out of the company growing by the month? Do you have an orderly scheme for keeping in touch? Beware if the answer to either question is no."
—Tom Peters

The second opportunity was a simple phone call I received. "I saw your article in the *Los Angeles Business Journal*, I would like to talk to you." That seems simple enough, but the history behind the fact that I have a column once a month in the *LA Business Journal* is a story of networking that goes back five years and involves hundreds of hours of contacts, referrals, and effort on my part and that of at least eight different people in five different businesses.

So, how do you get a network to deliver power?

Networking Tips

- Always carry business cards in your pocket or purse. Before you go to a group, decide what professional image you want to project, and dress accordingly.

- When you're at a large event and want to find a particular type of person—ask. Ask the people at the door, ask the president of the group, ask the speaker. They'll steer you to the right people—and you can use that referral as an introduction.

SOFT MARKETING?

For many people "networking" is a soft part of the marketing equation. Advertising seems more measurable on a cost basis and sometimes on a lead generation basis.

Every networking situation needs to be evaluated and structured within a framework that is "hard wired."

At times it may seem manipulative and cold— it can be! There is no substitute for looking out for number one. In the world of networking you have to be aware at all times: Who are you talking to? What do they do? Who might they know? What can you do with them? For them? And, of course, what can they do for you?

A NETWORKING SYSTEM

My type of networking is designed to obtain very specific, quantifiable results. Power Networking is built upon a system that contains specific action steps which build the hard wiring.

STEP ONE: DEFINING THE STEPS OF POWER NETWORKING

Defining the action steps in your Power Network is the first step. The word TIME provides an effective symbol for the individual elements that lead to a Power Network.

> **T** ime itself
>
> **I** dentifying influencers
>
> **M** arketing tools
>
> **E** nthusiasm, energy, expertise, and effectiveness

STEP TWO: UNDERSTANDING NETWORKING TIME

Several years ago I had a great year in ten months. By Halloween I had billed and collected more fee income that in any previous twelve-month period, but I was in trouble. Why? The problem was that I had done wonderfully, but there was absolutely nothing on the horizon. There was absolutely zero new business in the pipeline. Why? Because I had been so busy doing work that I had no time to get work!

This is the eternal problem that faces many businesses. How do you do the work and still have the time to get the work? It is a fine balancing act that can go off course any time. The better you are doing, the more likely it is that you will run into a disaster in a few months. It is not fair, but it is a fact.

The Pink Sheets: Real Goals

As my new business crisis developed, I decided to take action, "I know what I'll do, I will devote one full day every week to new business." That sounded great but three weeks later nothing had changed. Why?

November through January was not going to have any new billings, but I still had many demands on my time. The one day a week concept would not work.

While struggling with this dilemma I saw a pile of pink index cards on my desk. I thought, "What if I take a card and write down three things that I will do, for sure, to build new business?" Then what?

Key Goals

I decided that seeing the task was the key to getting things done. Being very compulsive about lists and tasks that are written down does not hurt, but anyone having to look at a list often enough will probably do something about it.

The pink card was installed directly opposite my full-page full-month calendar. That decision appears to be almost as important as the decision to make the short list in the first place. The combination of card and calendar put action and time together and forced me to get "things" done about new business.

That decision was the start of a total networking-new business system that has a pink 8.5 x 11 sheet as its focal point. Every week or two I create a new "Pink Sheet" with at least three items that have to get done that week.

Pink Sheets For Anyone

It even worked for my teenage son, after a fashion. He just took three weeks to get his car inspected while carrying around a list of six important items from his old man. He still has not gotten most of the rest of the list done, but at least he avoided penalties on that one.

Most of us non-teenagers are more driven and more compulsive about getting items checked off a list.

POWER NETWORKER'S "PINK SHEET"

Personal commitment: Each week do 3 "things" to develop new business.

No matter how busy it is, the three "things" listed below will get done. Review and revise this sheet at least weekly. Place it facing your daily calendar so you automatically look at it many times each day.

By definition a "thing" is: a phone call to a prospect, a lunch, a letter, a personal visit, etc., etc. By doing 3 things each week over the course of a year many new opportunities will develop. Keep track of how many of your "Pink Sheet" items turn into profitable volume for you and your firm.

The goal is clear...

more volume from more clients.

1._____

_____

_____

_____

2._____

_____

_____

_____

3._____

_____

_____

Other:

The sheet and the centralization of all new business efforts on one simple piece of paper makes the program work.

The process of creating the sheet gets my thoughts on networking and business development focused. The process of making the calls, having the lunches, writing the proposals, and all of the other "stuff" that gets onto the Pink Sheet is the most important and influential part of the Power Networking System.

But there is more...read on...

STEP THREE: IDENTIFYING INFLUENCERS

We all have them, friends or acquaintances who know people who can create opportunities for us. But, how do you take advantage of those indirect contacts? Or, how do you cultivate those contacts that can result in direct business?

A number of years ago a man named Lee called me and said that he had been referred to me by someone. He sounded pretty interesting so I said, "OK, let's get together and I'll listen to what you are saying about this seminar that I really don't want to go to." He thought that was cute and, knowing Lee, had already figured out that he had a lot to offer me besides the seminar.

> "There is no security in this life. There is only opportunity."
> —General Douglas MacArthur

The Power of One Key Contact

Well, we met and talked and I began to figure out who Lee was. He was about 10-15 years older than me, so about 55-60 at the time. He had owned a mid-sized advertising agency in Los Angeles for about 15 years. I owned one at the

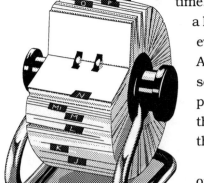

time. He had sold his agency and made a lot of money—a thought that I had every day that I owned my agency. And, he constantly called on people, selling them a seminar/consulting program. He let it casually be known that he often met people who needed the services of a company like mine.

Fortunately, I listened. That one meeting lead to my taking a seminar that I really did not want to attend. But I eventually learned a lot from it. And, more importantly, it also led to the development of the ideal influencer relationship.

My new friend Lee would travel all around the Los Angeles basin and from time to time would call me and say, "Write this down, kid, and call tomorrow. Say I told you to call, you are the guy I was talking about with the smaller agency that does great work, etc. It is yours to lose..." Those words ring in my ears. During the three or four years before Lee became ill and had to move from Los Angeles for the cleaner air of Las Vegas, he was a constant source of referrals.

Reciprocal Referrals

I learned to play the game very well. I had always had a great Rolodex™ and I put it to work getting introductions for Lee. It was his job, just as it was mine, to make the presentation and sell the program. But, I constantly opened doors.

I maintained a file of every referral that I gave to Lee and when we were together I made sure that I asked him about ones that he did not tell me about. It was clear to my friend Lee (we truly became very good friends) that I was working with him on a two-way street. He could count on me to supply leads constantly. And I knew that he would regularly call me for one of those sessions which would end with the words, "It is yours to lose."

A Hard-Wired Network

This type of "influencer" relationship is what builds Power Networks. A relationship like mine with Lee is truly "hard wired."

We were constantly working for each other with no money changing hands. We knew that during any year we would provide each other with X number of opportunities. We kept score in that we wanted to know how the other guy was doing with Bernie, Charlie, or Sharon, but we did not keep track of the dollars.

I don't know how much business Lee brought me. But I do know that one of the accounts he introduced me to subsequently became a long-term consulting client when I got out of the agency business. They helped support me as I built my new consulting-speaking business. This was three years after the initial contact.

How do you put a value on that type of introduction?

"Gentlemen, this is a power restaurant. If you want to discuss your families, please do so quietly."

Building Relationships

Building influencer relationships takes time and thought. Recently a new friend, who I met through some networking groups, visited with me over breakfast. We had not really done much with each other. We weren't too sure that we had much in common in terms of business, but we liked each other and had mutual respect.

> "Anything less than win/win in an interdependent reality is a poor second best...in the long-term relationship."
> —Stephen R. Covey

We kept talking through a lengthy breakfast and near the end I made a suggestion. "Why don't I send you 1-3 names every month at the beginning of the month. These will be people who I've met recently that I am not sure you know, but who I think you would want to know. [He is in the appraisal business.]. And, you do the same. I'll give you a 25-word-or-less briefing and you take it from there."

We have not been perfect with this "buddy system" but about 15 names have changed hands. And, most important, one of these names is currently a client of mine. I don't know if any of the names I gave my friend have produced anything. I'll ask him the next time we get together.

Work At It

There are times that it takes some reaching to figure out how to be an influencer for someone. I was having lunch with a young bankruptcy attorney from a very aggressive, well-known firm where I know one of the older partners.

This young man impressed me. I kept thinking about how could we develop a business relationship so that I could do some marketing and sales work with companies in Chapter 11.

(Interestingly, because of court control, you can almost always be sure of getting paid when the company finally goes into Chapter 11).

Finally, near the end of the lunch, he talked about the "top 20." I said, "What is that?" He explained that the court publishes the top 20 creditors list before a meeting of the creditors so that the creditors committee can be formed. He explained that their firm wanted to be counsel to the committee and influencing any of the major creditors would be useful.

"The first key to networking is to talk to everyone."
—Ken Blanchard

"Why don't you fax the names over to me," I offered. "I've been in business a long time in Los Angeles (25 years). Perhaps I'll know some of the people or the companies that are listed."

We have tried the system three times. Every time I have known someone or something that has been helpful to him. He has not sent me to see any companies yet, but I know that day will come. The influencer two-way street has traffic. We are building a hard-wired relationship.

STEP FOUR: MARKETING TOOLS ARE VITAL TO DEVELOPING TRAFFIC IN YOUR NETWORK

I'll define marketing as "any action or reaction by you or your company that impacts revenue." Therefore, anything from an advertisement in the local paper to a scratch pad is marketing. But before you start marketing you need to have an idea of what you want the results to be in both dollars of new income and in development of your network.

Sample Goal Setting

Here are examples of specific, quantified goals for an attorney.

1. Obtain the opportunity at least once a month to speak to a group of attorneys (a firm) at their office for 30 minutes on my specialty, labor litigation.

2. Identify four specific attorneys within my target list of 30 firms who definitely have the ability to influence business and get me appointments with their clients and those of their firm.

3. Measure my progress by the number of calls I receive for any information, follow up of any kind and the recognition that I get from attorneys who I have met/presented to. (I will always add every attorney who is in the audience to my data base and will supply 2-3 "things" per year by mail to every attendee for at least two years after I first present to him or her as part of the firm-wide group.)

Have Clear Goals

Quantification of goals is vital. A goal that can't be measured is not a goal.

Some people tell me that you can't quantify "image" or "influence." To that I like to respond, "How do you know when your image is good? How does influence impact your business?" Even the most skeptical person will admit that a good image results in the phone ringing and people recognizing your name when it is mentioned.

Clear focus is vital when you are organizing your networking plan. For example, if you are an attorney and you want to penetrate the accountant market, how will you measure your progress?

The Vital "Elevator Speech:" Presenting Yourself

As networking becomes more and more important and more and more people are involved in it, the ability to stand out in a few seconds is critical.

I call this brief overview of 60-90 seconds an "elevator speech." I get on your elevator. I notice a piece of literature, a bag, book, etc. that you are carrying and say, "Oh, that is really interesting. What exactly do you do?"

Your answer as we go from the lobby to the fifth floor in a fast elevator can spell the difference between opportunity captured or wasted. If you can tell me who you are, what you do and why you do it in less than 60 seconds, you may get the opportunity to get to know me more and get referrals from me.

Tools Make A Big Difference

I just got a call from a friend who told me to call a woman over at a company and introduce myself. The indication is that the company needs some help developing a written marketing plan as a part of their overall business planning effort.

After talking to Ms. Jones at ABC Inc., I am going to write a short letter, thank her for her time and enclose something to tell her about my firm and what I do. What can I send? The firm brochure is twenty pages long and out of date. The most

Dr. Revenue's Personal Elevator Speech

My name is John Haskell, but I'm better known as Dr. Revenue. I'm a marketing and sales consultant working with small and mid-sized businesses. I focus on written marketing programs and the implementation of new programs to generate immediate revenue. My job is to get things done in the market for my clients. I work with a broad range of companies in consumer products and services. Yesterday, for example I worked with four companies: a sporting goods manufacturer looking for a 25% sales increase, fast; an educational publisher packaging a new promotion for trade shows; an apartment rental service doing a marketing plan for national expansion; and a window treatment company seeking to help 24 independent distributor/fabricators grow and build profits. Dr. Revenue's prescriptions bring dollars to a company.

(Total speech: 129 words in less than 60 seconds!)

recent article that I wrote and published is technical and not at all directed toward the issues that Ms. Jones indicated are important to her firm.

The One Sheet—A Tool For All Reasons

The answer is a simple tool designed and developed to give the whole story on two sides of a single sheet of paper. We call it a "one sheet."

The one sheet has three goals:

1. Provide an overview which can be sent out in preparation for a meeting to learn about a prospective client and present our firm.
2. Provide a guide for presenting the firm.
3. Provide a more than adequate leave-behind piece that reiterates—loud and clear—the key points about your firm that you want the prospect to remember.

The one sheet is a series of bullets about you and your firm.

- How long have you been in business?
- What is the financial status [strength] of the firm?
- What business services do you provide?
- How do you personally fit into that package of services?
- Who have you done this for (client references; would a prospect know them)?
- How do you get paid for services? (e.g., retainer, fee, hourly, etc.)
- How cost effective is your firm? Prove it with examples.
- What hooks can you provide to get the client interested in the firm and your service program?

Build the one sheet from the bullets. If you have several in your computer, you can produce a one sheet customized for a prospect. For instance, you can tailor the references and testimonials to their industry.

It is best to think about it as a 10-minute presentation and as a handout after the presentation.

STEP FIVE: "E" TICKETS TO A POWER NETWORK

The "E'" on TIME stands for:

- Enthusiasm
- Energy
- Expertise
- Effectiveness

Your Power Network Needs All 4 E's

Enthusiasm must come through in every meeting, phone call, and letter. Without it, hard-wired networking is impossible.

Energy is vital to the networking p r o c e s s. You have to invest serious amounts of energy to support basic networking activities. Observing, learning, and acting are critical. As Yogi Berra said, "You can see a lot just by looking." Act energetically on what you see to build the relationship.

Expertise is part of what anybody sells in an information age. And it's 100% of what most professionals sell. But too often we are guilty of false modesty. You know that you know what you are doing. And you assume that everyone else recognizes it.

But how will they? Sell through case studies and examples.

Translate Personal Interests Into Effective Benefits

For example, for me one special interest is wine and food. As a result, my phone rings often with requests for "reservations." A lot more than "reservations" is the goal of the caller. He or she knows that I often know the chef, owner, and the maitre'd. Therefore, if Dr. Revenue makes the reservation at Le Cirque in New York, Rubicon in San Francisco, Everest in Chicago, or one of several hundred top-rated restaurants, he or she will get VIP service.

My restaurant and wine interest has been translated into a way to demonstrate effectiveness to prospects and influencers.

By helping with something as simple as a restaurant reservation I demonstrate a value that sets up a continuing dialogue with people in the network. I'm worth knowing, even if we don't do business together.

This makes your expertise concrete and helps them understand how you can help them.

Effectiveness is a descriptor for the part of you that goes beyond the degrees, titles, positions, and past successes. You are more than the sum of those parts. You are a person who has vitality, interests, and the ability to share yourself. You are someone who a prospective client or influencer can get to know through activities, symbols, and other personal evidence of who you are.

Your personal interests are a big part of power networking. Because they don't relate to business, many people don't see their importance. But they are authentically you. People know you didn't develop a special interest just to sell them something.

SUMMARY

Power Networking is a skill. It is a program. It is a way of life that is available to any business person (or anyone else). The key is understanding the elements.

T-I-M-E provides the symbol for the power of our "hard-wired" network.

You need *time* to do the things that have to be done. The *pink sheet* makes the network come alive. The pink sheet helps drive the networking system. The pink sheet is the focal point for all networking and business development activities.

Influencers are key to the program. Identifying and cultivating influencer relationships requires innovation, inspiration, and intensity. Working with someone to say, "How can I help you? Yes, you can help me, too." is key to building a power network.

Marketing as a discipline is part of the Power Networking program. The basics of marketing are absolutely essential to building a successful business development program.

Coupling a clear statement of your marketing goals with a simple "elevator speech" supported by good, clean, simple and effective one-sheets creates a powerful marketing mix that opens doors and retains interest between appointments.

Finally, there are the four Es.

- *Enthusiasm*—have it and people will be interested in you;
- *Energy*—invest it and you'll build a powerful network;
- *Expertise*—you have to be good at what you do and know how to present what you have in a way that demonstrates your skill and knowledge without making you look pompous; and
- *Effectiveness*—going beyond the basics to be something special to the people in your network.

Good luck and good Power Networking.

"Your influence is almost directly proportional to the thickness of your Rolodex™. Work the phone. Don't waste a single lunch. Go to cocktail parties. Who you know is still as important as what you know."
—Tom Peters

ACTION AGENDA

What can you do today to start hard-wiring your power network?

- First, copy the pink sheet on page 143. Then list a few networking tasks you can accomplish within a week.
- Clean out your Rolodex.® Start calling the people you leave in it.
- Attend group meetings to meet more people.
- Identify the influencers you know. Talk with them about how you can help each other.
- Develop your 60-second "elevator speech." (See also Chapter 1 about expressing your uniqueness.)
- Develop a basic "one-sheet" about yourself and your business.
- Call a few people now, or schedule calls.
- Recontact friends you've been meaning to talk to.
- Set up a lunch meeting.
- Call a supplier. Call someone!

Chapter 7

USING THE PHONE AS A SERIOUS SALES TOOL:
9 Steps to Success

Art Sobczak

Art Sobczak
has specialized in one area only for the last 14 years: providing real-world, how-to ideas and techniques that help salespeople use the phone more effectively to prospect, sell, and service—without morale-killing "rejection."

Sobczak writes and publishes the how-to tips newsletter, *Telephone Selling Report*. He authored several how-to telesales audio- and video-training programs, and wrote the books, *How to Sell More, In Less Time, With No Rejection, Using Common Sense Telephone Techniques—Volume 1*, and *Telephone Tips That SELL!—501 How-To Ideas and Affirmations to Help You Get More Business by Phone.*

He holds public training seminars nationwide and also customizes programs for on-site, in-house delivery ranging from one hour to several days.

Art Sobczak, Business By Phone, Inc., 13254–M Stevens Street, Omaha, NE 68137; phone (800) 326-7721 or (402) 895-9399; fax (402)896-3353. To hear a free recorded sales tip that changes weekly, call his Telesales Tip Line at (402) 896-TIPS.

USING THE PHONE AS A SERIOUS SALES TOOL:
9 Steps to Success

Art Sobczak

Regardless of what you sell, it's likely that the telephone plays a role in the sales process. Whether it is to prospect, qualify, set appointments, or handle customer contact, the phone is something we all must utilize in order to do business.

Unfortunately, most people use it very poorly.

Some people are scared to death of using the phone and therefore avoid it. Instead they shuffle papers or waste time on dead-end face-to-face cold calls. Others play the "numbers" game, smiling and dialing, burning through names with little regard for quality, hoping that the next contact will be the "yes" that they've been told—erroneously—will result after a certain number of "nos."

Using the phone professionally in sales need not and should not be painful—either for you or the prospect or customer. After all, you have something of value to offer, right? A product or service that will help make the lives of others easier, more profitable, less painful, less costly, or more pleasurable.

If you offer something of value, it should be a relatively simple process to communicate that to your audience.

For over 14 years I've shown sales professionals (and people who don't consider themselves in sales) how to use the phone to get what they want. They also help customers in the process, which I believe is the only way to sell professionally.

In this chapter we'll go through each part of the telesales call, building your call as we progress. Naturally we'll cover the material generically. It's up to you to mold, shape, knead, and adapt the ideas to your own sales process.

PLANNING FOR SUCCESS

Professional athletes make their performances look easy. What we don't see, however, is the lifetime of preparation they invested to reach their level.

Likewise, a great sales call seems to flow effortlessly. It too, is a product of preparation. This is one area that dooms many salespeople. They have no idea of what they want to accomplish on a call, other than to not get beat up too badly.

To ensure your success, and before getting close to the telephone, answer these questions.

- What do I want the prospect/customer to do at the end of the call?
- What should I be doing at the end of the call?

The answers to these simple questions might seem painfully obvious at first glance. But, believe me, they are usually not practiced. If you want to

THE BENEFITS OF "NO"

If you're prospecting, weeding people out is a useful outcome. A clear "no" saves you wasting time with non-prospects. Don't take it as a rejection. Be glad you can move on to likelier prospects.

set an appointment, fine, visualize it. If you want a prospect to accept a proposal, that's your objective. The important thing is to have a destination.

Notice that these questions require *action-oriented* answers. For forward movement to take place in a relationship, there must be action. You both need to *do something* as a result of the call.

Preparing Your Objective

Having a clear call objective is important. Your specific call tactics are based upon your strategic objective. After all, you wouldn't jump in your car without knowing where you were going. You need to know your destination, and the directions in advance. Your sales calls are the same way.

With your objective in mind ask yourself these questions.

- What do I know about this prospect?
- What do I need to know in order for them to take the ACTION I desire?
- What information can I get from people other than the decision maker (such as screeners)?
- If I reach voice mail, what will I say?
- What is my opening statement, and is the benefit strong enough for them to be sufficiently aroused to listen and share information?

Dealing With Voice Mail

Many salespeople consider voice mail a "black hole." Your message goes in and nothing comes out! Expect it. Prepare a dynamite message that gets a response. Tell them when to reach you and ask them to leave a good time to call.

- What specific questions will I ask?
- What is my fallback position? (Just in case you don't fully reach your primary objective.)

Does this preparation take a tremendous amount of time?

Not compared to the time that's *wasted* on calls where you don't have a specific objective. Wandering in no particular direction will get you quickly brushed off the phone due to lack of preparation.

WORKING WITH CALL SCREENERS

Often when you call your prospect or customer, you're put right through. Other times you encounter "screeners." How you interact with these screeners determines whether you're escorted in like a good friend, or cast aside like a self-interested peddler.

You might have heard this nonsense before: "Don't give the screener any information," and, "The screener can't buy from you, they can only get rid of you."

What bilge that is.

Screeners are some of the most important people you'll ever talk to. After all, they hold the key to the decision maker's door. The roadside is littered with the carcasses of sales reps who've been cast aside by screeners.

Screeners are not ruthless, Wicked-Witch-of-the-North-type characters that

"Screeners" Have
A Bad Image

How To Avoid Screeners

The "boss" usually works longer than assistants. One way to avoid being screened is to call at odd hours. Try 20 minutes before work, a half an hour after work, or during lunch. Or even take advantage of bad weather. When the roads are icy, the boss is the one who tends to make it in.

some sales reps envision and fear. For the most part, they're astute professionals who care about the value that you can deliver to their bosses.

Here's one simple way you can ensure you'll get through to more decision makers: know why the boss would be better off by speaking with you, and be able to articulate it very clearly. I term this a "Justification Statement." It's typically used when the screener asks the question, "What is this in reference to?" Here are a few rules for putting together your own effictive Justification Statements.

Justification Statements

1 **Talk about results, not about your products.** Normally I don't have my calls screened. But as I was rushing a newsletter to the printer, and also approaching a flight time, a call came in. Tricia, my assistant asked the caller what it was in reference to. The caller said she wanted to talk to me about advertising.

In other words, she wanted to talk about what she wanted to sell, not about what I wanted: increased sales, profits, customers. This is the very reason most sales reps get screened out. After all, who are screeners told to get rid of? Salespeople. Not individuals who have something of value to contribute to the company. You might indeed have tremendous potential value to contribute. But if it's not communicated clearly to the screener, you're lumped in with the pesky salespeople.

2 **Make delivery of the results contingent on speaking with the boss.** True, the screener can't buy from you. But she or he must buy into the fact that you do need to speak with the boss. Therefore, after mentioning the results you can deliver, suggest that you need to speak with the decision maker to determine how you could deliver these results. For example, " ...and to determine if this is something he'd like to take a look at, I'd like to speak with him about his plans regarding..."

3 **Ask questions of the screener.** I always preach on this. Always will. The more information you have, the better off you are when you speak with the boss. Say to the screener, "You probably work closely with Ms. Daffodil. I bet there's some information you can help me with first..."

Here are additional tips on getting to decision makers.

- Give full identification up front on your calls. Include your company name, and your name. "This is Pat Downy with ABC Industries calling for Terry Mudhen please." It answers the questions they most typically ask. If you're returning their call, mention that as well.

- Learn the screener's name, and use it on subsequent calls when they answer the phone. You immediately place them in a positive frame of mind.

- Recognize that a screener could be a user, influencer, and a co-decision maker. If after asking the screener a few questions, it sounds as if she or he is quite knowledgeable in the area, continue probing. You might be able to get the screener to become an advocate and give a personal recommendation and introduction to the boss.

- Be businesslike and professional on initial prospecting calls. Screeners roll their eyes and laugh at sales reps who think they're schmoozing screeners, when, in fact, they're being looked at very skeptically.

- Don't be stalled by the "Just send any information you have," request. This is a tool many screeners use to brush away unprepared sales reps. Respond by further justifying your reason for needing to speak with the boss. "As a matter of fact, one of my reasons for calling is to eventually send something to Ms. Crustacean. But I wouldn't want to waste her time sending things that didn't apply to her situation. So what I'd like to do is ask a few questions regarding…"

So the next time you encounter a screener, be prepared to work with that person as a resource. Explain why you have something that will make the boss's life better. You'll get through more often.

INTEREST-CREATING OPENING STATEMENTS

It's no wonder that many buyers greet a telephone sales call with the same enthusiasm they'd have for an IRS super-audit. Most callers invite and ensure resistance with abysmal call openings.

Bad Call Openings

Just look at a few of the gems I received at my office recently.

"I'm just calling to introduce our company to you and tell you about our products." *[I don't care about products, or companies. I'm interested in results … what's in it for me?]*

"If I could show you a way to reduce your long distance expenses, of course you would want that wouldn't you?" *[Reduce my expenses? Nahh. I think everyone should pay their fair share, so I send in a little extra every month with my bill. C'mon, give me a break! I can't believe people still use this tired, worn out salesy technique that manipulates the prospect into a corner.]*

"We have an advertising post-card deck and I saw your card, and want to talk with you about advertising with us." *[Oh? That's what you want? Hmmm, am I supposed to get excited about spending money on advertising? What I really care about is reaching proven buyers of my types of products and getting them to respond at an allowable investment per customer.]*

My list goes on and on. (I keep a file on these—it makes great material for columns and seminars!)

Start Strong!

I've been saying it for my 14 years in telesales. I still believe more strongly than ever that the opening statement is the most pivotal part of your call. This is even more true for the initial prospecting call.

Without an opening that piques curiosity, and puts the listener is a positive frame of mind to participate, nothing else matters.

The point you need to communicate in the first few seconds of a call is simple: "We have something that might be able to help you, and I simply need to learn more about you to find out for sure."

The key to success is to use the right words. You want to create an opening statement that generates interest, not resistance. Before you ever pick up the phone again, answer these questions:

- What do prospects want most as it relates to my type of product or service?
- What do they want to avoid? and
- How can I help them do their job more effectively?

The answers to these questions will give you a benefit you can plug directly into your opener. This is designed to get their attention and arouse their curiosity so they want to speak with you.

A Model Opening Statement

A general opening statement that has been tremendously successful for us is a variation of the following.

"This is ____ with ____. We specialize in working with businesses, helping them to ____. Depending on what you're doing/using/ buying in the area of ____, we might have something that could potentially help you to ____."

To make things even easier, since most everyone likes fill-in-the-blanks, paint-by-the-numbers, step-by-step recipes, I've created a template that my seminar participants use to build their own

openers. It's a formula with menus of word and phrase choices ready to plug in.

Naturally this is generic. But it can be customized by most anyone for their own industry and types of calls. That's what I suggest you do. Use this as an idea-starter for your own perfect opening.

More Examples

Once again, to set the stage, this is for an opening statement to a prospect you haven't previously spoken with. Let's look at some examples using this template. (Key phrases to be discussed are in italics.)

"Hello Ms. Dillon, I'm Dudley Denton with Able Supply. I'm calling today because depending on how you're now handling your receivables processing, there's a possibility we might be able to help you *cut down on the time* you spend *preparing invoices*, while also *increasing your cash flow* by *getting bills paid to you more quickly*. If I've caught you at a good time, I'd like to *discuss your situation* to see if this is something that you'd *like more information on*."

Here's another example.

"Mr. Grillo, this is Jill Nostrel with Slumlord Services. We specialize in working with multiple-unit property managers. Depending on how you're now tracking your accounting and owner reporting, there's a possibility we might be able to help you *cut down on the hassle and paperwork* involved in *those tasks*, while at the same time *enhancing the amount of useful information* you can put in a report, along with making them *easier to read*. If I've caught you at a good time, I'd like to *ask you a few questions* to see if this is something that you'd *like to take a look at*."

Try This One

Now here's the template you can fill in your-self using the sample words provided.

"Hello _____, I'm _____ with _____. I'm calling today because depending on what you're now doing/using/experiencing in the area of [fill in with your area of specialty] there's a possibility we might be able to help you [fill in with (1) Minimization Verbs] your [fill in with appropriate (2) Undesired Noun], while at the same time [fill in with (3) Maximization Verb] your [fill in with appropriate (4) Desired Noun]. If I've caught you at a good time, I'd like to [fill in with (5) Action Verb] your situation to see if this is something [fill in with appropriate (6) Ending Phrase]."

I must stress again, use this as an idea-starter...a place to begin when cobbling out your own opening. Be flexible with it. Don't use it word-for-word if you're not comfortable with it (although many people do just that, and have overwhelming success.)

Here's a final example with the key phrases marked.

"Hi Don, I'm Dale Fallon with Fishbreath Supply. My purpose for calling you is quite simple: depending on what items you're carrying now, there's a possibility we could help you *lower your costs on many of the same supplies you're stocking*, while at the same time *free up more*

More Opening Statement Tips

Here are some additional guidelines for opening calls.

• Create interest as briefly as possible.

• Write out your openings. Yes, script them. Everything else you'll say is in response to what they say, but the opener can be prepared, word for word. This way, you know it will work.

• Never *sound* like you're work-ing from a prepared opening.

• Look at your opening as if you were the person hearing it. If it doesn't excite you, scrap it and start over.

• Don't make a presentation, or ask for a sale or appointment— they're not ready yet at this point.

• When editing your opening, scrutinize every word and idea and answer this question: Is this adding to the effectiveness of the opening? If not, cut it out completely, or reword it. Be relentless in your editing. Better that you rip it apart than them.

Word and Phrase Menu

Use the following to fill in the blanks.

Minimization Verbs (1)	Undesired Nouns (2)	Maximization Verbs (3)	Desired Nouns (4)
save	costs	strengthen	profits
salvage	trouble	intensify	sales
free up	difficulty	reinforce	dollars
consolidate	problems	boost	revenues
minimize	restriction	increase	income
decrease	obstacle	expand	cash flow
cut down on	annoyance	add	savings
eliminate	inconvenience	grow	time
get rid of	time	maximize	productivity
reduce	expense	enhance	morale
lessen	charges	create	motivation
cut	taxes	build	output
lower	waste	enjoy	attitude
soften	hassle	ease	image
slash	burden	help	victories
shrink	work		market share
slice	drudgery		
trim	labor		
combine	effort		
modify	paperwork		
	bother		
	worry		
	anxiety		

Action Verbs/Phrases (5)
discuss
ask a few questions about
review
go through
analyze

Ending Phrases (6)
you'd like more information on
you'd like to discuss
that would be of value to you
that would be of interest
that would be worth considering
that would work for you

cash to carry other fast moving, high margin items. If I've caught you at a good time, I'd like to *ask a few questions* about your store *to see if we should talk further.*"

Lay the Groundwork for Follow-Up Calls

The follow-up is a continuation of previous contacts, on your road to your ultimate objective.

Your follow-up opener should:

- Remind them of your previous conversation,
- Mention what you both promised to do as a result of the previous call.
- State the agenda for this call.

It needs to be proactive to be effective. No nonsense like, "... and I was just calling to see if you got the literature, and if you had any questions." That's weak.

An effective example is:

"Kathy, it's Dan Adams calling to continue our conversation from last week. I've got some good news on the replacement parts research I did for you, and also I'd like to go through your thoughts on the proposal I faxed you..."

Calls to Regular Customers: Deliver Value

Do you like to be taken for granted? Or, do you like to be pampered, and made to feel special? The answers are obvious, but, why then, are so many customers treated with indifference. For example, "Hi Mike, it's Keith at Able Supply. Hey, you guys got an order for us this week?"

When your call is announced to your customer, you want him or her to say, "Oh, sure I'll take it. He always has great ideas for me." Contrast that with, "Oh, him again. Probably wants to know where my order is."

Every time you call, without exception, have a "Value Added Point" to make. It's anything that allows them to feel they've gained by simply talking to you. It can be good news, useful information, notification of a sale, ideas you have...anything they will perceive as useful. For example, "Sandra, it's Linda with Dino Services. I was studying what you've been buying from us over the past two years, and I've got an idea here for a program that might just make your job a little easier..."

Talk about ideas and results at the beginning of the call, not about products and services. People become curious about ideas and results. They resist the mention of products and services, because they feel they're about to hear a sales pitch.

Open calls by putting people in a positive frame of mind. Then move to the questioning phase of the call, and you're well on your way to success.

SELLING BY QUESTIONS

> "Find a need and fill it."
> —Napolean Hill (and others)
> Note that this old secret doesn't say *create* a need, it says *find* it.

Here's the secret of sales that can double your income: Get information before you give it. It's that simple.

Selling isn't *convincing* anyone of anything. It's helping them get what they want or need.

To enjoy gargantuan success in sales, you need to be a master questioner, able to open up your prospect and customer, unlock their needs, concerns and desires, and move them into a state of mind where they begin wanting a product or service like yours even before you begin presenting it. Think about it: offer someone a drink of water when they're not thirsty, and they decline. When they're parched, they seek out the water. Your job is to help them recognize the thirst. (See also Chapter 9 on SPIN® questions.)

Generating Need-Development Questions

People only take action when they are dissatisfied with their present situation, or want to avoid such dissatisfaction. You should structure questions to highlight specific dissatisfactions you alleviate.

Benefits are only benefits if the person hearing them perceives them to be. Here is a very effective exercise I recommend you engage in to help your questioning be as effective as possible.

I suggest you work backwards from benefits to create questions. Take a "benefit." Then think of what dissatisfaction it soothes, the need it fills, or the problem it solves. Then, write out the appropriate question you'd ask.

For example, an order-entry software program offers instant notification of out-of-

You Can't Pitch Without A Need

A cab driver a few weeks ago, after finding out what I did, said that he couldn't sell because someone gave him a test that asked him to sell a pen to a person who already had a similar pen. He failed miserably, and asked me what kind of pitch I would have suggested.

I responded that there's no possible way I would even consider trying to put together a "pitch" under those circumstances because you're predestined for failure. I told him that you'd first need to find out why and how the person uses pens, what he likes and doesn't like about them, ideally what he desires most and least when it comes to pens, and what value he places on that. Only then could you effectively tell him about your pen and have a snowball's chance of getting him to consider yours.

stock merchandise, allowing you to suggest alternative items.

But it's only really a benefit if listeners run into backorder situations and feel it's a hindrance because they lose sales, or have paperwork headaches, etc. Therefore an initial question would be, "How often do you run into backorder situations?"

You might follow by, "When do you realize it?" "Have you ever lost sales because you had to notify the customer later that their item was going to be late, and they just told you to cancel it?"

Notice that technique isn't simply, "Are you having any backorder problems?" That forces them to think too much. You want to help them recall and feel the dissatisfaction.

People Sell Themselves

People truly will sell themselves if you give them the opportunity. Do that with questions. After you've accomplished this on a call, then and only then are you in a favorable position to begin presenting what you offer.

Begin each call thinking of the dissatisfaction you can alleviate, and what questions you'll need to ask to determine if it exists. How will you help them recognize any latent dissatisfaction?

Additional Questioning Tips

Prepare your questioning plan. It's not enough knowing what questions you'll ask. The real pros know what they'll do with the answers—all possible answers. That's how you become *smooooth*. You can't script out an entire call; there are too many possible ways the conversation could branch. But you can be totally prepared for whichever artery it travels. As part of your preparation, take just one path at a time, and brainstorm every possibility. Just as a road is more familiar the second time you take it, so too will be your responses to questions, since you've already traveled that path in your mind.

Embellish needs. Again, people only take action when the dissatisfaction is strong enough. You probably have some need right now, but it's not major, so you let it be; you know, those "I'll get around to it" kind of things. With prospects and customers, you need to compound their perception of these needs. If they tell you they waste time now, ask how much. If they think sales are lower than they could be, ask how much lower. If they're losing money, find out how much. This gets them thinking about, and feeling, the pain.

Clarify the "fuzzy phrases." Don't get put off by an abstract phrase like, "We might do something next quarter. We'll take a look at it. Let's stay in touch." Ask questions like these to pin down what they mean:

- When you say "something," does that mean you'll go with it?
- What exactly will you be looking at?
- Does "stay in touch" mean I should call at a certain time?

PERSUASIVE SALES PRESENTATIONS

After we've asked questions to determine prospect/customer needs, the next step is the sales presentation. One key here is to present only what people are interested in, based upon what they told you in your questioning.

Some sales training spends inordinate amounts of time on sales presenatations. Not mine. I tell people I want them to talk less about their products or services. It's called "objection prevention."

Here's my simple process.

1 **Transition from your questioning.** Let them know you're done questioning, and spark interest—again—in having them listen to you: "Luke, based on what you told me about the existing insurance coverage on your business, and the added liability exposure you have, I believe I have something here that will cover you more, at about the same premium you're paying now."

2 **Paraphrase your understanding.** This is right out of Sales 101. Rephrase in your eloquently persuasive way, the needs, concerns, desires, and values they just related to you: "Let's just review what we've discussed so far to make sure I understand it completely. Bottom line, you feel you've been neglected by your present agent, except when it came time to renew your policy. And, you feel he's charging you an outrageous premium for the amount of coverage you now need since you're manufacturing toxic chemicals. Is that right?"

3 **Present the results of what you can deliver.** Only talk about what they told you they're interested in. Period. "Luke, by switching to my agency you would get the attention you deserve, and pay a reasonable premium for more than enough coverage. First, we would (present proof of each claim)..."

4 **Get commitment.** You're involved in a conversation at this point, either answering questions, or listening to buying signals. If the questions are buying or possession signals such as "That sounds good," or, "Do we pay the premium to your agency or to the corporate headquarters?", ask for commitment. "Should we get started?" "You can pay it directly to us. Should we prepare the paperwork?"

Make your recommendations conclusive. Leave no doubt as to what the person should do. You're the expert here. Don't just wish they'll come to the conclusion you'd like, and hope they volunteer to take action on their own.

I've heard reps leave things up in the air with a weak phrase

Tips To Help People Buy

Here are more tips to help you make powerful presentations.

- People buy results. I like the word "results" in place of benefits. People don't care diddly about the product or service itself, they get excited about the end result—the picture or feeling—they enjoy from owning or using it. Forget about your product or service, and concentrate on the results you deliver.

- Prepare sensory descriptions of your results. Think about how your results are seen, felt physically and emotionally, tasted, and heard. Remember, you want to help them experience, in advance, the results they can enjoy. "And just think how much easier it will be for you to prepare training. Instead of spending hours after work doing the research you said you hate, you can simply flip to the appropriate topic in your Leader's Guide for that month, circle the questions you'd like to use, and moderate while your reps learn through their own discussion."

- Preface results with a reminder. When presenting several results as part of your overall sales message, precede each with a reminder of the pain they want to avoid or eliminate, or the pleasure they desire. For example, "And here's what will help you avoid those lawsuits you were worried about..." Or, "And here's where you'll save big money..."

- Use exact numbers. People believe more thought and research went into arriving at precise numbers. Rounded numbers seem to be pulled out of the air.

like, "So keep us in mind when you feel you'd like to make a switch." Most people avoid tough decisions. State your suggestion explicitly so all they have to do is react to it—even if that means resisting. "Pat, based on everything we've discussed, you'd show a savings from day one on the program. I recommend I overnight the paperwork to you so you can OK it and have it back by Monday. Would you like to do that?"

It's quite simple. Make a presentation before you know what someone wants, and you're selling. Make it after, and you're helping them buy. Which would your prospect rather have you do?

CLOSING FOR COMMITTED RELATIONSHIPS

When clients tell me their reps need work on "closing techniques," I begin worrying. It's typically indicative of a larger problem: not moving the call and the sales process to the point where the "close" is appropriate.

"Sales advances take many forms, but invariably they involve an *action* that moves the sale forward...It's this action-oriented approach that characterized the successful people we studied...their success comes from how they set call objectives rather than from how they close."
— Neil Rackham, *SPIN Selling*

A couple of years ago I wrote in a magazine column that we ought to get rid of the term "close," and replace it with "commitment." I still feel that way. "Closing" implies an end.

What you really want is to open and build a relationship. To do that, you need constant movement on each of your calls towards an objective. This movement happens when your prospects or customers commit to doing something between now and the next call. This is central to getting sales.

The Commitment Phase Validates What Has Happened So Far

A football team doesn't throw the long bomb every time it gets the ball at its own 20-yard line. A man doesn't ask a woman to marry him after one date. Neither tactic is a high percentage play.

On sales calls, you shouldn't try to close on every contact. To achieve the objective, you need to move forward, enjoying small successes along the way. You build the relationship. The momentum is then with you. The ultimate commitment is much easier, since you've traveled nearer to the objective.

The "close" shouldn't be the major part of the call. It's the final validation of the customer's commitment.

Attitude is More Important Than Technique

Scan the sales section in bookstores or libraries and you'll find lots of nonsense on "closing
techniques." Many contain the tired old phrases
that cause people to bristle, like the guy from the
Better Business Bureau the other day who, after
his three-minute pitch about how I "qualified for
membership" (by virtue of having a business, I
guess) would like to drop by at "3:30 on Wednes-
day, or 9:00 on Thursday. Which would be better
for you?" Neither, I told him, since that would
imply I saw some value in meeting with him,
which he hadn't helped me realize yet. He threw
the long bomb too early, before moving the relationship forward, and tried to rely on a closing
technique known as the either/or close.

I say forget about technique, at least initially.
Work on your attitude. Get out of your
comfort zone, ask more, ask larger,
and you'll sell more. It's this simple:
Have an "asking" attitude and you'll
sell. Be shy about asking, and you'll
miss out. Maybe even lose your job.
Don't let that happen.

Get Commitments on Every Call

Never agree to place a follow-up call until you've gotten
commitment they'll do something between now and the
next contact. It can
be as minor as them
agreeing to review

Commitment Questions You Can Use

Here are ideas for commitment questions you can use or adapt to move the relationship forward.

- What will happen between now and our next contact?

- Are you comfortable taking this to the boss with your recommendation that you go with it?

- So you will have those inventory figures prepared by the next time we speak, is that right?

- You're going to survey your staff and get their input on what features they'd like to see, and you'll have the information by our next call, correct?

- By when will you have had a chance to go through the material so we can speak again?

- If you do decide to change vendors before my next call, will you call me?

- When you send out your Request for Proposals, may I be included?

Closing Questions You Can Use

When you've built the relationship, obtained commitments, and they have an immediate need, that is the time to ask traditional closing questions like these.

- Is this the program that you personally would like to invest in?

- The next time you need supplies, will you buy them from me?

- Shall we get started?

- May I sign you up?

- If the proposal contains all the items we've discussed, will you approve it and go ahaed with our plan?

your catalog and selecting items they would like to discuss next time. You can qualify a prospect by their level of commitment. If they won't do anything, they're likely not interested. And why would you waste time calling someone like that back? Of course, the ultimate commitment is agreeing to buy from you on this call.

Focus on moving your relationship forward, get in the "asking" habit, get commitments on every call, and you'll "close" more sales.

SETTING UP THE NEXT CALL

Do you ever have problems with follow-up calls, even after you felt the previous call went well?

Or, how about that gut-knotting feeling of staring at your prospect notes from a previous call as you prepare for the next one, searching for, but not finding, what you'll say on this call that's more inspiring than, "Well, ahh, I'm just calling you back to see if you got my brochure, and what you think?"

If you've ever been there—and most of us have—chances are that your previous call didn't end strongly, with a clear summation of that call. At the end of each call, clarify what is to happen next, both before the next call, and during it.

Ending a call with, "OK, I'll just send you out some literature, and give you a call back in a couple of weeks," virtually ensures your demise on the next contact.

And rightfully so.

There's nothing specific there, no connection between this call and the next. There's no summary of the problem, need or interest (if there was any established). There's no confirmation of what the prospect is doing next.

Ending Right

Here's what you should do at the end of your calls to ensure a fluid transition from this contact to the next. (By the way, all this presumes that you didn't get the sale. We're all pretty good at wrapping those calls up.)

Before ending the call you need to do an overview with your prospect or customer. Summarize:

- **The need or problem, and their interest.** Revisit what they are interested in, and why.
- **What they will do.** At the very minimum you should get commitment

they will read your material and prepare questions, test out your sample and evaluate it according to criteria you've both discussed, take your proposal to the committee with their recommendation, and so on. THIS IS CRITICAL! If you don't get a commitment for action, this person might not ever become a customer. Asking for, and getting some type of action commitment is my way of tightly qualifying people. If they're not taking action, why are you calling back?

- **What you'll do.** Review what you'll do, what you'll send, who you'll speak with, or whatever you promised.
- **When you'll talk next.** Don't say, "How about I call you in a couple of weeks?" Let them give you a date, and tie it to their commitment: "Carol, by when do you think you will have collected all of the inventory figures we'll need for our next conversation?" Not only do you have a date and time, but you have their commitment, that they'll perform their duties.
- **The next-call agenda.** Go over what's to happen next. It plants a seed as to what they should expect on the following call.

An Example Set-Up

"Let me go through what we've covered today. You feel that Advantage Inc. will provide you with better availability, you like our customer service policies, and you do want to get going with that new inventory program we offer. You need to wait to get funding in the next budget. I'll call you around the first of next month, when you'll know the budget priorities."

ADDRESSING RESISTANCE AND OBJECTIONS

When's the last time someone thanked you for telling them they were flat out wrong? It doesn't happen!

Everyone resents being told they're wrong. Yet most sales training suggests sales reps do exactly that—counter objections and resistance with slick, canned phrases. With insidious names like the "Boomerang Technique," they inherently tell people they're wrong and make them feel just slightly lower than topsoil.

You'll never change anyone's mind by preaching at them. For example, think about beliefs you feel strongly about: something

Canned Questions Lead to Canned Objections

political, moral, or even a favorite sports team. If someone simply started refuting everything you believed in, you would likely strengthen your stance, and think of why the other person is wrong.

You can, however, help someone to first doubt their beliefs, which is the initial hurdle in opening them up to your ideas. Get them to *question* their position regarding your offer or ideas. People believe *their* ideas more than they do yours. You can't tell them they're wrong and expect success. But you can help them to doubt their perceptions, which causes them to at least be open to what you have to say. You do this with doubt-creating questions. Here's how:

1 **Understand the objections you commonly hear.** Write them out. Then list reasons people voice that objection. For example, when they say "Your price is too high," does that mean they can get it cheaper down the street? Or, did they have a predetermined price figure in mind? Or, do they not have enough money in the budget? You'll need to know their rationale (their problem) before you can address the symptom: the objection.

2 **For each of the objection reasons, write out questions that uncover their rationale, and plants seeds of doubt.** For example, for the "price is too high," questions could be:

- Are we talking about just the price itself, or the long-term value?
- What are we being compared to?
- What price figure did you feel would be appropriate for what you're looking to receive?
- Take price out of the picture for a moment; do you like this unit better than any other you've seen?

Take the situation of a wholesale supplier trying to persuade a retailer to carry his product. The retailer says, "We don't need to stock any more lines." The wholesaler could use a canned "objection rebuttal," trotting out market share facts and figures that would prove the retailer wrong, but not change his mind. A doubt-creating approach would use questions:

- How often in the past month have people called and asked for this type of product and you were not able to provide it?
- Have you ever had a situation where someone called and asked about a product like this, but they didn't come in because they found out you didn't have it?

Approach objections in a non-adversarial way, and ask questions to root out the reasons. Go through this process, and you'll be better prepared to ask the right questions, open them up to considering your ideas, and soften their resistance.

SUMMARY

Marketing is anything you do to get or keep a customer. That's why you invested in this book. You also use the phone. And as long as you're using the phone, why not do it well?

As you've seen in this chapter, there's no need for salesy, "me"-oriented, techniques that make both the salesperson and prospect uncomfortable. Remember, you're helping people get what they want. That's the only professional way to sell.

ACTION AGENDA

Here are some ways to get started today to improve your use of the telephone for sales.

Analyze Your Current Outgoing Phone Calls To Prospects

1. What is your call objective?

2. Do you have a clear reason for calling that benefits them?

3. Do you know what information you need to get from the prospect to advance the relationship?

4. Do you have an interest-creating opening prepared? (Fill out the sample call template on page 170.)

5. List questions here that you can use to move the sale along to the next stage:

_____

_____

_____

_____

6. Summarize the major objections that prospects raise. List your questions to address them.

Objection	Question
_____	_____
_____	_____
_____	_____
_____	_____

7. Most sales take multiple contacts. What are the stages your buyers typically go through?

_____

_____

_____

What New Outgoing Calls Could You Make?

- Can you keep in touch with good customers? What can you call them about?
- Where can you get good lists of qualified prospects?
- When can you or staff make calls?
- When will you get started with more calls?

Chapter 8

THE NEW RULES OF SELLING:
Building Relationships

Jack Daly and Jim Pratt

Jack Daly (left) is an executive vice president for Fleet Mortgage Group, where he heads all production activities including retail, wholesale, and correspondent lending. He has more than 20 years of business, leadership, sales, and personal motivation experience. Daly is the former president of the Pratt•Daly Corporation, a consulting firm and training company that specialized in improved productivity through people development. Jack has served at the senior executive and CEO levels of several national companies including Security Pacific Bank; Glendale Federal Bank; GlenFed Mortgage Corporation; and Evans Products Corporation.

Jim Pratt (right) led the sales force of Northwestern Mutual Life, with 4,800 salespeople in 128 branches. As a co-founder and head of sales/marketing, Pratt built the sales force of PMI Mortgage Insurance Co., the nation's fourth largest private mortgage insurance company, subsequently sold to Sears Financial. He then became EVP of Imperial Savings Bank of San Diego and CEO of Ticor Realty Services in Los Angeles. Through his own company, The Pratt•Daly Corporation, Pratt has earned an international reputation for successful leadership, sales management, sales and team-building training.

Jack Daly, Fleet Mortgage Group Inc., 1333 Main Street, Columbia, SC 29201; Tel: (803) 929-7892; Fax: (803) 929-7962.

Jim Pratt, Pratt•Daly, 8380 Miramar Mall, Suite 107-109, San Diego, CA 92121; Tel: (619) 450-0300; Fax: (619) 455-1576.

THE NEW RULES OF SELLING: Building Relationships

Jack Daly and Jim Pratt

This chapter will give you the keys for selling in the 1990s, so that you can make more money with less work. Measure your activities against these standards and adjust your work efforts to build a more satisfying and profitable career.

Relationship selling means different things to different people. However, on this we should be able to agree: Successful career development depends upon how well we strengthen continuing business relationships with our customers.

WHERE DO YOU START?

Some salespeople have worked for five years, and have built numerous valuable business relationships.

Others have been in the business for one year, repeated five times—they do deals, but don't establish strong professional relationships with their clients and referral sources. An insightful measure into your success is how many "clients" you have developed. Clients give you 50 percent or more of their business.

Maximizing career growth starts with what we believe. Belief is the guiding factor, principle, passion, and faith that provides direction in our lives. We act in accordance with our beliefs. Commitment and passion for what we do come from a strong belief in our self-worth, our value to others, and a clear vision of our future.

We are all capable of so much more. None of us knows our true potential, yet we all know that we haven't challenged it. Our basic problems are lack of focus and an unwillingness to take on risk.

In this chapter, we'll focus on the "how to's" of building strong sales relationships with our clients. Then we'll wrap up with a summary of ten steps for successful action.

THE ANATOMY OF RELATIONSHIP SELLING

Your career growth depends on your ability to build strong, continuing relationships with top quality sources of business. Besides building these relationships, a professional salesperson is someone who:

- gets business from a prospect who is already committed to someone else,
- helps his or her business sources reach their full potential, and
- constantly upgrades his or her clientele.

And therein lies a problem. How do you gain the attention of these high producers?

How do you overcome their commitment to another supplier? How do you combat their indifference to wanting to see you? When two people want to work together, the details won't stand in their way. So you need to build a relationship where you want to work together.

Another key idea is that success with clients comes by giving "valued-added" service. You can accomplish this by delivering more than your client expected when he or she decided to try your service.

Be A Professional

Becoming a professional salesperson isn't that difficult. Experience shows that there are techniques which can allow us to earn more while actually working less. This helps you become excited about making sales calls, and ultimately enjoy your career more.

We start with several assumptions:

- We want to do business with attractive sources.

- We want to get most of our business from fewer customers and referral sources.

- By constantly upgrading the quality of our sources we will earn more with less effort.

- We need to create a positive environment in which prospects are receptive to our approach.

- We should invest in a computer and software to help us organize our marketing efforts and relationship maintenance. (See Chapter 14 for an example of computer sales automation.)

You develop customer partners because they discover it is in their best interests to work with you.

Another way to say this is that an account executive helps his or her clients be more successful. "Golden handcuffs" tie business sources to you. Your image, knowledge, sensitivity, attitude, and success create those bonds.

RELATIONSHIP SELLING

Prospecting

We start building strong business relationships by targeting a select number of prospects. A successful career as a salesperson is built upon maintaining a limited number of highly productive clients and not on seeing how many calls can be made in any week. "Focus precedes success" is a core concept of the process.

Regardless of our current success level or the amount of time we've been in business, we should write down a list of people we want to do business with. This target list may have as few as ten names for established, career-oriented account executives, and as many as 60 names for a beginner.

Have Specific Targets

Pre-selecting those we want to do business with because of their reputation, social style, and quality production is the foundation of our career.

Too often salespeople make calls in a territory and then work with whomever will give them a deal. Using this shotgun approach causes call reluctance, and is often disappointing.

Every account executive should create and carry a specific list of names who have been targeted as future business sources.

Target List

DataMagic
✔ *Magid & Assoc.*
✔ *ComputerShoppe*
MDI Plastics
✔ *Golden Printing*

In developing this list, use the following resources for assistance:

- Your manager
- Your support staff
- Your peers
- Your own observation

Consider your business niche when making your list. You want to identify those for whom you can bring the highest value. What strengths can you emphasize? Who generally are the best business sources for your company? High achievers then ask their current, satisfied clients for referrals to those whom they have targeted.

Your goal is to have a predetermined number of business partners. You must select them carefully because it is going to take some time to win them over. Additionally, you must get to know your target's managers, since they often either assist you or stand in your way.

You Need New "Clients"

Every salesperson, no matter how successful, should develop at least one new client per quarter. It is essential that we continually upgrade our clientele in order to increase our production. Since we can work with only a limited number of clients, they must be the best available.

> "If you want customer loyalty, you must be loyal to the customer."
> —Regis McKenna, *Relationship Selling*

Prospects are open to a new salesperson who will help them to be more successful. Despite this fact, most prospects are reluctant to change, and the more successful they are, the more this is true.

It is not cavalier to say, "Find out what someone wants and then deliver."

Doing so is far more effective than pitching your products in the hope that your prospect will respond. Top-producing prospects are too sophisticated for this selling style.

Before The Meeting

With your target list organized you are ready to set up an approach campaign. The key to a successful approach lies in creating a favorable image *before* calling for an appointment. Today's prospects are too busy or cyncial to respond to cold calls. We want to build an image which will cause the prospect to be willing, if not eager, to see us.

Building a relationship starts by overcoming their indifference toward you even before your first meeting together. You shouldn't call on a probable prospect unless you have "pre-marketed" yourself.

Pre-Market Yourself

A good approach campaign, in which you pre-market yourself, changes the acceptance rating considerably. The greater the positive image, the greater the success.

A pre-approach marketing campaign consists of mailing helpful information to your prospect about every four working days for up to six weeks before making an appointment. Systematically delivering useful business development ideas encourages your prospect to perceive you as a potential business associate, and thus someone who is worth seeing. (See Chapter 5 for an example of using newsletters to prepare the way for your approach.)

Provide Useful Information

These mailings do not need to be fancy or professionally prepared. But they should be legible, informative, and confined to one page. Attach your card with a handwritten note: "Thought you would find this interesting."

Send at least five mailings over a month, followed by a personal pre-approach letter with your résumé or bio attached. If you have a testimonial letter from someone whom your prospect

---

Pre-Marketing Campaign Boosts Sales

Our experience shows that different marketing activities result in appointments the following percentages of time:

	Success Rate
Cold call (no pre-marketing)	10%
Pre-approach letter	20%
Marketing campaign	40%
Referred lead plus campaign	60%

respects, mail that. Then call for an appointment. He or she will be excited about meeting you.

Every business source is looking for business relationships that are more beneficial to them. Every prospect is looking for the ideal professional sales partner.

This is hard to believe when we find Doberman Pinschers guarding the doors of our prospects, but it is true! No matter how committed customers say they are to another supplier, you can win them over with your professionalism.

Our job as professionals is to help our clients make more money. A continuing research effort should focus on what very successful clients are doing. Then share those concepts with others.

Call Reluctance

Determining who to call on and then initiating an approach are the most difficult parts of the sales process for most salespeople, no matter what industry they're in.

How often do we hide behind our desks doing unproductive work because we don't have a list of targeted prospects and a comfortable system for approaching them in order to initiate a business relationship? Once we have an interested prospect, we generally can proceed with confidence.

Call reluctance usually rises or falls in intensity depending on our current circumstances and recent results. But remem-

Keep Going!

A superstar should initiate one new approach campaign each week; a good producer needs to start two a week, and a beginning salesperson needs five per week. If you are already well-known, then reduce the number of mailings but not the number of new approaches.

ber this: Salespeople are paid more for their time than other professionals are because salespeople do what others are not comfortable doing.

> ## Look For Rejection
>
> We can say that we are in the "rejection business" because so many of our approaches have that result. But smart salespeople know that an initial rejection may well become a later acceptance.

Call reluctance thresholds are related directly to our self-esteem levels. A person with a healthy sense of self-worth is more willing to accept criticism, rejection, or even failure when pursuing a business relationship. While no one enjoys rejection, individuals with high self-esteem are able to overcome it and then move on to other opportunities.

Our major problem, then, is not the economy or our product line. It is our own motivation and self-esteem.

High achievers count only their wins, and ignore their losses. Outstanding success results most often after high levels of initial failure. The road to success is full of potholes.

WHAT TO AVOID

Too often account executives make frequent sales calls in an effort simply to be visible, hoping to find easy sales by being "in the right place at the right time." Being product pushers, such salespeople tend to "show up and throw up."

When meeting with a prospect they do an "information dump" of product features. Is it any wonder that some prospects place Doberman Pinschers at the front door when they see salespeople driving up?

KEEP UPGRADING

At times successful account executives slack off on new business development and "live off their fat." But when we fail to upgrade our clientele continuously, we risk a falloff of income if any of our clients quit using us.

This obsolete sales method perpetuates itself, since some successes can be found when using it. Yet it also is a prime cause of burn-out, which occurs when we don't establish career-building professional relationships.

If we aren't constantly developing new referral relationships and adding value to old ones, we will be forced to keep prospecting like a rookie. Remember, never quote price until you have established value.

THE APPROACH

You're now ready to call for an appointment. Here are a few hints on telemarketing:

- Concentrate on getting the appointment; don't discuss what you are going to talk about.
- Call from a place which has little background noise and where you won't be disturbed.
- Call on Thursdays for appointments next week.
- Identify yourself slowly so that the person being called learns your name.
- Do not ask, "Did you get my mailings?" Assume that he or she did.

Ask the professional question: "Did I catch you at a convenient time? Do you have a moment to speak?" If they don't, arrange a better time to call back.

Propose An Appointment

Once your prospect has said that he or she is

ready to listen, then state your purpose: "In the past few weeks, I have mailed you several items which I hope you have found helpful.

The purpose of my call is to arrange twenty minutes when we may exchange beneficial ideas. May I suggest next Tuesday—or what is good for your schedule?"

Selling The Appointment

If you get resistance, try a benefit approach: "I'm confident that twenty minutes together could be the beginning of a very beneficial business relationship."

Another response is, "Gamble twenty minutes of your time against twenty minutes of mine, and I promise not to stay a minute longer unless you invite me to do so."

Or, "I can easily understand that being as successful as you are, you're committed to another supplier. But I am confident you'll agree that no one has a monopoly on great ideas. Gamble twenty minutes of your time..."

Keep a record of your progress with the form on the following page.

These attempts to close on an appointment time will usually result in a commitment.

Before restating the time and thanking the prospect, suggest that he or she reserve the conference room for your meeting—since you have some things to show them.

Within 24 hours before every meeting, reconfirm the time of your 20-minute appointment. Restate your desire to meet in the conference room away from your prospect's desk.

A NEUTRAL SETTING

Every effort should be made to get a prospect onto neutral ground, such as the conference room or a nearby restaurant. Doing so avoids phone interruptions and gets him or her out from behind their desk.

Pratt • Daly
Corporation
Sales Builder

TARGET MARKETING
PROSPECT CALL LIST

Office/Location _____
Date _____
Call Rating ===========
(Best° 4-3-2-1 • Worst)

COMPANY	PROSPECTS NAME FIRST & LAST	PHONE #	TYPE OF CALL A B L C P S	OR	COMMENTS	ORDERS	TIME IN	TIME OUT

A-Appointment P-Purpose S-Status OR- Overall Rating
B-Breakfast   • I-Interview • N-New • A
L-Lunch   • P-Presentation • E-Existing • B
C-Cold Call   ○ S-Service • F-Former ○ C

TOTALS FOR DAY:

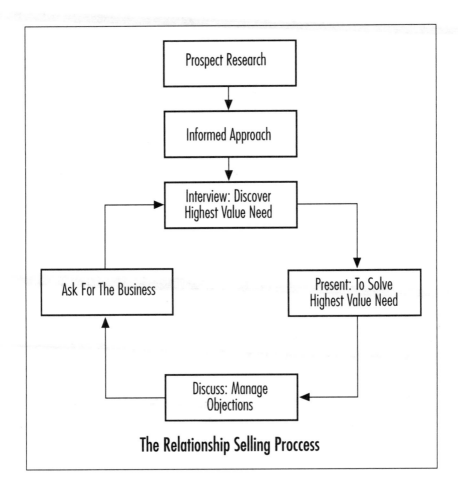

The Relationship Selling Proccess

THE INTERVIEW

Sales success begins with prospect research, shown both in the figure above, and at the bottom of the Critical Path pyramid diagrammed on page 201. Our first objective is to define the highest value needs of the prospect. To do this we must conduct a meaningful interview in a favorable environment.

Talk To The Receptionist

After arriving a few minutes early, ask the receptionist to announce you to your prospect. While waiting, interview the

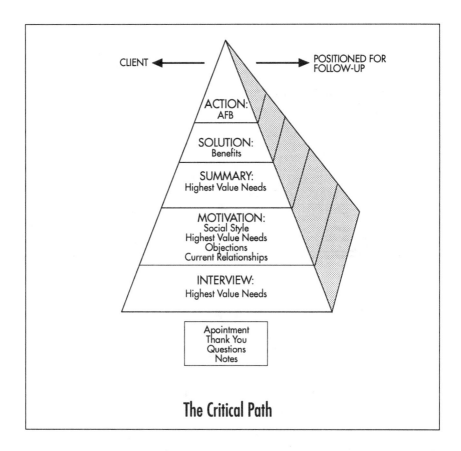

The Critical Path

receptionist. Find out the receptionst's name and how long he has been there. Ask what he did before; and perhaps even inquire about his career goals. Get to know the receptionist, because he can help you discover how to start working with an office.

When meeting your prospect at her desk, once again suggest going into the conference room. About half of the time this request will be successful. When seated, follow these four steps:

1) Thank her for the appointment, and reiterate your 20-minute commitment.

2) State that you have a number of exciting things to present,

"But would it be all right if I asked you a few questions first?"

3) After receiving a go-ahead, open your folio and ask permission to take notes. (This further establishes your professional credibility.)

4) Start with the first of the five questions that you have prepared for this prospect. Your prepared questions will be on the left-hand side of your folio.

You have now created the right environment—particularly if you were referred by a mutual business associate.

6 Reasons To Interview Your Prospects

Interviewing is beneficial because it:

- Creates rapport
- Builds trust
- Reduces tension
- Positions you for "adding value"
- Reduces objections
- Encourages interest

Diagnose First, Prescribe Later

Professionals never recommend an action until they have fully determined the problem, opportunity, or need in the relationship. How would you feel towards a physician who prescribed a medication prior to conducting a physical? Think of the environment when you visit your physician. Who does most of the talking?

You do, because your physician is determining your medical problem by asking questions.

Quality Questions

Questions will be repeated from different viewpoints. Many times your doctor will ask you to more clearly explain what you feel or think. Any physician who prescribes an action, a treatment, or a medicine before conducting a thorough examination is subject to a malpractice suit.

Any salesperson who shows up and then verbally "throws up" before determining the prospect's Highest Value Needs (HVN's) deserves the same lawsuit!

You need to make presentations and ask for the business. But to do that before establishing the needs to which you will respond is both non-professional and non-effective.

Your Goals

The prime purposes of the interview are to gain trust and interest while reducing indifference and rejection. To accomplish these goals we must follow a critical path of demonstrating our competence and determining the "Highest Value Needs" of the prospect.

Listen, Don't Sell

Our purpose now is to determine HVNs, and not to present our benefit statements. Do not let a question or statement by the prospect change the scene from an interview into a presentation. There will be plenty of time for presentations after we have determined the HVN's.

The questions you ask will define your professional competence, particularly when you very briefly indicate your experience between your prospect's answers.

Postpone making suggestions or asking for the business until you have defined the following:

1. The highest value needs of the prospect
2. His or her social style
3. Current relationships with other suppliers, and
4. His or her highest value objections

Incisive questioning and proactive listening will bring forth the answers we need.

Record the objections you're hearing, such as, "I'm already

committed to someone else."

If your prospect gives this excuse, respond with, "I'd be really surprised if someone as successful as yourself didn't have several established relationships." Then proceed with your questions.

We can build trust by demonstrating true interest in our prospect and by a sincere desire to assist this person. Our goal is to become her sales partner.

The bottom of the pyramid represents the point where we establish the relationship. It is done by determining the highest value needs of the prospect. We accomplish this by creating an understanding of what our prospect wants in an account executive, and by an awareness of what his or her goals are.

Selling is the transfer of trust. Therefore, ask questions and listen—*really* listen.

> **LISTEN**
> When you are in front of a prospect, how much time do you talk and how much time do you listen? It is important to remember that the listener controls the interview.

Buyer Social Styles

During this period, you should also estimate the social style which your prospect seems to have.

Each presentation must be planned to appeal to the social style of your prospect. Here are some suggested ways to stand out in the eyes of your prospect:

Driver Style: Use itemized action items that quickly get to the bottom line.

Expressive Style: Create a picture of a successful, supportive, and profitable relationship.

Amiable Style: Build trust and make the

change to using you safe and easy.

Analytical Style: Document every action suggested in order to increase trust.

Buyer Needs

Next, we must put the highest value needs of our prospect in order of priority. We then must decide how we are going to present our solution and benefit statements for each of these needs. Sometimes needs are equal in strength, and we meet them one by one. At other times there is just one overpowering need to address.

Here are the most common needs:

- Price
- Speed
- Quality

Price is always a consideration! Yet, the more professional and successful your prospect is, the less this will be a major consideration—as long as he or she knows you are competitive. However, inexperienced prospects tend to choose suppliers almost solely based on price.

How To Determine Highest Value Needs

Determine highest value needs by prioritizing what is most important to your prospect, and then defining exactly what she is communicating with each need.

For example, if your prospect states that service is her priority, you need then to ask her to define service. "What comprises good service by your definition?"

Commitment speed is another general need, even if a transaction may not close for some time. Time compression offers the greatest opportunity to differentiate ourselves from the competition. Wherever possible, we need to meet this need by re-engineering procedures to achieve this result.

Quality can refer to many things; but in our professional relationships, it is best summed up as "integrity" We define integrity as doing exactly what you say you will do, in the way you say you will do it, when you say you will do it. When combined with quality products and service, integrity makes us truly professional.

FOCUS ON THEM

A good question at this point is, "If you could design the ideal account representative for you, what would that person be like, and what would he or she do for you?"

When asking about a prospect's current business sources, find out the strength of those relationships.

Anticipate Objections

If someone surprises you with an objection, it is because you didn't ask enough questions, or you didn't listen during

Other Buyer Needs

Other needs of professional business sources are:

- An account executive who can be trusted
- A friend
- Someone who brings me business
- A salesperson who builds my reputation
- Someone who brings me profit-making ideas
- A business partner

Clients seldom will ask us for assistance with regard to their personal, work, organizational, or selling needs. Often our prospects think we don't "understand their business," or their egos won't allow them to make such a request of us.

But we often can help them in these areas if we present such assistance in a subtle and supportive manner.

the interview phase of the selling process.

If we know our prospect's needs, social style and objections, we are in a position to offer a solution that he or she will find not only acceptable, but also desirable. We can "motivate" this prospect to move in our direction.

Once we have defined our prospect's Highest Value Needs we must decide whether it's best to ask for a subsequent appointment in order to present our solution, or if we should suggest some immediate action.

We are influenced in this decision by how well we have determined needs, the prospect's social style, his or her present relationships, and what the likely objections will be. If in doubt on these issues, continue your interview. Or, if you're pressed for time, suggest making another appointment.

BE PREPARED

It's amazing how many experienced salespeople "wing it." Every sales associate should have a notebook full of concrete reasons a prospect should work with them and with their company.

UNDERSTANDING YOUR PROSPECT

Our next step is to present a solution which meets the Highest Value Needs of your prospect. You'll recall that during the interview we determined four vital pieces of information:

- The social style of our prospect
- His or her HVN's
- An awareness of anticipated objections
- What will motivate the prospect to work with us

Armed with this knowledge, we are ready to proceed. During our interview phase we have probably used the time allotment we asked for when making the appointment.

We then decide whether to ask for more time, which is usually granted, or if we should make a subsequent appointment permitting us to marshal our solution with greater focus and documentation. This is a "gut" call which must be made at the moment.

PREPARE FOR THE NEXT MEETING

Tell your prospect you would like to gather some information and ideas to bring on your next visit. Schedule the following appointment before leaving! Never leave an appointment without arranging the next action.

Generally the clients you want are already committed to some other vendor. You cannot expect them to sever their current relationship just because you have appeared on the scene.

On an average, it will take about five calls before you can expect results. Be patient, be professional, and be persistent—you'll get there!

DIFFERENTIATION THROUGH TRUST

If you want to become a top-producing salesperson, the key is to differentiate yourself and your company from the competing

How To Set Up A Second Meeting

Say something like:
"Thank you for your answers to my questions. What I'd like to do is gather some information from my office and meet with you again later in the week. I appreciate your courtesy and feel very confident that the information will be beneficial to you. May I suggest getting together Thursday afternoon?"

Having a break will give you time to prepare specific ideas and document them. Be sure to send a thank-you card reconfirming your next appointment. Also reconfirm by phone the day before your meeting.

salesperson your targeted prospect presently is doing business with.

Traditional selling—which focuses on presenting product features and then asking for the business, won't help you in this situation. Industry-wide pricing and products are too similar for you to rely on them to make a major impact on your prospects.

Instead, you should seek to develop a professional relationship which culminates in a transfer of trust. Most relationships with prospects never really develop deep-seated trust. Here we'll look at ways to make that happen.

HAVE FEWER CLIENTS

It doesn't matter how many sales calls you make. What's important is how effective each one is. See fewer people if you want to do more business, but be sure they are the right business sources for you.

PROMOTING TRUST

Every new relationship between two people contains an element of tension. For this reason many of us avoid cold calls, for the tension is highest in that situation. We suggest a process which will build a network of clients who give you at least half of their business. It isn't chasing after single deals.

BUILDING THE RELATIONSHIP OVER TIME

If you are not successful initially, continue to call on your targeted prospects. Your goal is more to move the relationship along than it is to concentrate on a single transaction.

When you feel the time is right to ask for your prospect's business, ask: "Considering what we have been discussing, do we have a basis for doing business together?" The answer will determine your progress and where the relationship is headed.

If you have demonstrated your knowledge, sensitivity, and constructive help, the answer will often be "yes" with some qualifications. Meet these conditions, and then you're on your way to building a business partnership.

PRESENTING

Now on to how to present solutions to those needs. Here are three steps to take:

1. Summarize the prospect's Highest Value Needs.
2. Gain agreement that your summary is accurate.
3. Present a practiced solution.

Decide beforehand what you want your prospect to remember after you've left. Focus your solution on four or five key points which meet prospect needs, and limit your presentation to these key issues. Your sales effectiveness will result from defining specific Highest Value Needs of each prospect, and then meeting those needs.

Customize Your Presentation

A suggested transition is, "Let's start by addressing your most important need."

Your presentation of solutions will be effective by following these guidelines:

- Tailor your presentation to each prospect's social style.
- Validate how you and your company can meet each HVN.
- Emphasize that your prospect will gain the benefits he or she most desires.

At times a prospect will create

"smoke screens" to keep from getting involved. These artificial barriers occur naturally. To tear them down we must build trust—quickly—and clearly provide beneficial solutions to the prospect's Highest Value Needs.

Trust Eliminates Barriers

Without a foundation of trust, prospects will keep bringing up objections, no matter how adept we are in answering them. Overcoming objections through power techniques is often perceived as manipulative and is therefore unacceptable.

It is far less effective to learn ten ways to "overcome" objections than it is to discover how to create interest and trust by building a positive image and practicing empathetic interviewing. We don't sell product, we help our customers buy our services.

DEALING WITH OBJECTIONS

While determining needs during the interview phase, you should learn of forthcoming objections.

A good interviewer will find out the prospect's concerns. Often they are simply a request for more information. When these issues are uncovered, a salesperson can decide whether to meet them during the interview, or whether to give them attention in the solution phase.

The best way to minimize objections is to define highest value needs and meet them. Despite our best efforts, we will still get concerns when we ask for the business — and ask we must!

PROSPECTS FEAR CHANGE

Prospects will hesitate to move from a known situation to an unknown. Many times prospects will show no interest, because they do not want to address the issue of change and the possibility of making a bad decision.

In fact, it's best to ask for the business in a way which will help us discover unmet needs.

Unmet concerns will resurface, and we must respond. There are only about ten common objections or concerns. We can thus prepare ourselves in advance for a sales meeting, thereby becoming a professional salesperson rather than one who "wings it."

> "There's a big difference between selling and helping people buy. Helping people buy matches their needs with proper solutions. Selling creates a sale. Helping people buy creates customers."
>
> —Michael LeBoeuf,
> *How to Win Customers and Keep Them For Life*

Practice Overcoming Objections

Create a "Success Guide." In it list each possible objection and how you will respond. Your purpose is not to memorize responses but to understand how to respond in the words that are comfortable for you.

Remember, never argue or disagree—don't meet force with force. Instead, try to understand your prospect's concerns.

Turning an objection into a question often will cause the prospect to elaborate on it. Usually, we then can determine how serious the objection is. If you did a good job in the interview, you are prepared to answer this objection.

> *Example:* "Your pricing is too high."
>
> *Response:* "Tell me why you feel that way. What has led you to believe that our pricing is too high?"

Remember that if we meet a prospect's highest value need, this will overcome most—if not all objections. Follow this model for dealing with objections:

1. Ask questions.
2. Prospect elaborates.
3. Respond empathetically.
4. Continue presentation to ask for the business.

Here's an example of how to proceed:

Objection: "I'm already committed to another supplier."

Response: "It's good to have someone to work with. How long have you been using him or her? Do you give him or her all of your business?

"I respect your loyalty and hope that soon you'll be as loyal to me. One thing is for sure: No one has a monopoly on ideas, don't you agree? Give me the opportunity to demonstrate what our team can do to help you to be more successful."

Another Response: "I respect your loyalty to (XYZ Company) just as I cherish my clients' loyalties to me. May I ask: Before you started using them, did you use someone else? Did you change because you perceived additional benefits? Was this change in your best interest?

"Doesn't it make sense that if you changed once for your benefit that changing again might provide you with even greater benefits? The only way to find out for sure is ... let's do some business together."

* * *

Objection: No interest or indifference.

Response: "I'm here to apply for the position as your business partner. You won't employ my services unless you're convinced that I can build your reputation. But if I can make you a real hero with your clients, you'll receive strong referrals from them. Isn't that right?"

"You impress me as being a very proactive and successful professional and that's why I called you for this appointment. Tell me about your current relationships."

DEVELOP YOUR OWN EXAMPLES

Each of us must use responses to objections that we find comfortable. Keep track of responses which are compatible to your style in your Success Guide.

Seek out your office's superstars and ask them what they say when they hear a specific objection. Also discuss specific objections at sales meetings. Your Success Guide should be dynamic—so keep improving your presentation skills by constant attention to key words and phrases that compliment your style.

SUMMARY

Our clients determine our success. Too many account executives waste their time calling on low-producing sources, when their time could be spent on more productive, targeted business opportunities.

DIAGNOSE BEFORE YOU PRESCRIBE
"Seek first to understand, or diagnose before you prescribe, is a correct principle manifest in many areas of life."
—Stephen R. Covey

To maximize our potential we must continuously upgrade our business by working with fewer but more-productive clients and referral sources. To reach these valuable sources and gain their attention in a positive way, we recommend conducting a pre-marketing campaign.

KEEP GROWING
"He or she who ceases getting better ceases being good."
—Anon

Directing your efforts toward these targeted sources will enhance your income, reduce your call reluctance, increase your professionalism, and help you enjoy a magnificent career as a sales professional.

A benchmark: Any calendar quarter in which you have not added a new, more productive client is a questionable quarter. A client is defined as someone who gives you 50 percent or more of his or her business. A customer is someone who brings you occasional business.

ACTION AGENDA

One of the best ways to end a bad habit is by replacing it with behavior which you recognize is good for you. Here are ten positive habits of top salespeople.

"Nothing happens until somebody sells something."
—Red Motley

1 **Make sure each of your calls has a purpose.** Many of your clients have various sorts of barricades to help them regulate sales reps and other callers.

Every call must have a purpose other than idle conversation. If there is not an immediately obvious one, it is up to you to create one.

A reason can be a product or price change, or news from the local scene. You can always bring something to give your call purpose. It is up to you to find it.

2 **Start analyzing your calls.** The best time to do so is immediately after leaving the prospect's office.

Ask yourself the following: "Did I make a professional impression? Did I talk too much? Did I uncover needs? Was my interview or presentation tailored to those needs, and the prospect's personality style? Did I address objections properly?"

Jot down several things you did right, then jot down several things you did wrong. Also, make certain you understand the next step with the client, and write that down as well.

3 **Start analyzing your clients' performance.** You cannot afford to spend your valuable time with customers who do not produce for you.

An office that used to be a big account for you may have lost a key player, surrendered marketing share to another firm, or had other difficulties. Be sure to recognize when this happens, and adjust your efforts accordingly.

You can afford to "carry" only a small number of low performers. Ask yourself these questions about your client base every 90 days:

- On a scale from 1 to 10, how has this client performed?
- Do we offer the right programs or products for them?
- How many suppliers do they deal with?
- Do I get my fair share of their business?

> "As a salesperson, keeping track of your time is the moral equivalent of a dieter counting calories, except you're monitoring your output, not your intake."
>
> —Harvey Mackay, *How to Swim with the Sharks...*

- How many calls have I made on them in the last 90 days?

Value each business source and constantly upgrade the quality of your clients. Stop calling on those who don't measure up to your standards. If you have internal sales support, turn over low-producing customers to your inside support team.

We must build clients, not hunt for transactions. Clients are those business sources which give us a significant percent—if not all—of their business. How many clients do you have? Add at least one high producer each quarter as a client.

> "You can finish school, but you can never finish your education."
> —Anon

4 **Become a student of people.** Just as an artist needs to understand the full potential of his range of colors, so must a salesperson know how to deal with the differences in people.

Most salespeople realize that people are different, and must be approached in varying ways. However, many do not realize that there are clues in observable behavior that can help you anticipate how others will react to certain situations.

That can be of inestimable value to a salesperson. Learn ways to easily identify some of these differences. Ask yourself early on in the interview, "What kind of person am I talking with?"

Stay With It

Learn to prioritize your time and tasks. This is fundamental to any time management system. There are a number of effective ways to accomplish it. Whether you use a day, week, month-at-a-glance type system, or just connect yourself with a "Things to do today" pad, the important matter is to stay with it.

---

5 **Get organized.** Time is a salesperson's most valuable tool. But using it to maximum advantage is often the salesperson's greatest challenge.

Salespeople tend to be ebullient, vivacious people for whom detail is a despised form of torture. Disciplined pros make and follow a flexible work schedule to maximize their selling time.

Generally that consists of office time, planned at the beginning and end of the week, and at the beginning and end of the day—with selling time for the rest.

Of course, you sometimes must be in the office to interact with your support staff, but it is not the place to spend your prime time hours. Do these things as bookends to your selling day—either early or late.

> "The secret to success is to do common things uncommonly well."
> —John D. Rockefeller

Remember, no time management plan will overcome lack of motivation to succeed. Do your work with enthusiasm and passion—success is sure to follow!

6 **Add the personal touch.** Use your individuality to do the little things that will make you stand out from the crowd. Writing personal notes to clients to thank them for their time, or to follow-up an appointment are examples. They need not be lengthy or complex, just sincere. (For examples, see Chapter 13 on thank you notes.)

Along the same lines, leave a brief note on the back of your business card when you miss key contacts in their offices. It's so simple, but hardly anyone does it. And it means that your card will get noticed among the many.

Ours is a people business, and creativity counts. Find ways to make your personality come through in your approach.

Keep Focused On Questions

When you find yourself tempted to rattle off the same list of programs that every other sales rep recites to clients, do yourself a favor and stop. Then take out something to write on and say: "Do you mind if I ask you a few questions?"

You are joining the elite 20% who do most of the business when they discover the power of effective questioning. (See also Chapter 9 on SPIN® Selling.)

7 **Create a notebook for presentations and objections.** A "Success Guide" will help you crystallize your thoughts before going into your presentation, and provide reminders for key points that will work with your client's social style.

An objective notebook helps you handle the hurdles every salesperson encounters along the path to getting a commitment. The amazing thing is that there really aren't more than ten objections out there.

Write down the objections that you hear the most, and answer them in your own words for future use. Also jot down a presentation idea or power phrase when one occurs to you. They provide effective refreshers, regardless of your experience level.

8 **Always conduct an interview before making a presentation.** This is the most fundamental rule in selling, but it is also the most frequently broken, even by the most seasoned professionals. You have to know what your prospect's needs are before you can do an effective job of meeting them. If it is as simple a concept as it sounds, why then do most salespeople opt to "shotgun" every feature, benefit, and aspect of their product line?

It is far easier to ask a few questions before

you target shoot. It's easy to do, if you listen. Don't just "show-up and throw-up."

Identify your client's Highest Value Needs. After you bring some of the client's concerns out in the open, then you can prepare a powerful and beneficial presentation.

9 Before you launch into your presentation, go over your understandings once more with the client—they may have changed. Sales take place over time. You might find your inspired solution to a client concern isn't relevant any more.

To avoid this, simply restate your prospect's highest value needs and ask for confirmation of them. Similarly, ask your prospect what she or he means before responding to an objection.

After making your presentation, ask for the business. Remember that we are interested in becoming a business partner, not just in getting one deal. A good way to find out how your prospect sees the relationship is by simply asking, "Considering what we have been discussing, do you see ways we could work together?"

10 Become a student of your industry. The best way to truly understand how to get business is to know how your clients do business.

Think like your customers, and you will seldom be short of ideas on how to serve them better. If you are to think like them, you must know the business inside and out—in some ways even better than they know it themselves.

"If your company is doing well, double your training budget; if your company is not doing well, quadruple it!"
—Tom Peters

Of course, that kind of knowledge does not come easily. Take courses and attend. Pick a client you know well and spend the day with him or her.

Find one or more successful professionals and model them to learn about your field, your role, and, ultimately, yourself. Sit at the feet of the masters.

TAKE ACTION

All of these ideas should cause changes in your everyday routine.

It will not do much good if you keep these ten Action Agenda items as vague goals. Give them a thorough evaluation. Implement the ones you believe can be helpful in revitalizing your career and recharging your batteries. A conscious decision to act and effect change is the most important step to take.

> "You miss 100% of the shots you never take."
> —Wayne Gretzky, hockey great

Everyone is looking for a better business partner. Build trust on every call and then be professionally persisent.

Chapter 9

SPIN® SELLING:
A Proven Sales Method

Bud Coggins

W.H. "Bud" Coggins
utilizes over 30 years of sales
and marketing experience to
helps small- and medium-sized
businesses develop and imple-
ment innovative strategies to enhance their success. His career as a salesman,
sales manager, general manager, and corporate vice president creates a solid
foundation for helping others create their own success.

After a twenty-year career in the broadcasting industry, and with two kids
in college, Coggins left the security of the corporate world (yes, in 1984 there
was security in the corporate world) to pursue his "passion" for independence.
He founded Coggins Sales and Marketing, Inc.

Coggins conducts workshops that help small business owners acquire the
necessary knowledge and skills to effectively market and sell their products or
services.

Coggins has a monthly column, "Bud's Bits," in the *Small Business Extra*
that provides marketing and sales tips, ideas, and stategies. Bud has always
believed that, "If your true purpose is to help others succeed, you will succeed."

W.H. "Bud" Coggins, Coggins Sales and Marketing, Inc., 8820 Six Forks Rd.,
Raleigh, NC 27615; phone (800) 394-9299, (919) 848-9299; fax (919) 676-
0666.

SPIN® SELLING: A Proven Sales Method

Bud Coggins

MARKETING VS. SELLING

It is important to understand the difference between marketing and selling. According to *Webster's Dictionary*, marketing is defined as: "the total of activities by which transfer of title or possession of goods or services from seller to buyer is effected."

These activities are many and various according to the needs of your business. Typical activities include advertising, public relations, networking, and methods of presentation of your product or service, i.e., brochures, flyers, letterhead, business cards, etc. (Many specific methods are covered in the other chapters of this book.)

The best way to determine the activities you should be involved in is to create a well thought out, written marketing plan. Through this process you will develop goals and objectives, and the strategies to accomplish them. Once you have completed your plan, the real key is to commit, implement, and periodically review your goals and objectives.

Marketing's Goal

The major role of marketing is to pave the way to the ultimate goal of transferring title or possession of your goods or services to your customer. A pitfall for many people is assuming that your targeted communication alone will convince your customers and prospects to buy what you are offering. Most products and services require a personal follow-up. That's where the selling process takes over.

The ultimate goal of the selling process is to finalize a transaction that transfers your product or service to a buyer.

The process is complete only when the buyers are satisfied, have remitted payment, and their checks have cleared the bank.

The question now becomes, "How do I acquire the attitude, knowledge, and skills to successfully complete a win-win transaction?" That question is the essence of this chapter.

> Marketing means first, anything you do to get OR keep a customer.
>
> Marketing can also be looked at as a funnel which channels prospects to the final, personal selling stage.

SELLING: ART OR SCIENCE?

In Arthur Miller's play, *Death of a Salesman,* Willy Loman's basic philosophy of selling was to "slap 'em on the back, tell a few jokes, and write the order." Selling was considered to be an art that could only be performed by fast talking, slick, personable, con-men.

Up until the 1970s, this philosophy worked pretty well. However, since that time, the selling process has evolved into more a science than an art.

What Sales Shouldn't Be

"Many of the major-account salespeople I work with complain that traditional sales training treats them as if they were selling used cars. What's worse, it treats their customers as simpletons waiting to be exploited by verbal trickery and manipulation."

—Neil Rackham, *Spin Selling*

RELATIONSHIPS PLUS

Because buyers and sellers are human beings, there will always be an element of art in selling. There will always be a place in the buying and selling process for a personal bond between buyer and seller. When all else is equal, that relationship can be the deciding factor.

More Is Needed

Unlike Willy Loman, sellers in today's marketplace must accept the fact that personal relationships alone cannot ensure an order for your product or service. With an unlimited amount of information available to buyers, their level of expertise has outpaced the expertise of sellers.

Most of the old methods of selling are inappropriate today. However, most sales training continues to teach these methods. Later you will be exposed to a research-based selling process. It is based on research, not theory, and rules out most of the traditional methods.

Is selling an art or science? Selling is some of both, with an evolution towards science.

Are some people born salespeople? Yes, some do have a "natural" affinity for selling. However, successful selling in our world today is achievable by first having a viable product or service. Then you must earn trust and help your customers solve their challenges by keeping your focus on their needs, wants, and desires.

SELLING IS AN ATTITUDE...A MINDSET

Yes, there are specific skills and personal characteristics involved in the selling process. However, your attitude is the key to your success. You possess the necessary personal characteristics and can acquire the skills to succeed...IF you have a positive attitude about selling.

UNDERSTAND YOUR MOTIVATION

Your first consideration is to define the importance selling plays in your personal and business success. If you determine, objectively, that your success is NOT dependent on the exchange of your ideas, concepts, product(s), or service(s) for something of value, such as money, then your attitude toward selling is unimportant.

The fact that you are reading this chapter is a good indication this is not your situation. The balance of this chapter will discuss success factors and share a proven method of selling.

Personal Attitudes for Success

Empathy (feeling the reactions of others)

Desire to serve (wanting to help people to win their approval)

Ego-strength (the need to succeed)

Self-esteem (the ability to cope with rejection)

—J. & H. Greenberg
What It Takes to Succeed in Sales

TEN CHARACTERISTICS FOR SUCCESSFUL SELLING

1 **Positive mental attitude.** This is an essential ingredient for everything we do in life, and is just as essential, if not more so, in selling.

2 **Good self-image.** In order for others to feel good about us, we *must* feel good about ourselves.

3 **Integrity.** Need I say more? Do you sincerely believe in the value of what you offer? You must be "for real."

4 **Self-motivation.** Self-motivation is created when we are truly enthusiastic about our product or service.

5 **Resilience.** Rejection is a natural part of the selling process. The key is to *not* take rejection personally but see it as a challenge to get better at what we do.

6 **Good listener.** When we ask the right questions and then truly listen to the response of our customer, we dramatically raise the odds in our favor for a successful outcome.

7 **Totally customer focused.** When your true purpose is to help others succeed, you will succeed.

8 **Real knowledge of your product or service.** Most people are acutely aware of whether or not you know what you are talking about.

9 **Determination.** There are many obstacles to overcome in the selling process. Successful people find a way to overcome these inevitable challenges. They turn these challenges into opportunities.

10 **Time manager.** We all are given twenty-four hours per day. How you use them impacts your degree of success. Maximizing your allotted time is a challenge. We *must* find ways to make time an ally, not an enemy.

As stated earlier, you already possess these characteristics for success. Understanding and evaluating the degree of their development provides a start for your next step on your journey of success.

NO MAGIC TO SALES

At this point you should be getting the message that selling is not a magic act. Unfortunately, a negative image of selling seems to get heavy exposure through the media and other venues. The fact is that everyday thousands of professional salespeople quietly go about helping their customers and prospects solve their challenges and maximize their opportunities.

Be enthusiastic about your product or service. Add a positive attitude about selling and a true belief that by helping others succeed you will succeed. Then you need only acquire the knowledge and skills to succeed.

The next section is devoted to exposing you to a proven selling process that will do just that.

SPIN® SELLING

Neil Rackham and his associates at Huthwaite, Inc. conducted a 12-year, $1 million, 35,000+ sales calls research project to evaluate effective sales performance. They had no preconceived ideas or formula to prove in this process. They simply accompanied salespeople on their personal sales calls, then observed and noted the behavior and results of the call. They looked at the data and came up with the "SPIN" process.

No other sales method is so completely backed by research. Huthwaite's findings are controversial because they, for the most part, go against the grain of conventional sales training.

The end result of this research and the powerful evidence presented should convince you. Using the SPIN® strategy can have a dramatic and positive influence on your quest for success.

The SPIN® process is both simple and complex. The following outline is intended only to give you an overview and motivate you to investigate more thoroughly by reading Rackham's book.

THE SPIN® STRATEGY

Small Sales

Huthwaite's research discovered that the reason many people still believe in some of the older techniques is because they still work for small sales. A small sale is defined as a sale which can normally be completed in a single call and which involves a low dollar value. If this describes the type of selling you are involved in, SPIN may or may not be of value to you.

> Statistics suggest that the average sale is made on the 6th contact—but the average salesperson quits after two attempts!

In the smaller sale, the customer is less conscious of value. Or you may be competing on price. As the size of the sale increases, successful salespeople must build up the perceived value of their products or service. The building of perceived value is probably the single most important selling skill for larger sales.

Most larger sales also involve an ongoing relationship with your customer. This underscores the fact that trustworthiness is essential to your success.

The Four Stages of a Sales Call

Rackham points out that every sales call, regardless of size of sale, goes through four distinct stages.

1 **Preliminaries.** These are the warming-up events that occur before the serious selling begins. This includes the way you introduce yourself and begin the conversation.

While first impressions do count, Rackham points out that, in larger sales, preliminaries have less influence on success than once thought. Less experienced salespeople are more prone to spend excessive time in this stage, delaying stating the purpose of the call.

As you gain experience, you sense from the behavior of your customer when it's time to move forward. Astute observation of the buyer's environment and hospitality dictates the time spent in the preliminary stage.

2 **Investigating.** This involves asking questions...the right questions. The purpose is to collect data important to your reason for being there. You need to uncover needs that can be met with your product or service.

Gaining more knowledge about the customer's organization and how it functions is also an important factor in this stage. Rackham points out that investigating is the most important of all selling skills. This is the essence of SPIN® selling.

3 **Demonstrating capability.** This is the stage where you provide conclusive evidence to your customers that your product or service is capable of solving their problems or needs.

4 **Obtaining commitment.** In a small sale you often get an order and finalize the sale at this stage.

A larger sale is quiet different. Because of the size of the commitment, your buyer may have to get approval from a higher authority, possibly a home office located in another city. Rackham calls these intermediate steps "advances."

It would be nice to gain a full commitment at this stage of every call. However, that is unrealistic. Your goal at this point is to advance the sale in a positive direction, exercising patience with the process and keeping focused on the "big picture"—the ultimate final commitment.

Continuations Are Not Advances

At this stage it is critical that you recognize the difference between advances and "continuations." Continuations are a kind of stall. They let you keep in contact but are usually an indication that the buyer doesn't perceive enough value in your product or service to make a commitment to buy.

It is also possible that you have not fully uncovered an explicit need, want or desire for your product or service. The SPIN® process will help you determine whether you have advanced the sale or continued it.

Time Per Stage

The amount of time you spend on each stage of the sale can be very different from one sales call to the next. Some determining factors are the personality style of your buyer (chatty or matter-of-fact), how many calls you have made on this customer, and the amount of information you need to establish a business relationship.

The key to SPIN® selling is to ask the right questions at the right time. You need to go with the flow, listen carefully and be observant of your buyer's environment and behavior. Learn from your experiences.

Huthwaite's research clearly showed

that success in the larger sale depends heavily on how the investigating stage of the call is handled. Since the investigating stage is centered on asking questions, the finding was that the more successful calls that led to an order or advanced the sale had more questions asked than the ones that ended with no-sale or advance.

Just asking a lot of questions alone will not be sufficient. The conclusion of years of study indicated that the nature of the questions and more importantly, the sequence in which they are asked, determines your success. Thus was born the acronym SPIN.® SPIN® stands for:

Situation
Problem
I mplication
Need-Payoff

SITUATION QUESTIONS

The "S" in SPIN® represents Situation Questions. Your strategy here is to get the "lay of the land." Find out what the prospect's situation is relative to the needs that your product or service can meet.

Let's say you sell office machines. Your situation questions may take this path:

You: "What types of office equipment do you use in your operation?"

Prospect: "We currently have three copy machines, two fax machines, and six computers."

You: "What plans do you have for additional equipment in the future?"

Prospect: "We will probably add another fax machine and replace two copy machines soon."

Situation questions establish facts about the customer's existing situation. They should probably be asked in earlier meetings, *before* you attempt to make the sale. Rackham says that, "In calls that succeed, sellers ask fewer Situation Questions than in calls that fail."

Gathering Information

In the real world this scenario may seem too easy to be true. The purpose here is to give you a clear understanding of situation questions.

In this simple example, you now know their current situation regarding their office equipment. And you see possible needs for additional equipment.

The key to situation questions is that they are specifically related to what you offer. They also begin to give you an understanding of the prospect's needs. Your impulse will be to jump in and say, "That's great, we sell fax machines and copy machines. Let me show you our catalog."

Big mistake.

At this point you have no idea why they "will probably" add a fax machine and replace two copy machines. While you may have a good feel for the situation, you don't have enough information to pursue the sale.

Keep in mind that you are the one benefiting from situation questions, not your prospect. She or he may have answered these same questions many times before and can become bored with an endless line of questions. Do your homework on your prospect

---

Plan Your Situation Questions

You will find that generic situation questions will apply to most sales calls. Take a moment now to write down some situation questions that you can use in your business.

• What types of needs do your prospects have? _____
_____
_____

• Who is your ideal prospect? Describe their situation. _____
_____
_____

before the call and plan your line of situation questions.

PROBLEM QUESTIONS

Problem questions are questions that probe for problems, difficulties, or dissatisfactions with your prospect's current situation. These problems have been hinted at by the answers to your situation questions.

Find Out Why

In our example we learned that our prospect is considering adding one fax machine and replacing two copy machines. Our focus now is to find out why .

Your attempt to uncover a problem through questioning may go something like this:

> You: "May I ask your reasons for considering replacement of two of your copy machines?"

> Prospect: "Our workload has steadily increased and the copiers are not as fast as we think they should be. It's not a big problem but we may do something about it in the future."

At this point you know the prospect's situation and that there is potentially a problem. Once again, there is the tendency to jump in and talk about how fast your copy machine is and how it will solve her or his problem.

Big mistake.

There appears to be a problem. But the prospect has only implied there is and doesn't see the problem as urgent enough to take action to solve it.

Rackham's research indicated that until the prospect recognizes and expresses an explicit

"Problem Questions probe for problems, difficulties, or dissatisfactions. Each invites the customer to state Implied Needs."
—Neil Rackham, *Spin Selling*

need, it's too early to discuss your solution. Had your prospect in this example said, "We *must* correct this problem as quickly as possible," she or he would be open to your offer of a solution. It is critical to listen carefully to your prospect and detect if there is a real sense of urgency to solve their problem.

Remember, it is not a problem that needs a solution until they have clearly expressed their need to solve it. Until this occurs it is too early to present your solution. Once again you must exercise patience and continue forward.

IMPLICATION QUESTIONS

Because of the fast pace of business and other influences, prospects often do not see that the problem really is bigger than they think it is. The purpose of implication questions is to help the prospect see that the need to solve the problem is bigger than they have realized to this point.

Your responsibility here is *not* to blow the problem out of proportion to satisfy your need to sell your product or service.

It is important that you understand your role at this point and don't feel that you are manipulating your prospect. You should feel an obligation to help your prospect see that the problem needs to be solved if they are to operate with maximum efficiency and effectiveness. This is customer focused. Continuing our example, you recognize that your prospect expressed an implied problem, but has no desire to take action yet.

Your implication questions may go something like this:

> *You:* "You mentioned your dissatisfaction with the slowness of your two copiers. Does that have a negative impact on your productivity?"
>
> *Prospect:* "Well, we are beginning to get heat from our salespeople in the field."
>
> *You:* "Why is the sales force giving you heat?"
>
> *Prospect:* "We are increasingly getting information to them late."
>
> *You:* "How does that affect their performance?"
>
> *Prospect:* "They say they are missing sales because of information their customers should have before our competitors provide it."
>
> *You:* "I assume that missing sales can create a lot of problems and negatively affect the profitability of your company?"
>
> *Prospect:* "Absolutely. It doesn't make the VP of Sales very happy either."

The caution here is to be careful that you don't use too many implication questions and cast a dark shadow on the performance of your prospect. If you raise their dissatisfaction levels, they may associate their negative feelings with you!

In our example we want to keep the focus on the inability of the copiers to meet the demand, not on the procrastination of the prospect in solving the problem.

If you have done your job with Implication Questions, the prospect now sees the issue differently. The prospect sees that the implications of what he or she thought was a minor problem make

> "Decision makers seem to respond most favorably to salespeople who uncover implications.... Implications *are* the language of decision makers, and if you can talk their language, you'll influence them better."
> —Neil Rackham, *Spin Selling*

a solution much more urgent.

Believe it or not, you are still not ready to jump in with a solution to the problem. Exercise patience.

NEED-PAYOFF QUESTIONS

Now you are ready to ask solution-centered questions. These build up the positive elements of a solution.

Need-payoff questions help create a positive problem solving atmosphere focusing on actions to be taken. They also get the prospect to tell you the benefit of a solution, which reduces the objections.

Continuing our office equipment example, you might say:

> *You:* "Is it important to you to solve this problem of inefficiency in your current copiers?"

> *Prospect:* "You bet it is. We have to provide our salespeople with timely information, keep the sales manager off my back, and keep our profitability up."

At this stage in the process you have helped your prospect see that the slow copiers have a major negative impact on his or her company. You have uncovered or clarified a need. You have helped your prospect realize that the problem is truly bigger than he or she thought it was. *Now* you are finally ready to present a solution.

Because of your earlier questions, you now know what features of your product are relevant to the solution. You only present those features that solve the problem. In this case speed of the copier and efficiency of operation are the only factors that matter. Any other features of your product are value-added features. A feature, or a benefit for that matter, has little value unless your customer sees a true benefit.

Product features can create potential advantages for prospects. These advantages may create benefits. As Rackham points out in his book, a feature of your product may only be an advantage, not a benefit. If the customer does not perceive the feature to be a true benefit to their needs, you can't use it to sell.

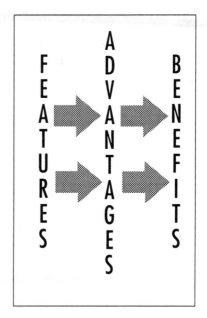

Be a Doctor: Have Sales "Patience"

The fatal mistake that many people make in the selling process is jumping in too soon with a solution to the customer's problem. *First*, you must uncover an explicit need and help the customer realize the negative implications if the problem is not solved.

An inexperienced salesperson will start bombarding the prospect with a long list of features and how they will help the prospect's business. When this occurs, prospects know that the focus is not on their needs. And their perception —which is their reality—is that the cost is going to be too high. In either case the salesperson has set a tone that will probably result in an unsuccessful sales call.

Rx Channel your eagerness into helping the customer solve a challenge or opportunity, not toward making the sale.

The simple office equipment example should help you understand the nature of the questioning process and the importance of the *sequence* in which the questions are asked.

It should be obvious that patience is truly a virtue in selling. In most cases, your urgency to sell is not matched by the buyer's priorities. Your eagerness should be channeled into helping the customer solve a challenge or opportunity, not toward making the sale.

Keep in mind that you are not only competing with those who offer a similar product or service to yours. You are competing for the dollars that a company has to spend for ALL their needs. Your product or service may be unique, but, your customer ALWAYS has another option.

OKAY, WHAT'S NEXT?

Now that you have an overview of SPIN® Selling, what do you do with it? First, you should agree that a client-oriented attitude about selling will enhance your journey of success. Get serious about acquiring more knowledge to help customers, and USE it.

ACTUALIZE YOUR POTENTIAL

Rackham says that one of his favorite words, is *entelechy*. This is a little known word that means the actualization of what was potential. It involves turning something into practical usefulness, as opposed to theoretical elegance.

In other words, put to use what you learn.

Too many times we look for the "quick fix." To properly use the sequence of SPIN® questions takes a lot of practice. You have to make a strong commitment to changing your approach. And you have to work hard. Even with a wealth of natural talent, any great athlete will tell you that they never stop working on the basics. Practice makes athletes—and salespeople—better.

HOW TO IMPROVE YOUR LEARNING

Huthwaite's research indicated that most people can greatly improve their ability to learn skills if they commit to four simple rules.

Rule 1: Practice Only One Behavior at a Time

Focus on one behavior at a time until you get it right. Do not try to incorporate the entire SPIN® process in your next call. For example, you may want to develop your portfolio of situation questions. Gain confidence with these before moving to the next skill.

Rule 2: Try the New Behavior at Least Three Times

Just as a new pair of shoes is usually uncomfortable at first, so is a new skill. You have to "break in" your new skill as you do new shoes. Practice one skill until it becomes a natural part of your process. Never judge whether a new behavior is effective until you have tried it at least three times.

Rule 3: Quantity Before Quality

Focus on the number of times you practice a behavior, not how well you do it. By using this approach, the quality will come.

Rule 4: Practice in Safe Situations

Don't use important sales calls to practice your newly acquired skills. That would be a terrible mistake at this point. Very few hit shows open on Broadway until they have performed in an "off Broadway" venue. Practice in situations where there is minimal impact on your outcomes.

Following these rules will help you create a solid foundation that you can build upon. The keys to making SPIN® work for you are dedicated practice, evaluation of your results, and constantly fine tuning your skills.

BECOME A "SOLUTIONIST"

"Trust—or the lack of it—is at the root of success or failure in relationships and in the bottom-line results of business, industry, education, and government."
—Stephen Covey

Most of the people you do business with today are extremely busy. They are often stretched to their maximum capabilities. To really be successful, you must become a "solutionist." You help your customer find solutions. The pledge of the solutionist is as follows:

- I am 100% focused on the NEEDS of my customer.
- I will demonstrate by my ACTIONS that my customer is my #1 priority.
- I know that when I help OTHERS succeed, I will succeed.
- I will ASK my customer, "How are we doing for you?"
- I will ASK my customer, "WHAT can we do to better serve your needs?"

There are times when you must face the reality that you cannot solve the needs of your customer or prospect with your product or service.

This is where your integrity is tested. Do you sell to the customer anyway? Is the short-term gain of compromising your integrity worth the irreparable damage to your character in the long term?

The answer is a resounding "No!" As Stephen Covey clearly states in his book, *Principle-Centered Leadership*, trustworthiness is the foundation of trust. Trustworthiness is based on character—who you are, and competence, how well you do what you do.

By becoming a true solutionist you earn the trust of your customers and prospects. This provides a solid foundation for your successful marketing—and life!

SUMMARY: A SPIN ON SPIN

Selling is an attitude...a mindset. Only you can make the final choice on how you think and feel about selling. Your feelings about selling may not be objective reality, but they are your reality. Take control of them to benefit yourself and your customers.

> "If you think you can or if you think you can't, either way you are right."
> —Henry Ford

Incorporate solutionism as the foundation of your relationship with your customers and prospects. Your sales mission should be to build a relationship with your customers founded on trust, identification of needs, presentation of solutions, and recommendations for action.

When you truly help others succeed, you will succeed.

Acquiring knowledge, skills, experience and, most importantly, putting these into ACTION, can help you achieve a level of success you never dreamed possible.

As Oliver Wendell Holmes said, "What lies behind us and what lies before us are tiny matters, compared to what lies within us."

ACTION AGENDA

Selling should be building long-term relationships. What can you do to enhance your relationships with the key customers who should give you most of your business?

- Who should you recontact this week to show that you're interested in more than the quick sale?
- Who should you build a non-business relationship with around mutual interests like sports or a hobby?
- Who should you send a surprise gift to now?
- Who should you send a thank you note to? (See Chapter 13)
- Who should you be sending referral business to?

In order to meet customer and prospect needs, you need to practice the SPIN® questions.

Where will you practice these questions?

Situation: Find out about the current situation.

Problem: Probe for potential, unrecognized problems.

Implication: Help people see the implications of their situation that can be improved.

Need-Payoff: Show people how you can meet their needs.

Unlike most selling systems, the value of these types of questions has been proven. But without use, the best information is of no value. The last two types are not used well by most people. When and where will you practice them?

Chapter 10

HOW TO SELL EVEN IF YOU'RE NOT IN SALES:
The 7 Secrets of Heartful Selling

Marc Fine

Marc Fine
is president of Voice Activated
Systems Technology, Inc.
    Fine has worked with a
variety of companies and in-
stitutions, including Diasonics, Procter & Gamble, Upjohn, SRI International,
Planned Parenthood, The American Heart Association, La Clinica de la Raza (a
nonprofit Community Health Center), and several high-tech firms in Silicon
Valley. Over the past 20 years, both as an executive and as a consultant, he
has created or reshaped corporate cultures at numerous companies.

    In 1989, he traveled to India and became familiar with Buddhist concepts.
He began to ask himself how he could translate these concepts into the language
of business. He decided to heed the advice of the Dalai Lama, and others, who
encouraged him to "Take home with you what you have found useful, and leave
the rest behind."

    Along with his experience as a company founder and consultant, he is a
pilot, musician, filmmaker, inventor, and world traveler. Fine lives in Santa Rosa,
California with his two sons.

Marc Fine, Voice Activated Systems Technology, Inc., 349 College Avenue, Santa
Rosa, CA 95401; phone (707) 537-0915; fax (707) 454-2650; e-mail
MTFine@aol.com.

Chapter 10

HOW TO SELL EVEN IF YOU'RE NOT IN SALES:
The 7 Secrets of Heartful Selling

Marc Fine

"When one sees that everything exists as an illusion, one can live in a higher sphere than ordinary man."

—The Buddha

The purpose of this chapter is to show you how to sell from a new perspective. I've studied how Tibetian Buddhism applies to the "normal" world of sales. By combining this ancient wisdom with common sense, you'll become better at sales, even if it's "not your job."

The Buddhist culture places a strong emphasis on Karma. So it is natural for Tibetans to conduct each exchange in a way that, when the process is complete, all parties to the transaction have benefited equally.

Tibetans try to view everyone they meet as having been their kind, loving mother in a previous life!

They certainly don't want to generate any negative Karma by

cheating anyone. Based on their philosophy, it only makes sense to treat others with total honesty and respect. This philosophy gives them a different perspective on the simple process of buying and selling!

FOR PEOPLE WHO "AREN'T IN SALES"

Most people don't think of themselves as being in sales.

One reason is probably because they don't have the word "sales" in their job titles. And if the truth be known, most people *really dislike* the idea of selling.

"I like inventing, (or designing, or building things, or providing services), but I *hate* marketing and sales."

I've heard people say this time and again.

"Well, who's going to market and sell your product or service for you?" I ask.

"Oh, I'll just get somebody else to do it. I can't stand that part of the business."

"SELL" Is Not A 4-Letter Word!

I have had this conversation about "someone else" doing the selling many times over with engineers, inventors, and other professionals who are considering starting a business.

I maintain that whether you work for yourself or for a large corporation, produce a product or a service, are an engineer or a receptionist, you are involved in sales in one form or another. And guess what—it's a good thing, too!

Sales is what fuels any business enterprise. Just as you can't drive a car without gasoline, you can't drive your business without sales.

Everyone Is In Sales

Typically, people who aren't in "sales" believe that sales is something distasteful that someone else does. Sales is beneath them.

An Evil Mirror?

Why is it that many people shudder at the thought of being involved in sales? Perhaps you fear that you will look into the mirror one morning and see a loud-mouthed, obnoxious, person selling Florida swampland staring back at you!

That attitude is one of the more prevailing and damaging misconceptions in business. People simply don't understand what sales is all about. Thus, they fail to realize how vital it is to the success of each and every enterprise.

Once you learn to live with the fact that one of your jobs is to be a salesperson, you will be a far more effective businessperson. And you will learn to have a great deal more insight and respect for this vital function.

IT TAKES BOTH TYPES FOR SUCCESS

It is important to acknowledge that different professions tend to foster dissimilar personality types.

It is not uncommon for companies to have a polarization between "quantitative" people, such as engineers and accountants, and "qualitative" folks, such as salespeople and marketing people. This polarization causes friction within a company. This creates a fractionalized, inefficient work environment rather than an harmonious team.

For instance, the thought process of the "quant" type often goes something like this. "I went to graduate school for umpteen-zillion years. I sit behind a desk for 60 hours a week, and I have designed a revolutionary product which is going to make the company a lot of money.

So why is this lower life-form without a high school diploma, wearing a silk monogrammed shirt opened to his navel, and a twelve-pound gold chain with a pendant that says 'Damn, I'm Good' making four times as much money as I am? Especially given that he has no integrity, and if you put his brains in a shot glass you'd still have room for a double martini. To add insult to injury, he's out playing golf three times a week and taking clients to fancy restaurants on the company's expense account."

Maybe I'm exaggerating a bit.

The way the "Quals" sometimes see it is that a bunch of dweebs with pocket protectors and tape holding their glasses together have no respect for them. They don't speak their language. Further, they are conspiring to hold up product shipments, and have no understanding of what it's like to be "out there" in the real world. They don't appreciate that sales pays their salaries.

You Must Work Together

The reality is that both groups need each other and can help each other. In order to be effective team members, non-salespeople need to understand the sales process as much as the people with "sales" in their titles.

"As we continue to grow and mature, we become increasingly aware...that the higher reaches of our nature have to do with our relationships with others... Interdependent is the paradigm of we—we can combine our talents and abilities and create something greater together."
—Stephen R. Covey

It would be beneficial if everyone spent some time in the field with sales staff. They need to understand that sales cover their paychecks. And they need to know that every employee, including the "quants" represents the company in "sales" as far as many customers are concerned.

For the sales types who have no respect for the non-selling people in the company, consider having them spend time in the office going over operations and manufacturing details.

They can benefit by learning some of the technical ins-and-outs of the product they are selling. This will also reinforce the fact that without the accountants, there'd be no paychecks. Without engineers and designers and the people who make and ship the products, there would be nothing to sell.

Without mutual respect and understanding, your company will not function as a team. Everyone has to learn to work together. Once everyone in your company realizes the important role each and every person plays, they can invest their energy in being effective, rather than fighting among different departments.

THE 7 SECRETS OF HEARTFUL SELLING—
FUNdamentals Of Selling

These tips are for both non-salespeople and professional sales-people.

I've been in both roles. The only difference I could see is that salespeople make more money than people who don't think they're in sales!

If you follow these guidelines, your business will be more successful and you will find the selling process considerably more enjoyable than you find it now.

1 **Everyone in the company (including you) is in sales, or better be.** No matter how hard you might try, you can't avoid selling. Selling is something we're always doing. When someone

calls your company, whoever answers the phone is projecting an image of the company. He is "selling" the company. And so are you, whether you're an engineer, a receptionist, or someone with the actual word "sales" in your title.

It is important to realize that everyone in the company can influence whether or not a sale will be made.

> ## Show Users
>
> I used to regularly bring my engineers into the hospital where our medical products were being marketed. What better way to learn what it takes to make their designs sell better? And to see the value of what they made. Sounds obvious? No one else used to do it.

An example of this principle demonstrates what can happen when the people in your company don't understand that they are part of the sales team.

I was evaluating some software development tools for a voice recognition system my company wanted to buy. I called IBM, Kurzweil, and Dragon Systems, the three companies which marketed these tools. I asked each one, in turn, to help me chose which system to buy, and what made their system better than their competitor's.

Not one of the people I talked with even attempted to tell me how their system was different or better. They just read some of their product specifications.

This was a huge lost opportunity for each company. (See Chapter 1 on the value of uniqueness.)

What Do Your Callers Hear?

As an experiment, you should try calling your own company. Pretend to be a potential customer

Everyone Projects The Company's Image

One of the first customers for a medical imaging system I designed insisted on talking to everyone in our company: the president, engineers, the service department—even the secretaries. He wanted to make sure he would be well supported if the product ever needed service. He was impressed by the dedication and professionalism of everyone he met, and decided to buy our system.

Because he loved the system, and appreciated the way we took care of him, he promised that he would be our greatest supporter. And boy, was he! At conferences, he would grab his colleagues and drag them over to the booth where we were exhibiting our equipment.

I think he sold more systems than my top salesperson! I love it when we all win. This would have never been possible had he not first been impressed with our company from the ground up.

and ask the person who answers the phone why you should buy their product. I hope you aren't unpleasantly surprised!

The solution to this problem is that everyone in the company must be trained. They must practice expressing the benefits of the services and products you are offering.

It may be that you provide the best support, or have the highest quality, or offer the lowest price. Whatever the benefit, each and every one of your employees must be skilled and proficient in communicating these benefits to potential customers and clients.

2 **The president has to sell the first one.** Tradition holds that the President of the United States throws out the first baseball on opening day.

The same rule should hold for selling the first product a company produces.

You may ask why the president of a company should bother herself with sales.

The answer is simple. The president, more than any other employee, has to understand exactly what it takes to sell the product.

The president has to stay in touch with the market (that is, customers), and be able to respond realistically to the needs of the sales force. The only way the president can do this is by actually going out on sales calls. She needs to listen to the street, and be part of, rather than above, the process. The same holds true for management, engineering, marketing, and manufacturing.

Apple Was On The Street!

Steve Jobs and Steve Wozniak sold the first computers they designed out of the back of a car in a parking lot! They certainly refined the concept of "getting close to the customer." Nobody was better at staying in touch with the market place and the needs of their customers. That is why Apple grew, in a few short years, from an operation started in a garage to one of the largest computer companies in the world.

Know The Value of Sales

I am not implying that everyone should go immediately into sales full time. What I *am* saying is that sales is the lynch pin which holds all business together.

Every employee, including the president, must take a hands-on approach where sales is concerned. If that means getting down and dirty from time to time, so be it. If that means sending management on the road from time to time, do it.

Al Waxman, President of Diasonics, sold the first ultrasound imaging system the company produced. He was the best salesperson we ever had. By meeting with physicians, he was able to stay in touch with their needs and produce a system they would buy. This made Diasonics the leader in the field for many years.

In every successful company, you will find the president out selling and talking to the customers.

They need to learn as much as possible about the comings and goings of the market place. Informed decisions begin at the top.

Here's a suggestion for people starting out in business. If you want to move up in management, take a sales territory for a year. You don't have to make it your career, nor do you have to be the best. But it is an experience that will give you insight into your products and the market, respect for your sales force, and respect from the people you are about to manage.

3 **Know your product or service inside and out.** This should be obvious. How can you communicate the benefit of what you have unless you understand what you are offering?

Take Borrolo's Pizza in Santa Rosa, California. The owner knows everything there is to know about making pizza. He's been doing it all his life. He was in the pizza business in New York, and when he moved to California, he decided he was going to make the best pizza around.

Borrolo's didn't advertise, and wasn't even listed in the phone book when they started. Yet, they are one of the fastest growing pizza parlors in the area. Their growth is a direct result of satisfied customers who know a good pizza when they taste one, and recommend the pizza to their friends. Without a lifetime of experience in the business, I doubt Borrolo's would have survived in this competitive market.

4 **Communicate the benefits of your product or service.** Selling is nothing more than communication. Whether you are talking to a potential client, customer, or fellow employee, you are communicating about your values, yourself, and your company.

> He who knows nothing else knows enough if he knows when to be silent!
> — Japanese Proverb

You are always selling who you are and what you stand for. So it is important to be mindful of what and how you are communicating.

There are two components of effectively communicating: listening, and speaking. Most of us like to talk, but don't always effectively communicate the benefits of our products or services. This takes practice and confidence.

The biggest obstacle most salespeople have is their inability to listen closely to the needs of their customers. If you don't understand what your customers' needs are, how can you present your product or service in a way that makes sense to your customer?

Buddhist Listening Skill

The Buddha used *skillful listening* and *skillful speaking* to get his message across to varied groups. He understood the uniqueness of individuals and always tailored his talks to meet the particular needs of his audiences. He understood that people

Critique Your Listening Habits

Are you a good listener, or a pushy person, impatiently waiting to speak? Test yourself by checking these traits of a poor listener:

- You help others finish their sentences when they pause too long.
- You do *all* the talking.
- You step on people's sentences by starting to talk before they have completed their thoughts.
- You don't maintain eye contact with others when they are talking.
- You give too much vague feedback by mumbling a lot of uh huhs."

—*Sales & Marketing Management* magazine

come from different cultures and have different backgrounds.

People's ability to hear the Buddha's message depended on his speaking their "language." He was so effective in helping people because he had the ability to first listen before speaking.

Close To Customers

Ten years ago in her garage, Mary Hughes started her own company, Mary's Futons. As a young, inexperienced businessperson, Mary was determined to produce only the finest furniture. She was committed to quality and customer service. One day, I asked her how she explained her success.

"I really know what my customers need," she blurted out, without even stopping to think.

She knows her market intimately, because she spends so much time listening to customers. She invests significant time and resources on employee training to make sure they listen carefully, as well.

She went on to explain that she sees her business as an extension of her personal desire to provide a service to her community.

"Community involvement," she stated, "is critically important to my business. You know, fund raisers, charities, social events, local advertising. I try to do it all. Everybody knows me because I'm really out there. Most

Values Help Marketing

Mary also provides a good example of how Karma, or what goes around comes around, applies to sales as well. I have found that being socially and philanthropically active in the community you profit from is the best way to guarantee a long lasting and healthy give-and-take relationship.

of my customers don't even know my real name, they just know me as 'Futon Mary.'"

Mary is successful in all the ways that are important to her: she is profitable, loves her job, and has made people happy. Her customers are her friends.

Mary is proof that effective communication is the most effective and least expensive way to increase sales.

5 **Buying and selling are basically irrational activities guided by rational thought.** Human beings operate on two levels: the rational and the irrational. Most of the decisions we make are basically irrational (i.e., emotional). But for some twisted reason we hate to admit it.

Think about it. When was the last time you bought a car or some clothing, or decided what movie to go see? Did you make your choice based on some rational, objective criteria? Or did you choose simply on the basis that it made you feel good? It may have been a combination of the two, but I'd wager more on the latter.

The rational side of us needs to flex its muscle by analyzing and rationalizing and justifying what is essentially an emotional decision. That way, we tend to feel better about our decision because we are, after all, being rational.

By understanding the hu-

"Nothing, thanks. We're just deciding if we want a boy or a girl."

man need to be rational, you can quell your customers' fears and doubts about being irrational by providing them with objective data. The more sound, objective, concrete data you can supply your customer with, the easier your customer will be able to come to grips with having to make what ultimately is an emotional decision.

In Buddhist terms, you are balancing the rational with the irrational, the yin with the yang. This creates a guilt-free forum for your customer to buy or not buy. And that allows both of you to do your jobs under the best of circumstances.

Even For Scientific Purchases

You might agree that purchasing a new car or a suit is an emotional decision. How about buying a million dollar super-computer?

I was visiting a friend who works at Apple Computer a while back, and he was proudly showing off their newly purchased Cray Super Computer. I asked him why Apple would spend that much money on what I perceived to be essentially a new "toy."

"Well, it will pay for itself if it can shorten the design time for our next system by even a few months," he explained, while laying out the statistical and quantitative data demonstrating the specific cost savings.

"Besides, we're the first computer company in Silicon Valley to get one. And we've got another one on order!" he bragged.

He then took me into the special air-conditioned room that housed this futuristic-looking machine, and explained how it required a separate power plant and a team of technicians just to run it.

"It was available in a choice of 256 different colors, but we chose a custom color," my friend explained. "We just like to be different."

After he was convinced that I was convinced of the utility of the Cray Super Computer, I asked him point blank how much of the decision to buy the Cray was rational, based on objective need, and how much was motivated by purely emotional factors.

"Oh, about fifty-fifty," he admitted, with a sly smile.

The engineers just wanted one because it was cool. And fast. And expensive. And amazing. And management wanted it because no one else in the industry had one. But, he added, it is doubtful that Apple would have bought the computer without first being sold on its overall utility.

6 **Nothing happens until a sale is made.** This is the fundamental rule of business. Without sales, there is no revenue. As I said earlier, this means nobody gets paid (including you). This means there is no office to go to, no product development, no services, no engineers, and no company. It is imperative to keep in mind that sales, making rain, or whatever you want to call it, is the bottom line in business. Without sales, you have nothing.

7 **Ask for the order**. Say these words: "Do you want it?" And then be quiet and wait while the person decides.

By asking "Do you want it," you take the last essential step in the sales process. It may sound

---

We Fail To Deal With The Market

CYMaK Technologies was a computer graphics company I helped to start. It is a classic example of "nothing happens until a sale is made." We started the company because we had a great product and the spread sheets showed plenty of room for profit.

But no one had focused on the customer. We completely missed the boat on the market. As it turned out, even though we had a super product that we could produce quickly and cheaply, we could not sell it. We were never able to convince the customers of the benefits of the product. Not surprisingly, the company was short lived.

simple, but, ironically, asking is the hardest part of sales for most people. Nobody likes to hear "no," because "no" feels like rejection.

But Buddhist principles say that unless you are willing to live in an "uncertain place,"— to risk rejection—no magic can happen. You have to be willing to give people the opportunity to choose, to say "no" before you can hear the great "yes."

Remember, there is a difference between being direct and having bad manners. You don't have to be manipulative, or dishonest to be an effective salesperson. But you do have to ask the question, "Do you want to buy this?"

Many times, a customer wants to buy, and is just waiting to be asked.

So ask. Even if you have the greatest product or service in the industry, and your communication skills are unmatched, you still have nothing unless you are willing to ask for the order.

A NEW PHILOSOPHY OF SELLING

The Hard Truth About The Soft Sell

Most of us have a tough time with the idea of the "hard sell," because it seems manipulative and pushy and so—hard! Basically, no one likes to be pressured. It makes us uncomfortable.

But is the "hard sell" any worse than some so-called "soft sells?" When a salesperson acts overly nice, chummy, and manipulative, I duck and hold onto my wallet.

Whatever approach is used needs to focus on satisfaction for the customer. Otherwise the end result is an unhappy customer. And chances are you will have to clean up the mess later, probably by way of a returned product.

Selling The Middle Way

Jim Montgomery is the best salesperson I ever met. He possesses all of the fundamental skills necessary to do his job. But what makes Jim truly amazing is his belief that selling is just a means for meeting people, connecting with them, and providing a service. The actual selling of a product is secondary to Jim! Of primary importance, to him, is how he conducts himself in the business world.

To Jim, selling has become a way for him to express his spirituality. He is the essence of a Buddha in a business suit.

A Middle Way

There are unscrupulous salespeople in every industry. But they will never be effective in the long run.

Buddhism suggests following the "Middle Path." Don't get stuck in the role of what you think your job is supposed to be. And don't stick anyone else in that role. Just concentrate on service to others, and you will succeed. The Buddhist Middle Way will guide you to find the right balance between being "hard" and "soft" in your approach to selling.

To be effective, you must be honest and straightforward and tailor your presentation to meet the needs of your customer. This is because selling is about relationships.

Understand how a product or service will

benefit the customer, and skillfully communicate those benefits. This can only happen within the context of a healthy relationship.

And don't be shy about selling. If you believe in your product or service, you should be willing to tell people. It is both honest and effective to say: "I've got a great product, and I believe that it will benefit you. It is my privilege to let you know about it, and I encourage you to try it!"

Reputation Is Everything In Business

Whether a company or an individual, if you have a reputation for honesty and providing great service, you will flourish.

Conversely, if you have a reputation for poor service or ripping off customers, you will not last long.

How often have you recommended a business or service to your friends if you didn't feel you were treated fairly? And how many times have you become an evangelist for a product, service, or company that you thought was outstanding? It's funny how something so obvious is so often ignored by people in the business world.

 Take Linda Payne, the proprietor of Biscotti Mio, an Italian bakery and espresso bar. She opened the bakery and espresso bar because she genuinely likes people. It is a social event just to drop by her store. She is constantly chatting with customers, bickering with suppliers on the phone, and rushing off to personally deliver orders.

She never stops moving, and she never stops selling. She is always asking customers if they want a refill of coffee, another Biscotti, or perhaps some treats to take home with them.

Would Linda characterize what she is doing as selling? Probably not. She would, I believe, think of it as socializing. Whatever you want to call it, she treats all of her customers with the same kind of warm, friendly, vivacious energy. It is obvious she loves her job, which is serving her customers. Her reputation is impeccable.

Because everybody likes Linda and her products, her customers have turned into her sales force, recommending her products to their friends.

HEARTFUL SELLING FOR SERVICE

Many people approach sales with the attitude: How can I get what I want?

Unfortunately, this thought process is backward. The more you concentrate on getting, the less you will receive. The magic is understanding that the more you give, the more you get back.

For a Heartful Manager, selling is about service and communicating. The process starts with creating a dialogue between you and another human being. This generates an understanding of what that person needs, and what benefits you have to offer.

The benefits may be in the form of a service, a product, or an idea. It doesn't matter. Have the intent to serve. Be willing to be generous by sharing yourself. Then chances are you will be successful. And chances are that all parties to the transaction will benefit.

Buddha, Jesus, Gandhi, and Martin Luther King were all superb salespeople. They sold their philosophies worldwide, even after death! As long as your intent is true, and you are committed to helping others, you'll be in good company.

A SERVICE MISSION SELLS HOTEL

by Stephen R. Covey

I wanted to find out how this organization had created a culture where people bought so deeply into the value of customer service. I interviewed housekeepers, waitresses, bellboys in that hotel and found that this attitude had impregnated the minds, hearts, and attitudes of every employee there.

I went through the back door into the kitchen, where I saw the central value: "Uncompromising personalized service." I finally went to the manager and said, "My business is helping organizations develop a powerful team character, a team culture. I am amazed at what you have here."

"Do you want to know the real key?" he inquired. He pulled out the mission statement for the hotel chain.

After reading it, I acknowledged, "That's an impressive statement. But I know many companies that have impressive mission statements."

"Do you want to see the one for this hotel?" he asked.

"Do you mean you developed one just for this hotel?"

"Yes."

"Different from the one for the hotel chain?"

"Yes. It's in harmony with that statement, but this one pertains to our situation, our environment, our time." He handed me another paper.

"Who developed this mission statement?" I asked.

"Everybody," he replied.

"Everybody? Really, everybody?"

"Yes."

"Housekeepers?"

"Yes."

"Waitresses?"

"Yes."

"Desk clerks?"

"Yes. Do you want to see the mission statement written by the people who greeted you last night?" He pulled out a mission statement that they, themselves, had written that was interwoven with all the other mission statements. Everyone, at every level, was involved.

RIGHT LIVELIHOOD SELLING

The Buddhist concepts of *Right Action* and *Right Speech* have much to offer in the way of guidance along this path.

Right Action is the term for being mindful of the effects of all of our actions or inactions. The test for Right Action is to ask yourself: Is what I am about to do going to benefit or harm others? Don't act unless you examine the consequences of your actions.

The practice of Right Speech requires that you communicate honestly, skillfully, and effectively. The test for Right Speech is to ask yourself: Is what I am about to say truthful? Will it benefit the person I am talking with? Will it harm anyone?

Serve Others

I know it is tempting to slant what you say to give you an advantage in business. It can be tempting to put your own needs first.

A better approach, in the long run, is to put your customers' needs first. See what that does for your sales, not to mention your peace of mind.

The ultimate test of Heartful Selling is whether you'd sell this product to your mother. If you

A Trusted Consultant

Bruce B. is a successful salesperson. Yet he often steers his customers to another supplier if he thinks their services or products are more appropriate. In the short run, he loses some business. But in the long run Bruce gains the respect and trust of his clients, who in turn buy his products whenever they can. They know he is looking out for their best interests.

Bruce carries over his *Right Speech* approach to sales even though he works in a very competitive industry. It is not unusual for the competition to make disparaging remarks about his company's products. Bruce always tries to compliment the competition, and point out the worthwhile attributes of their products while stressing the special benefits of the products *he* offers.

This positive approach works well for Bruce. Year in and year out, he is consistently one of the top performers in his region. Nice guys do finish first.

aren't willing to sell it to your mother, then ask yourself why you would be willing to sell it to somebody else. And if it's good enough for your mother, why would you be shy about offering it to others?

CONCLUSION

It takes discipline, commitment, hard work, and courage to be a professional salesperson committed to Right Speech and Right Action. This is especially true given the fierce competition to make a profit in today's saturated markets where margins are slim.

To many salespeople, the easy road appears to be cutting corners, taking cheap shots at the competition, and selling the product regardless of the consequences. The end result of engaging in such conduct is always the same: confusion, animosity, lost opportunity, and lost profit.

By following Right Speech and Right Action, the end result is also always the same: clear direction, goodwill, opportunity, and long term profitable relationships.

ACTION AGENDA

- List all the ways in which you "sell" your products and services.
- List all the ways you sell yourself, your ideas, etc. to your spouse, your kids, your friends, etc.
- For an entire day (or for an hour, if this seems too much) try to be aware of every word that comes out of your mouth. Without judging yourself, notice whether your words are: truthful, kind of truthful, not too truthful, hurtful, helpful, optimistic, pessimistic, etc.

Is there a pattern? That's all you really need to do. Don't try to change, or even to worry about it. The awareness is more than just a first step. It is the catalyst for change.

- How do you communicate the benefits of your products or services to your customers? How do you listen to them? Are you able to hear what they really need?
- In a few short sentences, describe how your products or services benefit your customers. Practice, practice, practice. Do this in front of a mirror, or have a friend video tape you.
- Review each of the seven secrets and decide how they can apply to your situation.
- List the things you do which get in the way of selling your products or services. What are you committed to doing about them?

ONLINE MARKETING
New Technology for
New Results

Rick Crandall

Rick Crandall
is a speaker,writer, and consultant, specializing in talks
and workshops on marketing
and sales, creativity, and
change. He has spoken for *Inc.* magazine, the American Marketing Association,
Autodesk, Chambers of Commerce, and given many keynote presentations.
Crandall has presented approximately 1000 seminars on applied business,
marketing, entrepreneurship, etc.

Crandall is the author of *Marketing Your Services: For People Who HATE
to Sell* (1995). In addition, he serves as editor and marketing columnist for
Executive Edge newsletter (a popular middle management newsletter), and as
editor of *Ken Blanchard's Profiles of Success* newsletter (containing top management case studies).

He is the founder and executive director of the Community Entrepreneurs
Organization (since 1982). He is the recipient of an SBA Small Business Award,
and is listed in various *Who's Whos*. With a PhD in Group Dynamics, Crandall
taught business, research, or psychology full time at the University of Michigan,
University of Illinois, and Texas Christian University in the 1970s.

Rick Crandall, c/o Select Press, PO Box 37, Corte Madera, CA 94976-0037; phone
(415) 924-1612; fax (415) 924-7179; e-mail 731220,3531@compuserve.com.

Chapter 11

ONLINE MARKETING
New Technology for New Results

Rick Crandall

"That's an amazing invention, but who would ever want to use one?"

—President Rutherford B. Hayes (after trying an early telephone in 1876)

HYPE AND HOPE

Since 1994, we've been hearing more and more hype about the "Internet," the "Information Superhighway," and the "World Wide Web." Most of the articles about online business tend to be positively biased about the potential of this new medium. Amidst all this hype, is it possible to come out with the "truth" ?

In brief, I think that the Internet has been largely hype to-date. But it represents the first major new marketing medium to come along in many years. It will be important in the future.

This chapter will briefly discuss online history and technology. Then it will cover ways to do online marketing.

Self-Fulfilling Prophecy

In addition to the unique qualities of online marketing, there is a self-fulfilling prophecy at work. When enough people say that online marketing has great potential, it causes others to take action. Sign-ups on the commercial services and for direct Internet connections have been skyrocketing.

Sometime in 1994 it became expected that if you were in a high-tech business, you'd be online and have an e-mail address. Sometime in late 1995, it began to be expected that many people would have e-mail addresses, not just those in the high-tech industry.

I predict that by late 1996, if you don't have an e-mail address, it will become embarrassing, just as it would be if you didn't have a fax number.

Online growth may be as high as ten percent every month. Even the media that compete with it, are hyping it. When TV programs, newspapers, and radio stations all list their World Wide Web addresses, it supports the self-fulfilling prophecy.

The Internet Highway

The idea of an information superhighway leads to an obvious analogy to the regular highway system.

In the early days of the automobile, they were largely curiosities. People drove mainly for pleasure.

At first, cars were slower and less reliable than horses. The roads were rough. Many cars would be pulled over to the side and you'd be patching your own tire. Yet, if it hadn't been for those early pleasure drivers who liked the novelty and were willing to endure the hardships, the automobile wouldn't have been able to develop into the more efficient vehicle it is today.

Similarly, for the online highway. The early users for 20 years put up with a lot of inconveniences, had to know something about programming, and had to do a lot of patching themselves. Even in 1994 when it began to boom, the largest uses were still for games and pornography.

Early users helped create the infrastructure of better "roads," better tools, and better software. They made doing business online more practical.

We haven't yet reached the superhighway stage for online, but we're a lot closer to it, a lot faster, because of those pioneers who were willing to "patch their own tires."

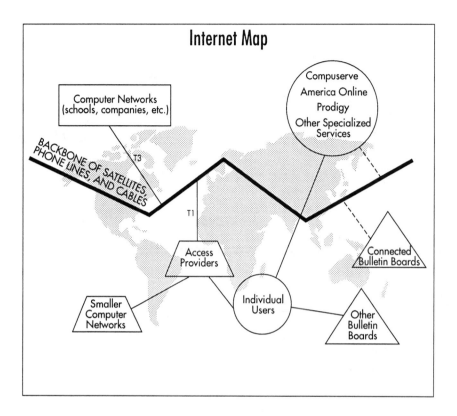

Internet Map

Computer Networks (schools, companies, etc.)

Compuserve America Online Prodigy Other Specialized Services

BACKBONE OF PHONE LINES, SATELLITES, AND CABLES

T3

T1

Access Providers

Connected Bulletin Boards

Smaller Computer Networks

Individual Users

Other Bulletin Boards

So while online marketing has been more hype than substance, acceptance of it is gaining fast.

THE ABCs

Before we get too far let's cover some basic definitions. One of the problems in this area is that there are many overlapping terms that mean the same thing.

The constant profusion of initials and unusual names makes it easy for online marketing to be treated like secret knowledge shared only by a few. In fact, the basic idea of online business is rather straightforward.

The **information superhighway** is a term for a theoretical infrastructure of communication cables, wires, and satellites that would allow us all to be hooked up in some inexpensive way.

The **Internet** is a very crude interconnection of networks of computers with a backbone of telephone lines, cables, and other ways of transmitting digital information from point to point. The Internet, because of its major growth and popularity, has essentially become a crude, de facto version of the idealized information highway.

The **World Wide Web** is the most active part of the Internet with the biggest potential. It's a system that rides on the connections of the Internet and allows a number of additional things besides the transmission of text and data. The Web, so-called, allows the transmission of graphic images, animation, and video. It also allows hyperlinks. This means that with one push of a button, using a hypertext format, you can bounce from computer to computer or from page to page of a computer file.

A **Web Site** is someone's file on the Web which, itself, is on the Internet. The **home page** sometimes is used to mean the entire Web

SAMPLE WEB PAGE

Community Entrepreneurs Org

CEO Community Entrepreneurs Organization

Hi! Welcome to the Community Entrepreneurs Organization (CEO). CEO is a nonprofit organization made up of consultants, business owners, lawyers, accountants, inventors, and those considering self-employment:

• Meetings are held the first Tuesday of each month, from 7:30 to 9:30 pm. The public is invited. Cost is $5. See calendar for a listing of upcoming events.
• Membership is $25. Find out how to join and membership benefits.
• Read our online newsletter for articles on marketing. Another useful site is Select Press.

CEO, c/o Select Press (415)924-1612, SelectPr@aol.com

site but originally had a more restricted meaning of the first page of your Web site.

"Semi-Independent" Services

Operating independently of the Internet for many years were **commercial services** like CompuServe, America Online, and Prodigy. They have broad ranges of services from discussion forums to data bases. There are also specialized services like Lexis-Nexis for specific groups. Think of the commercial services as simply large computers that you can dial into to search their various databases, interest groups, chat lines, etc. These services are often costly, but they provide many unique resources.

Now, because of the overwhelming popularity of the Internet, these services have added connections to it. A number of smaller or newer commercial services such as those started by Apple Computer, Microsoft, etc., have decided that they are unable to make it as independent commercial services. They have either closed or switched over to free Internet access.

Also independent of the Internet, were about 10,000 **bulletin boards**, usually run by one person in a basement. Interested users call in, post messages, and share files and information. Now, more and more of them are also hooking up to the Internet. Like the commercial services, the bulletin boards often charge money to join. Similar services on the Internet or on a commercial service, are called news groups, usenets, mailing lists, etc.

The **intranet** is Internet technology *within* a company. Using the same approach, it saves printing costs and allows better distribution of information. There are expected to be more intranet users than Internet users soon.

In retail, **electronic data interchange**, or EDI, has been growing strongly for several years. Independent of the Internet, many large customers like Walmart have been requiring that their suppliers hook up electronically to them so they can automatically reorder online without paperwork, etc.

After an initial investment, this saves time and money all around and is one way that the Walmarts of the world are getting better service and better pricing. The Wal-Marts look at it as a way of getting faster service and better pricing, thus, EDI has tended to be driven by large customers.

As a smaller business, you might look at EDI as a way of serving your customers better, and a way of getting information from them. When you're hooked up to their inventory computers, you can tell exactly how your different lines are selling so that you can get much faster feedback for retooling your lines or output. It is now being done using the Internet.

MicroBiz issued an ultimatum to dealers: Get connected electronically, or get lost. Everyone cooperated and their phone bill was cut in half.

WHO'S ONLINE?

Estimates of the number of people online have been greatly exaggerated. As of the beginning of 1996, estimates were ranging as high as 30 to 40 million people. But more carefully-conducted, random surveys showed about five to six million people on the Internet who were active users. Maybe another four million were on the commercial services such as CompuServe. This gave you a total of about ten million.

The Numbers Are Exaggerated

Even this number was exaggerated for business. Many of the regular users were at universities. They received free accounts and were not likely to spend much money.

These numbers were also exaggerated by the fact that many users have accounts with at least

Who's On The Web?

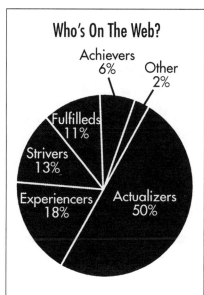

ACTUALIZERS: Highly educated (technical professionals, scientists, professors, etc.).

EXPERIENCERS: Innovative, stimulation seeking, fashionable.

STRIVERS: Technically sophisticated young professionals and students.

FULFILLEDS: age 35 to 45, information-hungry, active purchasers, and users of consumer information.

ACHIEVERS: Stable, upscale, family-oriented individuals (white-collar sales and management).

OTHER: Includes Believers, Makers, and Strugglers, typically lower income, lower education, with a general suspicion and aversion toward technology.

The above data are from a study by SRI International. The categories are part of the VALS 2 (Values and Lifestyles) psychographic system.

two commercial services such as America Online and Compu-Serve. Some will also have direct accounts through Internet service providers. So there's probably a great deal of redundancy.

Demographics and Psychographics

Demographic studies have agreed that the majority of users through 1996 were male, perhaps as many as 75 percent. Of those who aren't college students, it's easy to believe that users are above-average in income because they are computer users. Studies of Web users show that, psychographically, 50 percent of users are "actualizers." They are only 10% of the general population. They are highly educated professionals with upscale tastes. In the future, other groups like "achievers" should increase on the Web.

E-Mail, Not Shopping

E-mail was the most common use. This means that most people are simply sending messages back and forth to each other, not browsing the Web and virtual malls looking for information and bargains.

Many people only use e-mail or one usenet discussion group. This means that, as of early 1996, there may have only been a few hundred thousand serious online users who were also buyers.

Real-world comparison studies support this conclusion. When companies make a commercial offer on both the Internet and a commercial service such as CompuServe, their sales were just as great on CompuServe as they were on all of the Internet. CompuServe during these studies had about two million users. Sales might only come from a few hundred or thousand people. This suggests that relatively few people were buying on the Internet.

> ## Mostly Computer Sales
>
> Studies show that, as of early 1996, more than half the purchases online were for hardware and software. Less than 5% of all households had ever purchased anything online.

The Growth Is Exciting

No matter what the numbers of active users, passive users, occasional users, etc., one thing is clear. If the number is growing at approximately 10% a month, this means the number of users is more than doubling every year.

Because of all the publicity about business potential, more of these new users are going to be trying to do business online. This means that there will be more and more things available for people to purchase.

Again, we have a self-fulfilling prophecy. Online will be a fast-growing marketing medium, at whatever level it started.

HOW DID IT ALL START?

Where did the Internet come from? Why are we're hearing so much about it since 1994?

What we have had is twenty years of groundwork being laid for the Internet to spring up as an "overnight success."

The Internet actually started as a Defense Department project (ARPNET). In the 1960s, a few major government computer sites were tied together with telephone lines. The original intent was to allow communications to continue in the event of a nuclear war, even if major parts of the network were knocked out!

Fairly quickly, the National Science Foundation started funding this project. In order to help spread the costs, they brought academic computer networks onto the network. Then the first international hookups to the Internet came in 1973 in England and Norway.

At many universities in the 1970s, and in particular the 1980s, all students and faculty had free access to this communication link. Many academics began to exchange e-mail and set up various interest group lists on Bitnet, the academic version of the Internet.

Early Notes

By 1973, computer-savvy academics were able to exchange files essentially free. I knew a case where an academic at Michigan and an academic in California were writing a paper together. They'd each have the file on their computer. They'd make their changes on their mainframes, and then squirt the paper to the other party who, the next morning, would open up their computer and have the paper with changes included.

Today all this can easily be accomplished with Lotus Notes and many other e-mail technologies. But in 1973, this was cutting-edge.

The "Modern Era"

In 1994, there was a big change. The National Science

Foundation decided they couldn't keep supporting this free computer network forever, so they opened it up to commercial users. This is when most of us heard about the Internet as a new commercial medium.

The fact that the Internet was born with an academic and technical background accounts for most of the cultural differences online.

For instance, the dislike of blatant promotion and marketing comes from the time when it was forbidden on the Net. University users had little need for marketing. Because it was subsidized and largely academic, everything on the Internet tended to be free. This accounts for other parts of the Internet culture.

Even into 1995, the technical aspects of the Internet made it hard for the average user who wasn't computer literate.

Up to that point there was a Catch 22 to working online. In order to get most of the browsers and other tools to help you navigate online, you had to be online! As the tools became easily available to create a Web page and navigate the Net, it grew even faster.

Technology Accelerates

Forget the technology involved.

Even if you know it well, within a month, there will be major changes. Basically, anything you can think of that could be put through a phone line or through a computer is possible on the Internet, either now or it will be soon.

10 ADVANTAGES OF ONLINE MARKETING

Online marketing has many advantages that make it appealing.

1 Online marketing is **inexpensive**. It's also easy entry. Simple marketing can be done with nothing but your time. You can contact large numbers of people at very low cost with e-mail. And unlike other media, your costs don't necessarily go up as you provide more information.

2 Online is **faster**. You can post up-to-date information for your customers and prospects immediately. You can even send it out automatically to your list.

3 Online is **simpler**. You can save steps, both for you and the customer. If you're reengineering your marketing function, using online as a model will suggest a number of ways to simplify your processes, cut out middlemen and streamline your marketing.

4 Online marketing is **customizable**. Customers can be presented with individualized information that speaks directly to them. With new tools discussed later, custom Web pages can be created "on the fly" as customers ask for specific information.

5 Online marketing gives a lot of **control to customers**. In a world of one-on-one marketing, where customers want personalized service, online leads in that direction naturally.

6 Online marketing is **interactive**. Much like the personal sales process, you have a chance to get feedback from users, prospects, buyers, competitors, etc. It can involve your customers more closely. A related benefit of doing business online is that it allows direct contact with customers. This may have some dollar benefits in cutting out middlemen costs. But the greater benefit is simply allowing more people in your company to get direct, unfiltered input from customers. It won't just be your sales force or your customer service force. Everyone in your company can communicate directly with customers now.

7 Related to several of the above points, online marketing is **information-rich**. Pictures, video, sound, and text can provide more information than any other single marketing medium. Two way communication also adds to the richness, as does the virtually unlimited space for information.

8 Online exposes you to a growing and **diverse audience**. While it does not reflect the entire country, many types of people are online. By looking for specific interest groups, you can find representatives of almost any type of person.

9 Online marketing is **international**. While commercial transactions internationally are very small, you have immediate access to an international audience, whether for sales or feedback or ideas. It's making us more and more of a global village as predicted in the 1960s.

10 It's a **24-hour medium**. People can respond when they want. You can post information around the clock. If you're trying to run a fast company or a 24-hour company, this is the tool that will get you there. And, even if you're not running 24 hours, customers at least have the sense of interaction 24 hours because they can access information any time. And when someone sends you their name or asks for in-

The Homeless Online?

While the poor and uneducated tend to not be online, there are exceptions. Schools and libraries are beginning to make Internet connections available widely. So are programs targeting underserved groups.

The most dramatic example of individual initiative I've heard of was in Northern California. A homeless man was found under a freeway underpass because he had stolen car batteries from road maintenance vehicles. He was using them to power his portable computer and wireless connection to the Net!

formation, your computer can automatically send them a response with a note, even if you're asleep at the time (autoresponders).

Now let's look at some of the details of marketing online.

YOUR WEB SITE OVERFLOWS WITH POTENTIAL

Marketing is anything you do to get or keep a customer.

Your Web site embodies aspects of many types of marketing. The major sub-categories of marketing I prefer are *advertising*, *publicity*, *customer service*, *research*, *sales*, *planning*, and *merchandising*. But there are hundreds of specific types of marketing, such as brochures, networking, etc.

A Web Site Combines Approaches

Your Web site has some aspects of almost all of these traditional types of marketing. For instance, a brochure is something that you create which explains your business, has services lists, pictures, etc. Your Web site can do exactly that.

Even better than a printed brochure, people seek it out and "custom design" it to fit their needs. By moving through your Web site differently, each person can find the pieces that are of interest to him or her personally.

The Web page should be your master marketing file. It should include all your brochures, catalogs, philosophies, testimonials, customer lists, and everything that a customer might want to see.

You need to funnel people to your Web page through your other marketing, advertising, and sales contacts. A Web page address on your business card can be a status symbol. This also is important for marketing your Web page. For instance, when you talk to somebody new on the phone, invite them to check out your Web page. It's a way of showing that you're "with it" and a way of getting them looking at more detailed information so that they can sell themselves.

Your Web Site Does Many Things

Let's look at the seven marketing areas I mentioned and see how they apply to online marketing.

THE NEW ADVERTISING?

Advertising is the most common marketing tool that most people know. It's typically defined as paid, mass-media exposure.

The model of advertising is generally that you distribute a message about your product or company, and a small percentage of the recipients respond. It's considered a mass-medium because you're unable to target it. For instance, TV and the newspaper reach lots of people you don't care about.

Multiple Ad Forms

We have advertising online in a number of different ways. But it very quickly begins to overlap with more targeted approaches such as direct mail. For instance, you can place an ad for your company or service on other people's Web pages, or on CompuServe or America Online. You can also buy ad space on some of the browsers and other tools that people use to "navigate" the Internet or the Web. Thus, when they call up the tool, your ad will be there on their screens.

You can also look at your own Web site as an advertisement.

When people dial into your site, you can provide them with everything from copies of your print or video ads to more general material. The

HOW MUCH BUSINESS IS THERE? As of mid-1996, there was more talk than spending online (perhaps $120 million). Your trick is to entice customers to return to your site over and over by offering regular new material.

first page of your Web site is much like the headline of an advertisement. It has to get their attention. Then they'll read further and consider developing a relationship with you.

Advertising revenues on the Internet were estimated at about $40 million in 1995. In about the same time period, television advertising revenues alone were close to $40 *billion,* or a thousand times more for that single medium.

In one way, $40 million is a lot of money. In another, it's tempting to wonder how fast, if ever, online marketing will grow to the volume of television advertising. Online marketing combines some of the advantages of television with the more targeted advantages of direct mail Some estimates are that there will be $50 billion in online ads by 2000!

High-Tech Billboards

Billboards are a specialized form of advertising. You can look at your Web site as a billboard. Just as you drive by a billboard on the highway, people surf by your Web page. It's a quick shot. If it gets people's attention as they're clicking around, then they'll stop and want to learn more about you.

Unlike a billboard that has to rely on a few words and a quick attention getter, you can have more depth to your billboard once people stop to look.

It's like a billboard at the front of a store or rest stop. Once their interest is grabbed by the billboard, people can enter the store and go to any department for additional information.

You can see how a Web site combines many forms of marketing. A discussion of advertising takes us to billboards, retailing, and direct mail.

"Hot Links"

Another way to advertise online is to connect your Web site to other people's sites that would appeal to the same types of people.

These so-called links, or hot links, or hyperlink connections, can be worked out on a mutual basis for free. Or you can now pay a number of services which will provide links to your page on hundreds of other pages.

Measuring The Action

If you put up a Web site, you'll want to know how many people visit it. So naturally a number of products have evolved, free and otherwise, that can count "hits" to your site. There are also advertising services which will do custom analyses of the types of inquiries to your site. They can even capture the e-mail addresses of people who visit your site.

LEGAL LINKS
One legal consulting firm has 42 links to its site from other legal sites. Only 12 of these sites requested a return link!

PUBLICITY AND PUBLIC RELATIONS

Your Web site also serves as a PR outlet. You can literally post press releases and news about your company.

To be successful, a good press release has to have a "hook" that attracts the interest of journalists and, "ultimately," readers. Likewise, in order to

FOR IMMEDIATE RELEASE

NeXT Computer Web Objects

Steve Jobs is demonstrating the new Web tools at a live press conference. These tools allow the creation of instant custom Web pages.

Hear us live on Real Audio.

Download the product now from www.next.com

get attention at your Web site, you need to have interesting material, newsworthy material, novel material, funny material— something that attracts people to you. And if you follow the PR model, you have to continually update, so there will be "news" for people to check in on.

Live And Online Press Conferences

At a 1996 news conference, Steve Jobs of NeXT Software (co-founder of Apple Computer) announced new tools for building Web pages. The conference was simultaneously broadcast over the Net by Real Audio.

As Steve was doing a live demonstration, his company server was swamped because people online were downloading demonstration copies of the software he was demonstrating!

In other words, there was an immediate response from users, as he was making the introduction. This wouldn't have been possible at an old fashioned press conference.

E-mail PR

You can also use your e-mail to send out press releases electronically, just as you would in the mail. Services such as PR Wire and Business Wire will also send out press releases electronically to different news media for you.

CUSTOMER SERVICE SUPREME

Your Web site is a great place to communicate with your customers. Customer service may be its best use.

> ### One-To-One Marketing
> High tech allows a return to small town service. Old time stores knew their customers. Personal solutions could be worked out. High tech can help a return to that "high touch" service.

E-mail is the most used part of online connections right now. It's perfect for customer service. Customers can post their questions directly to your customer service staff, sales staff, technical staff, etc.

The questions and answers can also be posted for permanent reference and indexed so that new customers can come and look up standard answers and standard information (FAQs—Frequently Asked Questions).

Because of the immediacy of e-mail, it can provide faster, more detailed customer service than is now available in general. It can also be connected to automatic response systems so that customers can download documents, software, and catalog material.

Catalogs

Your Web site can provide customers with all the information you have available. You can present a complete catalog of everything you offer. And unlike a printed catalog, added length adds little to your costs. Once your site is up, adding extra pages costs very little. In addition, unlike a four-color catalog, your printing costs are minimal.

Users pay to seek out your information and download it to their own computers.

Your catalog online has additional advantages, just as CD-ROM encyclopedias have over bound ones. First, you can list infinite detail. Second, you can have video, audio, programs, etc.

Perhaps most importantly, you can arrange information "hierarchically." Readers can use an index, and get a brief description. Then you can set it up so they can click and get all the technical specifications, the details of who invented it, or anything. You could essentially put ten pages of material explaining each item in your catalog if you wanted to!

> **THEY'LL PLAY GAMES ONLINE**
> Online game shows, trivia contests, and the like are the way to get people to register at your site and tell you their interests.
> —Seth Godin, *e-Marketing*

THE NEW RESEARCH

Market research is a great application online. You can collect custom information at your Web site by asking users to fill out a form or register their interests. (Many will be too impatient to do so unless there's some reward for taking the time.)

You can also do research by surfing online yourself. There's a lot of information out there. Certainly larger than any libraries that are easily accessible. Unfortunately because much of the information is free, the quality is sometimes lacking and organization is currently poor.

What's Really There?

Many promoters of online marketing like to say that anything is available online. This is not true.

As of 1996, less than two percent of the information in the world is online. However, much of the new information that's being created is being created in a digital age. More and more of this new information will be posted online as it's created. So the research capabilities can only grow in this new medium.

Wheat and Chaff

Not unlike other sources of information, when you do a search, you'll end up getting as much as 95 percent that isn't what you wanted.

You'll occasionally find things you hadn't known to look for. So the waste factor depends on your attitude toward browsing in the library or through trade magazines. Hopefully, intelligent agents will make it more and more productive to do research. (See page 308 for more on artificial intelligence.)

Online Focus Groups

Another combination of research and customer service is to do online focus groups. By posting questions to users or prospects, you can get a lot of information.

It's more exciting to convene a group and have a live online chat, much like a focus group would convene a live group. Companies have had some success with this, getting large volunteer participation.

Because they are online, people are less shy about speak-

Build Relationships with Customers and Prospects

One type of information that can help your marketing is to learn about personnel changes in your customers' and prospects' companies.

Why not be the first one to send an e-mail note of congratulations to the new person who would be purchasing your products? Or why not send a note to the outgoing person, who may have gotten a job at another potential prospect for you?

It's as if you had your own computer intelligence agents tracking people and topics that are of greatest interest to you.

ing out. Thus, you get more input and one person's opinion is less likely to dominate the group or bias the outcome.

Competitive Analysis

Another area where online research can be of value is for competitive analysis. A lot of material gets posted online which can give you valuable insights into your customers and competitors.

For instance, if your competitors are public companies, there are specialized accountants who can break down their financial statements. Based on knowledge of your costs for different lines of products, you can now make very good estimates of costs and profits for your competitors' information.

Clipping Services

Another way to keep up to date is custom clipping services. Clipping services were named for people cutting out articles from newspapers, or "clipping" them, and sending them to you.

Online, you can set up your own clipping function. You can also pay to have someone create a custom newsletter or newspaper for you every day or every week of just the types of articles that you specify.

SALES CALLS ONLINE

Sales is usually considered a face-to-face or one-to-one activity. It's now possible online to run seminars, live chat groups, and so forth. It's also possible for members of your company to develop one-to-one relationships through e-mail, the In-

---

AN OFFER THEY COULDN'T REFUSE

SBT Internet Systems does free Web pages for Chambers of Commerce. The Sausalito, California Chamber used their new ability to add pages for members as a sales tool to greatly expand membership.

ternet telephone, etc. You can have a relationship built and a sale created.

When you add online telephone to live video, you have more and more of what's involved in the give and take of personal sales. But right now this area, from a traditional definition, is not as well developed as some of the others.

FIRST GET THEIR ATTENTION

Merchandising is an area of marketing normally devoted to retail displays. In a store, being at eye-level can double or triple your sales. Having your product displayed over a broader area of the shelf can improve sales.

Merchandising can also cover packaging—for instance, using design and colors to attract attention.

Merchandising rules apply to your Web page—how you use color, graphics, sound, and movement. Anything that gets attention and holds the browser in a retail store may be usable on your Web site. For example, to get people's attention or to highlight specific material, use a special offer. New technology like "frames" is making new effects available for your Web site every day.

Some of the first major commercial sites created online were shopping malls.

These are virtual malls where companies buy space. Consumers or businesses might look for a "mall" that specializes in computer material. And then, within the virtual mall, there are Web page "stores" that specialize in various kinds of software, hardware, etc. They're trying to create an analogous shopping mall.

10 WAYS TO MARKET ONLINE

In addition to applying the major aspects of marketing discussed above, there are many specific ways that you should know about how to market yourself online. Here are ten of the key ones.

1 **Your signature.** When you send a letter, you sign your name and possibly your title. For online e-mail communication, it's traditional to have your name and an additional line which can be a mini ad for what you do.

For instance, a signature could say, "John Smith, Construction Marketing Specialist. We help you impress architects and owners."

Your signature can also relate to your "domain name" if you have a Web page. For $100, you can register a name for your site for two years. If your name is a great one, this can be a valuable marketing tool on its own.

Even in the "netiquette" where self-promotion is sometimes frowned on, your signature line is acceptable and can become one of your best marketing tools. Of course, it works in conjunction with other forms of marketing such as sending people messages.

2 **Give away advice.** Giving away free advice to various interest groups, chat groups, and mailing lists allows you to build relationships.

When contributing to an online discussion, learn the rules of the group first. "Lurkers" are people who read or listen to discussions but don't make any contributions. If you lurk forever, you're not contributing your share. However, "newbies," newcomers to a group, are told to lurk before they jump in and interrupt the flow.

By observing for a while, you can understand the types of questions that are appropriate and the level of discussion. Then you can contribute at the correct level.

Another way to do this is to look in the FAQs file. Frequently Asked Questions are things that come up all the time. Rather than deal with them over and over, a group or expert will simply refer you to FAQs. So in addition to "lurking" during live discussion, reading some past frequently asked questions can bring you up to speed very quickly in a new area.

> ## Online Networking
> In about 1984 when online bulletin boards were still scarce, a friend of mine became "pen pals" with someone on a bulletin board in Milwaukee. He was in California. He never met her, but they exchanged information and ideas about marketing. She eventually referred him to a friend of hers for whom he wrote a number of marketing materials. But he had never met either the referrer or the ultimate customer.

Build Relationships

Think of e-mail as a chance to build relationships, just as you would have by letter in the old days.

E-mail combines the features of the phone and writing. One reason is technical. Some e-mail programs don't allow you to make corrections. If you dash off a message and then see an error or decide you haven't expressed it quite right, you have no easy way to go back and edit. Thus, e-mail often has a less-polished feel than might a letter that you had a chance to edit and think about.

Of course, I recommend that you use an e-mail program that allows you to edit easily. Everything that you produce should represent you just the way you want it to.

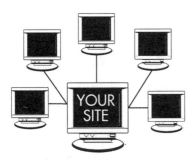

3 **Obtaining links.** One of the major features of the Web is hyperlinks. You can create hot buttons where, with the click of a mouse on a word or graphic, someone can move to another area of your page or to another page anywhere in the world.

There are two ways to use these links to market yourself. One way is to link your site to other sites that people like your customers will tend to go to. This makes your site more valuable, so that people will visit it more often.

Your Web page becomes the central resource. By constantly adding interesting site links, people will have an incentive to come back and see what's new.

Exchanging Links. The second way to use links is to get other sites to provide links to yours. Then when people find a related site, they'll be able to find you too. And, of course, a link from another site is an endorsement that your site is worth visiting.

Links are often exchanged where each of you will have a button that can take people to the other site.

These links on the Web are why people call it "surfing the Web." You can click-click-click and be three different places around the world, often without knowing where you've been.

If you don't catch people's attention and capture their name, you've lost them. Even if they'd been intending to come back, something in your page can take them to another page, something in that page takes them to another page, and so on and so on. Pretty soon they've forgotten where they are, if they ever knew. This leads us to method #4.

4 **Encourage bookmarks.** Bookmarking is a way of recording or indexing the Web pages you've visited. Tell people

on your first page that if they like your page, bookmark it so that they can get back easily to see updates.

You might want to mention this several places on your site, especially near material that is updated regularly, or near your best material. By reminding people to bookmark your page, with a key word, they can find you again under that subject.

5 **Web page design.** The problem of people surfing through your page and forgetting you brings us to how you can use good design to improve your online marketing.

Proper design is aesthetically pleasing. Desktop publishing brought design power to every computer, but not design talent! This is even more true of Web page design. How you use color and space can make a big difference in your page's effectiveness.

Title Your Graphics

Graphics make your Web page look nice, but they are responsible for most of the time wasted online. Many people turn on the "ignore graphics" option in their browser. This means no graphics are loaded and all the viewer sees is "[graphic]" in the place the graphic would be.

HINT: Construct your Web page using the "ALT=" feature. This allows you to include a one- to four-word description of the graphic. Instead of seeing "[graphic]", viewers will see "[CEO photo]" or [New Product Front View]. That way viewers can decide if it's worth turning the graphics import feature back on.

Practical Tips

In addition to the general value of "good design," there are some specific things to use.

One design issue is how you link to other Web sites. You don't want to put links on your first page. You want them to only leave your page after they have read something valuable on yours.

Another simple point is to remember to put

Reasons To Visit A Site

One direct mail consultant has a "critique of the week" on his page. He takes a mailing he receives, scans it in and tears it apart. He also has data bases of marketing statistics and an index of articles people can order. By constantly updating all these, people have lots of reasons to visit his page regularly.

your name, address, phone, fax, or e-mail on every page—as the computer presents them to readers. If browsers print any page, everything they need to contact you will be right there.

Remember that not everyone uses the Netscape browser. Look at your page using different browsers to see how the presentation looks. For instance, your type is read and presented different ways by the various browsers. People on slow modems can't wait to download complex graphics, and some overseas users often can't read graphics at all.

Offer options, like text only, sketchy graphics, and complete graphics. This means you'll probably create three separate files. This is also a simple variation of the customization mentioned below.

6 **Updates.** I've already mentioned the importance of updates. If you aren't constantly adding new links, new articles, new research, etc., your page becomes old news.

A static page that just sits there becomes a "cobweb site." When there were few pages, they were a novelty. But we're far past that point now. If you expect repeat visits, you need to stay fresh.

7 **Custom pages.** What's the best material you can think of for your surfers' pleasure? It's material that is created specially for them.

By linking your Web page to a data base, some

some programs let your computer create custom material for each person who visits you. For instance, NeXT Computer's Web Objects uses a car dealer page as an example. You specify the color, type, price, etc. of the car you want to see. Their program presents that information, creating a Web page only for you. (A free version of their program is available at http://www.next.com.)

8 **Directory listings.** One of the best ways to be found on the Web is to get yourself listed in all of the many directories and indexes. Some directories try to cover most Web pages, like Yahoo. These combine directories and search engines to help users find resources that they need. There are also services that will list you in multiple directories. (Promote It! at http://www.cam.org/~psarena/promote-it.html.) Don't forget to check the directories to see if you really got listed.

Key Words

This brings us to the idea of key words. Most directories and search engines look for key words and combinations of words. It's an important marketing decision what you name your Web page and what key words you use to describe it. You have to think in terms of the user. What are they going to be looking for? How can you help them find you?

Content Is King

Content is where I expect much of the real money will be made on the Internet, just as it was in broadcasting...The Internet allows information to be distributed worldwide at basically zero marginal cost to the publisher.

—Bill Gates, Microsoft Corp.

Don't call it "Rick Crandall's Web" page.

No one but your friends will search for that. Call it the "online marketing, consulting, advertising, publicity, merchandising, retail, customer service page from Rick Crandall"!

9 **Give away information**. Implicit in some of the points made above is another one. People like free things. When you can give away valuable information, data, ideas, graphics, etc., people will remember your site.

If you give away information you've developed, it is a work sample demonstrating your expertise. It can also be a free sample encouraging further purchases. For instance, several people have given away the first chapter of a book and sold the rest. Or they've given away one version of their software and sold upgrades (e.g., Netscape's browser).

Sampling is an old retail marketing technique. If your product appeals to people, getting them a sample can turn them into loyal customers. This may only work for 10% of the samplers. But even 1% could be highly profitable if your costs to give out the samples are low as they are online.

10 **Spamming.** Spamming means sending an e-mail message to "everyone," without concern for how it fits their interests. It is the net's junk mail. Spamming was made notorious by lawyers Laurence Canter and Martha Siegel. In 1994 they posted ads for their immigration services in every Usenet group they could find. People hated it and the lawyers' computer service was closed down from the "flames" and "mail bombs" they received. But they claim that they also got $100,000 of business from it. And they wrote a book.

When 10 million e-mail addresses are available almost free, it's tempting to try to communicate with people who you don't know much about.

Netiquette

This brings us to an important topic, both marketing and otherwise. Netiquette is a term developed from the word "etiquette" and the Net or network. The online world was originally populated by nonprofits. Most material was given away. It was considered in poor taste to actively promote yourself or to impose yourself on users.

In addition, much like junk faxes, users were paying for their accounts and paying for their time online. If you left them messages or otherwise contacted them, they were having to pay for your marketing.

Junk mail is not as accepted in this universe as in your mailbox at home. But it's already common. This is an area where there will probably be lots of conflict and evolution. As millions of e-mail addresses become available, there's bound to be misuse and problems. At the same time, it does give you almost free distribution to a wide audience.

"Professional" Spamming

At least one person specializes in spamming the Net for you. For about $500, Jeff Slaton (501/821-1945) will send your message out to 6 million e-mail addresses, or 7000 groups.

Let's be clear here. His accounts have been closed many times by providers who were clogged up by the hate mail he receives. In fact, he recommends you set up a front account that you will abandon after you get your payoff. Otherwise, you'll never be able to show your ID online again! Providers may also try to charge you extra for problems you create.

NEW MARKETING MODELS

We need to develop new ways to invite people to receive more information from you without offending them enough that they flame you in return.

THE ONLINE TWO-STEP

We don't have to reinvent the wheel here. In direct marketing, advertising, and telemarketing, they have developed two-step marketing. This is probably the best model from traditional marketing to apply to online marketing. In fact, online will probably end up popularizing three- and four-step marketing programs.

It's all a matter of building relationships with people. For instance, let's say you have a list of e-mail addresses of people who you think might possibly be interested in your product or service. Or, even worse, you have a large list of e-mail addresses who you know nothing about. You're tempted by the fact that it may cost you a little time and $5.00 to send them all e-mail messages.

You can send out 100,000 e-mail messages for the cost of a few stamps. So you give in to this temptation. If you send them a commercial message, you'll be guilty of spamming. You'll get flame-mail and your service provider may even disconnect you!

Step 1: Try an Invitation

Is there another way to open the relationship? What if you sent people an invitation that said, "I wasn't sure if this was appropriate for you, but if you're interested in information on XYZ, please send me a message and I'll get you more information free. If you don't respond, I'll take you off the list and not bother you again. Thank you for your time."

Try to offer people something of real value.

If you got a half or one percent response that was typical of junk mail, without getting flamed to death, you'd be way ahead. The 500 to 1000 responses cost you $5.00 instead of $50,000 for mailing 100,000 envelopes.

You'd not only get it 10,000 times cheaper, you'd also get it faster.

Step 2: Start a Relationship

Now comes the second step. For the people who actually identified themselves as interested, the second step is to send them the material you promised them.

You'd start off by saying, "Here's the information you asked for on XYZ." Then in a low-key way, you would explain the proposition to them. Because these are selected prospects, you might get a 10% response, or more. And some of the others would buy later.

Multi-Step Marketing

Where it would become three- or four-step marketing is you might not even ask for the order at this time. You might say, "We're very interested in getting input from new people and seeing what they like in this area. We'll keep you informed with free reports and other material that becomes available in this area, unless you send us an e-mail message that says you don't want to hear anything more from us."

First they had to "opt in" to get on your list (they had to make a positive response). Now they have to "opt out" to get off your list. It's like the continuity book clubs. They'll get more information unless they explicitly ask to be removed.

The Relationship Builds

You can now put these new people on your newsletter list or press release list or other non-pushy communications which builds the relationship. This allows them to get used to you and build potential trust. Then, at some point, it will become appropriate to make them an offer.

For instance, your newsletter may have interesting articles and information. It may also have a flyer attached to it that says, "Special this month. If you'd like me to critique your internal policies manuals for the newest HR law, send them to me." Or you may say, "We've just written a book on this topic and we have a free report or we have a paid report." Gradually it becomes more and more natural to offer recipients things that they could pay for.

TECHNICAL DETAILS

Your Computer

What sort of equipment do you need to surf the Net?

There's nothing wrong with starting with the equipment that you have. There's no point in going out and buying a new machine if it turns out that you don't really like working online. So try it with what you have until you find your way around, and then upgrade as appropriate.

Most of the current computers being sold today are Pentium-based. These are plenty powerful in terms of processors. You can get by with slower machines, but as programs get bigger, it's probably recommended that your internal RAM be 16 Mb rather than 8 Mb and that your hard drive be over 250 Mb.

If you want to download visuals or videos, you'll want an even larger hard drive. Video files take up a tremendous amount of space.

Your "Modem"

The most important variable for happily surfing the Net is your modem or other connection to your online service providers.

A 14.4 baud modem is now considered about the slowest that you'd want to use. A 28.8 baud modem makes a noticeable difference. It's two to four times faster than 14.4. When you're downloading visual images, which are a distinctive characteristic of the Web, your modem speed makes a big difference.

Technical Connections to the Web

A *shell account* is the slowest way to be connected to the Web by your modem. It's also the cheapest of course. In a shell account, your address is joesmith@AOL.com, or something similar. This tells people that AOL is handling your Web page or e-mail.

A *virtual server* makes it look like you have your own personal (expensive) server. It uses an address like sallysmith.com.

When you really had to have your own hardware to have an address like this, it had a lot more status than the shell account. It meant you'd made a serious investment ($50,000 up).

Virtual servers are usually attached to *slip accounts*. They are now common and considerably faster; almost the same as being directly connected to the Internet. A PPP account is faster still, with each costing more.

The phone companies offer ISDN lines which are about four times faster than the currently available modems.

If you're at a larger company, you may have dedicated T1 or T3 lines to your service provider or to the Internet backbone directly. These are much, much faster as well. Your local cable companies are going to be offering a super-fast modem con-

A New Moore's Law?

The Internet is serving as the keystone to drive new technologies, and faster speeds. Services like ISDN have been around for a long time, but nobody wanted them until now.

Moore's law basically says that computer chips will get twice as powerful and half as expensive every 18 months. Now, with the online growth, Moore's law should begin to apply to online connection technology too.

nection through your cables, and various wireless alternatives will be available as well.

The $500 Boxes

The new $500 "Internet box" is also coming. In a sense, the Internet can be looked at as one large computer system. So theoretically you don't need much processing power in your computer that's connected to it.

This is something of a "back to the future phenomenon."

In the old days, this would be a dumb terminal connected to a large mainframe. This model of dumb terminals and centralized computing has largely been displaced by powerful desktop computers and distributed networks between them. But for some purposes, the central mainframe and dumb terminals are more efficient, even if less popular.

The Internet is going to now have competing pushes. On one hand, people want more powerful, faster machines so they can surf faster. On the other hand, an inexpensive box using programs online may be coming back as sort of a dumb terminal approach.

The $500 box will not include a screen. It will be a useful potential tool to be hooked up at schools, libraries, and other areas to make the Internet accessible to everyone. People will simply have enough computing power to sign on. Then they will

The "Pippin"

While not yet promoted as a cheap Internet box, the Apple Pippin is an inexpensive game box *and* Internet connection. Available now in Japan, it should be the first of many inexpensive boxes.

access a program online, free or otherwise, that does what they want to do.

Artificial Intelligence (AI)

Another technology, mentioned earlier, that's being resurrected because of the power of online is artificial intelligence.

Some years ago there was great hope that we'd be able to create artificial intelligence programs that did everything we needed. They would think the way we did and become "smarter" by learning our preferences. Some were created. But the field has not developed as hoped years ago.

There have been successes with programs that mimick therapists or are able to perform other "higher-level" tasks like beating a Chess Grand Master. But in general, artificial intelligence as a programming approach has been disappointing.

www.search.com

A new Web site offers links to *hundreds* of search tools. As newer and better search engines become avilable, they will be included.

Better Searches

One thing that's needed on the Web or in any search tool for computer databases, is something "smarter" than keyword or title searches. A number of "spiders" and other intelligent agents are beginning to be developed which can act the same way you might. They can spend hours screening material. If they could do it just the same way you would, then the remaining material that they present you would be cleaned to your specifications.

As it is now, if you do a database search on a typical service, you're going to get 95 percent material that you don't want and maybe five percent that you do. *You* can usually tell what you want very quickly by going through the titles or abstracts or descriptions. But the average search engine or search parameter, even using Boolean logic where you say it must have "marketing" *and* "sales" in the title, still gives you a lot of chaff compared to the wheat.

While I'm not aware of one that performs at a high level yet, artificial intelligence agents look like a good potential bet here. As they become capable of making the same judgements you would about the value of what they find, the field will leap ahead.

SECURITY

Another major concern that people have about doing business online is security.

Actually, the security issues are no worse than giving your MasterCard number to someone over the phone or to a waiter at a restaurant. Both have the potential to misuse it or add other charges to your card. Perhaps online is more frightening because it's new.

If your actual credit card is stolen from you now, MasterCard and Visa cover the charges. As of this writing, the charge card companies have now agreed on a new security protocol for online transactions. Soon, online consumer transactions with credit cards will be "insured" too.

One thing that makes people nervous about online security is that, since the beginning of computers, there's been a group of "hackers" who broke into computer systems for fun. Some have created computer viruses to wreak havoc in pro-

SECURITY TIP
Always maintain a back-up set of files on your own computer separate from Internet files.

grams. A few hackers do no damage. They are responding to the technological challenge of entering a locked system. But there has been a lot of damage done to computer systems.

> There are now approximately 35 million-dollar plus electronic thefts every year from banks and similar networks.
> Banks don't publicize these because they don't want to encourage people!

As of this writing, there have been no documented instances of an individual's credit card being stolen and misused online. For most of us security isn't an issue.

Firewalls

There are a number of ways of minimizing security risk. Most of these are called "firewalls." Firewalls are a combination of hardware and/or software products that cut off access to your computer.

Check Your Provider's Security

If you're not a big business or institution, you probably will have your files on a server connected to the Internet that belongs to someone else. Hackers might be able to break into that server. Then, if they have the editing commands for the server, they might be able to break into your file, destroy it, corrupt it, plant a virus, or make alterations. A practical protection is to set your files up on the server as "read only." Then they can't be edited online.

Firewalls can be expensive so you'll want to ask your online provider about their security precautions. An example of careless security is that some Internet service providers leave the default password that came with the system in place. This means that anyone familiar with the equipment will also know the password!

Check Your Security

Independent of your service provider, there are a number of things you can do to improve security.

Some security solutions are hardware-based. For instance, you can have a dedicated computer that has your files on it. It's not hooked up to other computers within your company. Or you turn your computer off when you're not using it online.

A software firewall would have a similar intent. Through a series of passwords and command structures, it would seek to eliminate access from outside or by unauthorized people.

Of course, most security violations or breeches in computer systems have internal help. Many of your staff give away passwords or are careless about changing passwords and this sort of thing.

PROGRAMMING YOUR WEB PAGE

HTML was the first major programming language for Web pages. It was designed to be a very simple-to-use method for giving your page the power to have hyperlinks, graphics, sound, etc.

HTML can create a simple page in half an hour. The chart on the next page shows the basic commands for starting a Web page. By simply writing between the designated elements, you can create a crude Web page. (See the disk for more examples.)

Questionnaire

How old are you?

What product do you like?

What color do you prefer?

How many people are in your household?

How many people would use this product?

More Expensive Pages

Some major companies are spending hundreds of thousands of dollars to create Web sites.

To get this:	Do this:
Page start	<HTML>
Page end	</HTML>
Start of header	<HEAD>
End of header	</HEAD>
Create page title	<TITLE>your title here<TITLE>
Start of body	<BODY>
End of body	</BODY>
Start address	<ADDRESS>
End address	</ADDRESS>
Bold type	<B>your text here</B>
Italics type	<I>your text here</I>
Underline type	<U>your text here</U>
Smallest type	<H5>your text here</H5>
	<H4>your text here</H4>
Medium type	<H3>your text here</H3>
	<H2>your text here</H2>
Largest type	<H1>your text here</H1>
Line break (carriage return)	
Line break with blank line following	<P>
Line break with blank line and horizontal rule	<HR>

Basic HTML Commands

One of the things that adds expense to a Web page is the use of forms. Forms are a device where people can fill out information which is then captured by you. If you want to have some interactivity where people fill in the blanks of a form, this is a more complex programming structure.

The example mentioned earlier of the NeXT program is another example. Connecting your page to a data base to create custom pages is expensive.

Another popular tool that is sweeping the Web as of 1996 is Java. It and other such programming applications allow you to have video, animation, and motion. Java creates sub-units of programming code, sometimes called "applets," which can make your page more interactive and more complex. Java received lots of good press in 1995, but was not actually released until early 1996. Competent Java programmers were scarce at that time.

CONCLUSIONS

The good news is that, as of 1996, you are still on the ground floor of a major new business medium. There's still time to take advantage of it, despite the fact that others have been experimenting with it for 25 years.

If you're concerned about your dollar return from online, you have to fall back on the old marketing wisdom to test.

Test Before You Spend

Not only can you test different ads or offers, but you can test different places to publicize them. You can track from which directories your inquiries come by using different e-mail addresses (equivalent to post office boxes in direct mail). You can post notices to different groups using different name codes or e-mail addresses. You can begin to understand where actual business or viable inquiries come from.

In other words, just because online is a new and exciting medium doesn't mean old rules don't apply. Find people who need what you have to offer. Track your responses. And build relationships to do lots of business over time.

Those are the basics of good marketing. They will apply to any new medium.

ACTION AGENDA

If you're new to online, find a friend who can show you the ropes. Then get the free trial disks from commercial providers. When you've had enough practice, work your way up to the Web.

If you're more experienced online, start systematically applying what you know:

- Put up a simple Web page.
- Add new keywords to your page.
- Register a dynamic name that will attract people.
- Have lots of e-mail correspondence.
- Visit user groups.
- Get on mailing lists.
- Improve your signature line.
- Arrange links with other related sites.
- Improve your Web page with forms, and applets.
- Make sure you're in every possible directory.

Have fun and see the computer disk for more details about online resources.

Chapter 12

10 REASONS TO MARKET BY FAX

Bob Bailey

Bob Bailey
is a technical strategist who helps businesses plan and implement high tech tools to improve operations, save money, and boost profits. Bailey says, "It's not what the tool can do but what the tool can do for you that's important. You have to match the tool to the problem." His combination of technical expertise, business experience, and ability to explain concepts to real people is the perfect mix of skills to provide practical business advice and planning for using technology.

Bailey was one of the first to own a personal computer and frequently buys hardware, software, or uses a service just to see what it can do. He is curious about technology but there is a practical, business-oriented side: as the owner of a whitewater kayaking school he used his computer to schedule and track business. As a consultant he constantly uses high tech tools in his business.

Bob Bailey, ebiz, 528 Ashford Road, Silver Spring, MD 20910; phone (800) 707-ebiz; voice, (301) 587-3447; fax (301) 587-3299; email, ebiz@aol.com

10 REASONS TO MARKET BY FAX

Bob Bailey

The fax machine has already revolutionized the way we market products. And it has just as much potential for services. With faxes becoming available on every computer, we've only scratched the surface of fax marketing.

We already fax product descriptions, price lists, and invitations to events. We can build relationships by faxing cartoons, articles, questions, answers, etc. Virtually all of your business customers have fax capabilities. And faxes are being installed in more homes every day.

FAX VERSATILITY AND SPEED

While the Postal Service steadily increases the cost of mailing documents, the cost of faxes steadily declines. While the mail gets slower, the ease and speed of fax delivery has steadily increased.

In the past, announcing a new product or service to your customers would take weeks if not months. A bigger competitor with a larger budget could get there first and eat your lunch. No more! With broadcast fax you can reach your customers overnight and at a fraction of the cost of a mailing.

You're Invited! Free seminar on what the new tax changes mean to your business.

santax 100

There is a lot that you can do with fax marketing, and it's cheap, fast, and easy. You can use fax to contact existing customers, keep in touch with current prospects, and initiate contact with people whose names you have gotten through a referral. Here's what you can tell them:

- Announce a new product or feature.
- Follow up a sales call.
- Distribute a value-added newsletter about your product or service.
- Conduct a fax-back survey with easy-to-use multiple choice answers.
- Confirm appointments.
- Just ask, "How are things going?"
- Build the relationship with a clipping of interest to them, a cartoon, or other informal material.

WHAT FAX SOFTWARE IS

Fax software is dramatically changing the way we use the fax.

We no longer have to create a document, print it, and then feed it through a balky scanner. We can simply sit at our PC, call up a suitable cover page, create our message, establish the distribution list, and send the fax. All of this can take less than a minute! (Contrast that with sending a letter via US Mail to a hundred people.)

In its simplest and cheapest form, a stand-

When NOT To Use Fax Software

The only time *not* to use software for outbound fax is when you have an original document that is outside of the PC. Even then, you may want to scan it into the PC and throw away the document. It's easier to find things in computers than in filing cabinets.

alone fax machine combines a scanner a fax modem, some storage, and some programs (a.k.a. software) with a low-quality dot matrix printer.

A PC with a fax modem and fax software replicates a fax machine without the scanner. The main difference is flexibility. Where a fax machine can do only one task and stands idle much of the time, a PC can do many chores when it is not working on faxes.

Fax Features

All fax software packages can send and receive faxes. Most software can and should do much more. The difference in cost between a merely adequate and a robust package is likely to be less than $50. In my judgment, this is a trivial amount when you consider the length of time you will be using the software and the potential productivity gains.

Invest in the features for the future even if you don't need them now. The following are the essential features for any fax software package:

Address book. An address book is a place to keep names, addresses, and fax phone numbers. The address book also lets you create groups of people to receive broadcast faxes. If you already have a contact manager or PIM such as Act! or Ecco, a really good package like WinFax PRO lets you use that phone book in addition to its internal phone book.

With most software you can also do queries

on the address book. This can take the form of a single query like "Tom Jones." Or, you could search for everyone named "Tom" or by company name, area code, or any combination. Having found the subset of people or companies that you want, you can use the list to create a group.

Cover pages. Cover pages are forms with places for addressee information as well as sender information. Some packages such as WinFax include hundreds of pre-made cover pages and a cover page editor. The ability to create an individualized cover page is essential, since this presents the image of your business or personality. Many cover pages have a box for inserting a message, so that you need only one page for cover and content.

In-box, out-box, sent log. An in-box is the repository for all the faxes that you have received but not printed, filed, or deleted. You can also use it as a to-do list.

The out-box is the file of outgoing faxes that you have prepared but not yet sent. Faxes can be in the out-box because they are on hold, scheduled for future delivery, or scheduled for off-peak delivery. Some packages have an automatic off-peak scheduling capability that can cut phone costs significantly.

The sent log is the repository for all the faxes that you have sent but not filed or deleted. You can also consider it a follow-up list.

Attachments or stock pages. Attachments are pages that have been created in fax format by a word processor or a scanner and filed with the software package. Typically, attachments are stock pages or boilerplate that are sent to many clients or customers, but not at the same time like a broadcast fax (see below). Attachments can be reused over and over but usually cannot be modified without being recreated.

When I run public seminars, I typically create a number of attachments and fax them to clients at various stages of the sign-up process (see p. 327). The ability to print to the fax software is very important and an essential feature of any package you'll use to create attachments.

Printing to fax. Most software lets you direct the print to more than one printer. You may have a printer on your desk and also have access to a network printer. Or you may have two printers attached to your PC, each performing a different function. Fax software packages include a driver that looks like a printer to your other software but is really sending the print output to fax. The fax software then creates an outbound fax or an attachment.

Broadcast faxes. Broadcast fax is simply sending the identical fax to everyone on a list. This is one of the primary functions of fax software and should be part of any package you buy.

OVERVIEW OF REASONS TO MARKET BY FAX

1. Beating the rising cost of postage.
2. Faster, easier mail.
3 Direct mail from concept to delivery in hours, not weeks.
4. Conducting a survey fast, cheap, and easy.
5. Receiving faxes on the road.
6. E-mail for folks who don't have e-mail.
7. Fast file transfers for people who aren't hooked up to the Internet or online services.
8. Broadcast faxing.
9. Fax on demand.
10. Sending newsletters and other news to customers.

10 REASONS TO MARKET BY FAX

1 **Saving on postage** (a.k.a. snailmail). Using fax, you can get more impact for less money in your communications.

A first-class letter now costs at least 32 cents, no matter where it goes in the US. A local fax from a personal phone line can cost as little as nothing! A long-distance fax costs about 20 cents per page during the day and a dime a page if you send it overnight. Contrast this with an overnight rate of about $10 from the US Postal Service and more for Fedex.

International fax is an even better deal if time is a consideration. Airmail to an international destination can take over a week and costs 60 cents for one page. Overnight charges overseas range from $15 up. International phone rates from the US are such that a fax costs about a dollar a page. But the fax gets there now.

What's crazy about this upside-down cost picture is that even though it's generally cheaper, the fax gets more attention when it arrives! Fax technology is still novel enough that people take notice. And you're not competing with piles of junk mail.

Is the US Postal Service going to disappear? Probably not. The Mail is enough of an institution that it will survive for quite a while. And *someone* has to deliver all that junk mail that nobody reads!

2 **"Speedmail."** To send a message to a colleague in a distant state via the US mail you must:

- Write the message either longhand or by keyboard.
- Address an envelope (assuming that you have one handy)
- Put on a stamp—make sure it's enough for the latest rate hike!
- Lick and seal everything.
- Trot down to the local post office to mail it or wait for your pick-up.

At this point your message is still at least two days from the recipient.

Let's replay this story using the fax. The same message has been entered into your computer via the keyboard. (If you normally type letters this is already done, right?) If your PC has fax, all you have to do is:

- Have your word processor print to the fax software.
- Address the fax in the fax software.
- Press "Send Fax."

Case Study:
Fax Builds Membership

Tycon Toasters started as toastmasters club in a single company, which made marketing and communications easy. We could schedule the meetings on the company's e-mail system, send e-mail reminders to all members, and use the company phonemail system to spread the latest news.

But then things started to change—which was good news and bad news. The good news: We were growing fast and taking in members from all over the area, over half of whom were not company employees. This was great for diversity, and we heard some terrific speeches. The bad news was that our communications system no longer worked. We could not keep a phone tree together for long, and not enough members were connected to e-mail to make that viable.

We solved the problem with fax. All but one member (who was temporarily unemployed) could be reached by fax. After every meeting each member receives a fax. The cover page is a form letter, but it can include news and schedule changes. Also included is a list of the home and office phone and fax numbers of all members. Most important, it includes a master schedule showing all meeting dates, special events, and who is in charge of each meeting.

Such is the power of creative faxing that our attendance has skyrocketed, membership is booming, and no-shows are way down.

Your message is instantly on its way to the recipient!

Even if you don't have fax software in your computer, you can still take advantage of the speed and low cost. Simply print out the message and slip it into the fax machine. It's on it's way!

3 **Fax as direct mail**—in hours, not weeks. Almost as soon as there was fax, somebody started sending junk fax. Most of the original junk fax tried to sell fax paper! And why not? You created demand for your product while advertising it!

Congress quickly put a stop to this and created some very

Don't Send Junk Faxes

- Before you send a fax to some-one, be sure that you make a connection with them. The connection can be through a third party, but it must exist and you should establish the connection in the first paragraph.

- Don't send junk faxes to titles; use real names when possible.

- Don't buy fax number lists. People resent incoming faxes that tie up their machines and waste their paper if that fax is coming from someone they don't know.

- At the top or bottom of your first fax to someone, clearly indicate that you will take them off your list if they fax the page back to you with the box checked to do so.

reasonable rules for business use of fax. The formal rules are embodied in a million words of legislation and regulations buried somewhere in Washington, but a few practical guidelines are listed in the sidebar.

Fax Software. Fax software on a PC is best for direct mail efforts. Create one message and send it out to multiple customers. Avoid naming customer names in the fax; instead use the generic "you." Open the fax with "Hi!" or some other form of non-specific greeting. Some packages allow the use of a name field in the body of the message, but the time spent making this work may offset any advantage gained. Keep it simple!

Use the features of the fax software to make life easy for yourself, and use the recipient's machine at a time of day when it is likely to be idle. Schedule the outbound fax for evening hours, 7 to 10 pm for example. Some target fax machines may be in private homes in bedrooms that double as offices: ringing phones at 3 am won't be welcome.

Keep It Brief

Don't wax eloquent. Keep your message short. One page is usually enough to say anything that needs saying; two pages tops. This has the added advantage of forcing you to be clear and concise.

If it takes more than two pages, it probably wasn't suited to a fax message in the first place.

Fashion a cover page that has plenty of space for the message and includes essential information such as your name, phone number, fax number, and address. (Ever get an anonymous fax?) Remember the cost of a fax is based on the length of time it takes to send it, typically about a minute per page. A two page fax costs twice as much as a one page fax. If you send that fax to hundreds of people, well,...

Be careful about using graphics, especially graphics with a lot of dark space. Dark space lays down a lot of ink and makes the paper wrinkle—plus it slows down the transmission, tying up everyone's machine and increasing your costs. Is the graphic an essential part of your message? Does it dramatically increase the impact of your fax? Will it show up at the receiver's end looking as wonderful as it does to you? If not, lose it.

4 **Conducting a fast, easy, and cheap survey.** Using the fax is a great way to do a survey. For instance, to find out whether there were the sort of problems that I suspected in an industry, I used the fax to get some ideas and confirmation of my hypothesis.

First, I thought about and wrote down what I wanted to know. Then I turned those ideas into questions. I had to be careful to avoid biasing the answers with the wording of the questions. Next I created a broadcast fax to all the members of an association where I am a member. The fax was one page long,

> ## Let Us Know What You Think
>
> Some of you have requested that we offer appointments during nontraditional business hours. In response to these requests, we are planning to expand our hours. Please rank order the following options:
>
> _____ Weekdays, 9 am - 5 pm
> _____ Weekdays, 6 am - 9 am
> _____ Weekdays, 5 pm - 9 pm
> _____ Saturdays, 9 am - 2 pm
>
> FAX YOUR RESPONSE BACK TO US AT 555-5555. WE VALUE YOUR OPINION.

Case Study: Saga Of A Seminar

When you just start a business, any business, you always have more to do than time to do it. This has been true of every business I have started; ebiz consulting and speaking are no exception. I presented my first seminar for free. I just wanted to find out what my audience was doing and what they were interested in.

But giving away a seminar is no easier than selling one. In fact, it may be harder because participants have no vested interest in attending. My problems were to make time for selling, keep track of who was coming, and make sure everyone had all the information they needed when they needed it. Here's how I managed using various properties of the fax.

All my prospects were already in my database, but so were a lot of non-prospects. The first step was to identify every potential prospect and put the names into an electronic folder.

Next, I inserted the names of those prospects who, for whatever reason, seemed more likely or desirable than others into a subfolder labeled "Prime."

Then I started making phone calls. When I couldn't reach people by phone but had their fax number, I would send a fax explaining what I wanted and requesting a good time to call them. Some prospects responded and signed up by fax; we never spoke directly!

As part of my preparation, I used the facilities of my fax software package WinFax PRO to create stock documents. I made up standard one-page faxes to confirm registration and send more information. I had a one-page flier describing my seminar stored as a fax image. When I needed to fax a confirmation or additional information, all I had to do was pull the cover page and the appropriate document. WinFax is smart enough to connect to my database and retrieve the phone number.

I was so successful that I had a waiting list. I also broadcast fax another reminder the day of the seminar.

The results: 95% attendance at the seminar! I had written no letters, published no forms, licked no envelopes. Sending the broadcast fax took less than a half-hour including writing, selecting addressees, and following up (busy signals, bad connections, etc.). I created the faxes early in the morning, scheduled them for a time when I would be out, and followed up later in the day. Except for a few folks who lived relatively far away, all the faxes were free local calls!

the questions were generally only one or two lines with all possible answers included below the question.

I suggested in the first paragraph that the recipient answer the survey at once and fax it back to me now. In other words, I made it fast and easy.

Most surveys get about a 20% response rate that takes weeks. I got a sixty percent response, fast, and spent only about $5 for a few toll phone calls!

"Next year couldn't I just fax you my list?"

5 **Remote retrieval of faxes.** Road Warriors are people who travel so much they think of hotels as home and the maid as family. They have been known to show up at home in a rental car, having left their own car in the airport parking lot!

If you are in a place where you can plug your PC into a phone line and receive the fax through a fax-modem, here is an option: WinFax PRO can dial in from your laptop to your desktop fax PC and download your new faxes. This has been a missing link for Road Warriors who never again have to call in and have a secretary read them their faxes or refax them to their hotels. (These refaxes, of course, arrive after they leave the hotel.)

Remote retrieval works well because the communication is handled by two copies of the same software, eliminating compatibility issues. Security becomes a concern, though. To address it I recommend the following steps:

- Disable remote retrieval when you are not on the road.
- Use a password not found in the dictionary like "zippitydoo."
- Do not use obvious passwords.
- Change your password after each road trip, if practical.

Receiving Multiple Faxes on the Road

If you need to receive lots of faxes on the road, another system is available for you.

One drawback with fax is the point-to-point nature of the technology. Normally, a fax device is fixed in one place and attached to a single phone number. If a fax comes into a machine, it is printed and there it sits.

An excellent solution is to subscribe to a fax mailbox. You list the service as your fax number and receive all your faxes at that number. The mailbox can be on an 800- or standard line. Periodically you dial in using a fax machine or fax-modem and retrieve all of your faxes or selected faxes. You can also arrange to be notified via pager whenever a fax is waiting.

Some services provide voice mail as well as faxmail on the same mailbox. You can simplify operations by having one 800-

Fax Mailbox Services: What They Cost

This service, like many services involving technology is not cheap. A typical basic rate structure:

- Fax mailbox: $10 per month.
- Additional charges for fax retrieval: 35-50 cents per page depending on volume.
- Voice mailbox: $10 per month.
- Additional charges for message retrieval: 35 cents per minute.

number that is never busy and can take any incoming call, whether fax or voice.

When To Use A Fax Mailbox Service

Consider a fax mailbox service if:

- You are on the road a lot.
- You receive a high volume of faxes or calls and are allergic to busy signals.
- You need confidentiality.
- You need an overflow capability for your regular fax number.
- You require pager notification of incoming faxes.
- Missed faxes mean lost revenue.

6 **E-mail for folks who don't have e-mail.** Everybody talks about e-mail and many people print e-mail addresses on their business cards. Some people have more than one e-mail address; as of this writing, I have six!

E-mail is growing fast. But the fact remains that only about 20 million or so are actually hooked up to universal e-mail. Not everyone has a connection to a service provider and not everyone is willing to pay the connection fee such services charge (about $10 a month). Moreover, not everyone wants e-mail. Some people are unprepared to do business that way.

But everybody has a phone. And almost everyone has access to a fax at work. Even the corner deli accepts orders by fax!

Fax e-mail

And the availability of desktop fax can transform every PC into an e-mail terminal. There are over sixty million PCs in the US alone, almost all of which are ready candidates for fax software. Moreover, there are over ten million fax machines in the US, some of which are shared by up to ten people.

Consider this process: I have desktop fax and so do you. I compose a fax on my screen and have WinFax PRO send it to you. The phones latch up, the fax is sent, and you are looking at my message on your screen. Nothing has been printed. The whole process took only five minutes or so. Sounds a lot like e-mail, doesn't it? Try it, you'll like it.

E-mail Gateways

Another way to reach people who don't have e-mail is through a fax gateway. Major e-mail service providers such as MCI and CompuServe feature a fax gateways as part of the service. A fax gateway is a special address within the e-mail service that receives the message and the sends it out via fax. Examples of CompuServe addressing for fax:

Name	Address
Bob Bailey	Fax: 301-587-1234
Bob Bailey (in Germany)	Fax: 41-75-123-4567

CompuServe's fax service is not cheap; a one-page domestic fax runs 75 cents.

Internal computer networks can also have a fax gateway service. The e-mail is addressed to the gateway which extracts the phone number and other information and then sends the fax. The e-mail service provider may also offer standard mailing lists such as all of the members of Congress. If you are part of a private, internal network, contact your network administrator to find out what services are available.

Gateways are also useful if you are hooked into an e-mail service provider but don't have access to your fax software. This can happen if you are on a digital phone service or in certain overseas locations.

7 **Fast file transfers without online service connection.**
Sometimes sending printed text is not really what's needed. Sometimes you need to send the word processing file complete with all the formatting. Or perhaps you need to send a complete spreadsheet file to a project collaborator. Or maybe the printed text is just plain too long to fax. There's a solution using fax.

With the right software, most new fax modems can send a file to another user who also has similar capabilities. This feature is called Binary File Transfer or BFT.

What is BFT anyway? Faxes work by sending a stream of codes that determine whether a spot on the page will be blank or black. In practice, it's a bit more complicated than that, but not much. Each fax machine knows what the code is and follows it. A few years ago somebody said, "What we are really sending is a file." Bingo! Why not send all kinds of files? BFT was born.

How do you make it work? First, the fax-modem must have the ability to understand that it is a file and not a fax. Only Class 1 fax-modems have this ability. Next the software must be able to do file transfer. Many packages on the market today can do this. Finally, you decide to send a file and then follow your software's instructions.

File transfers like this will become more and more universal as modems and software are upgraded. For example, with WinFax, you select Attach File from the Attachment panel which is selected from the Send dialog, WinFax then prompts you for the file name to send. The receiver's software must be able to handle BFT.

8 **Broadcast faxing.** Assume I've convinced you of the value of using fax to reach your customer base. But you have a lot of customers and you can do some simple math. To reach all of your customers overnight at a page a minute will take, say, six fax machines and no busy signals. Bummer. But wait, there is a solution.

When To Use A Fax Broadcast Service

- Solution for: Faxing to thousands of destinations overnight.

- Marketing: product and promotion announcements.

- Time sensitivity: financial services, law enforcement, other notifications.

- Direct mail: ideal for maintaining customer contact.

- Press releases: assure concurrent release.

- Associations: cheaper than mailing a newsletter.

- Political action: reach your members and activists fast.

There are a number of commercial services that do broadcast faxing. You provide the document and a list. They provide the phone lines, fax hardware, and software to get the job done. Moreover, the cost is reasonable, comparable to using your own fax machine. Typical charges for domestic transmissions are 50 cents per minute during peak business hours, 35 cents per minute off-peak. Most service providers offer volume discounts based on number of destinations or dollar volume.

9 **Fax on demand.** Fax on Demand (FOD) is, in effect, an electronic filing cabinet or a document vending machine with remote access. You create a directory of documents that you wish to sell or give away, and then you create a catalog listing those documents.

Next you publish the access number or numbers to your customers, clients, or prospects. You can include the number in marketing material, ads, on you Web page and catalogs - anywhere you would normally refer someone to a source of additional information. Distributing the fax number of your FOD system is a very important step. If your FOD number is only available in the phone book do you think you'll get a lot of calls? Not very likely.

Anyone who knows the phone number can dial in and have a selection of documents faxed back to them. You set the parameters for how often someone can call and how many documents they can have at once, and whether they're free.

Selling Products

Once set up, the arrangement requires no intervention. The inbound call can be a direct call billed to the caller or on an 800-number. Given sufficient capacity and phone lines the Fax on Demand System can accept credit cards, verify card numbers, and collect payment. All this can take place while you go out to dinner!

By setting up certain documents as products, you can sell direct, accept credit cards, verify them, issue a fax confirmation, and submit an order for your staff to fulfill. All this happens while you are on the road (having fun?).

Fax on Demand systems cost from $2,000 to over $20,000 depending on capacity and speed. Your mileage will vary.

Fax On Demand: Try It!

Want to check out some Fax on Demand systems for yourself? Here are some fax numbers to call:

- US Commerce Department Hotline: (202) 482-1064.
- US State Department Travel Advisory : (202) 647-3000.
- Para Publishing: (805) 968-8947
- IBEX Technologies: (800) 573-IBEX.

Here's how to do it: First, using the voice handset, call the fax number from your fax machine or your fax line connected to your fax software. Listen for instructions and be prepared to take notes. If the Fax on Demand offers a catalog, make that selection, receive the fax and then read the catalog or instructions. Simply follow the directions and receive the faxes you are interested in.

At some point you will be asked to press start. If you are using a fax machine, press the start key. If you are using a software package, select Receive and then Manual Receive Now or the equivalent.

A Fax Catalog Supplement

A catalog's job is to be exciting and grab the reader's attention. Catalogs are expensive to produce and expensive to deliver. Fax on demand can help.

Copious quantities of dry text and tables don't belong in most catalogs. But some items are technical sells that require information beyond the short paragraph in the catalog. What to do?

One answer is a Fax on Demand system with an inbound 800-number. The catalog has references to the FOD system and includes the phone number. Each catalog entry has an identifier that relates to an entry in the FOD setup. The prospect calls from a fax machine, enters the code, and instantly receives the document with the additional information needed to make a purchase decision.

Competitive Advantages

If your competition relies on the US Mail or a manned telephone, you gain significant advantage by making your information available seven days a week, 24 hours a day. You can accept an order at 4 am on Sunday without staffing a 24-and-7 operation. You provide better service by making information available at all times to all of your clients.

10 **Publishing newsletters.** Newsletters have many advantages as a way to keep in touch with customers and prospects. But there are drawbacks as well. Not everybody is interested in every newsletter, people move and don't tell you about it, it's expensive to print, etc. (Also see Chapter 5.)

By publishing your newsletter by fax, you save printing costs and create a sense of immediacy for recipients. You can either publish on a regular schedule, or put out "flash bulletins" when you have something to say. You don't have to use expensive multicolor layouts. You can encourage people to respond to you by fax. You can keep it short to preserve their fax paper.

You can also combine a fax newsletter with either your Web page (by posting it there archivally) or with the prior section. You can set up a Fax on Demand system that has each article as a separate document. Publish the newsletter via fax as a single-page index to the articles on the FOD system. Clients can call and retrieve only the parts of the newsletter that appeal to them. The possibilities are endless.

Flash Bulletin

The Tax Reform Bill was just passed by Congress. Here are some strategies to consider in your year-end tax planning:

• Take capital gain profits from stocks and other assets to offset any losses.

• If you are in an alternative minimum tax situation, prepayment of state income tax is not advisable.

(Page 1 of 3)
Please call us at 555-5555 if you have any questions or would like an appointment to discuss your situation.

SUMMARY: THE FACTS ABOUT THE FAX

Almost everyone will soon have access to fax technology—including most homes. By the year 2000, fax coverage in homes via either PC or stand-alone unit will exceed 50 percent.

People will discover the low cost and fast delivery of the fax for personal communications. They will write letters, conduct dialogs with businesses, place orders—without waiting on hold. Along with replacing the mail, the fax will continue to replace a lot of regular voice phone calls. The fax has already started to replace US Mail for newsletters and broadcast letters.

Fax is already important for direct mail communication with customers in business-to-business marketing. This will accelerate, again replacing the mail.

Fax on demand (FOD) will become a major channel for marketing material. It will give consumers and business the power to receive complete information on topics they choose.

IS THE FAX A PERFECT MARKETING MACHINE?

Like any new software or hardware product, you'll need to invest some time to use fax capacity just the way you want.

Of course, there are many things you can't do with your fax. However, new fax options are becoming available every day. If there's something you can't do now, it will probably be available soon.

You probably already use the fax to exchange basic messages. Hopefully, this chapter has suggested other ways you can use it to build your business. Perhaps the most important is as a tool to improve communication with prospects and clients. The fax can help you now to build and cement long term relationships.

ACTION AGENDA

What can you do to use the fax in your marketing now?

- Evaluate your fax capabilities. Do you need to upgrade your fax software?
- Fax your current clients a note next week.
- Obtain fax numbers for people you don't have them on.
- Investigate new fax lists available for possible prospecting. Are there directories with fax numbers you can use? Are fax lists available for sale or rent?
- Is there a quick survey you can do that will give you useful information?
- Can you set up a fax-on-demand system?

Part III: Marketing Specifics

The Power of Personal Notes: 35 Ways To
Say "Thank You" And Stay In Touch
Wajed Salam

Implementing Marketing Programs:
A Sales Automation Example
Fran Berman

Chapter 13

THE POWER OF PERSONAL NOTES: 35 Ways To Say "Thank You" And Stay In Touch

Wajed Salam

Wajed "Waj" Salam is president of Foresight International, an international training and consulting firm with offices in Tampa and London, England. He is a peak performance consultant to individuals and organizations. He is frequently called upon to speak to and to develop company's field sales teams. Before founding Foresight International, Salam was, for five years, the number one field Sales Manager and Trainer for Anthony Robbins Seminars.

He has delivered over 3,500 talks to large and small corporations, educational institutions, and nonprofit organizations in North America and Europe. Foresight International also offers a turnkey thank you card system for personal and professional use.

This chapter is dedicated to Borbhai, my eldest brother, who after my father's death, had to leave school at age 21 to take the responsibility of educating six brothers and sisters. Without his selfless sacrifice I wouldn't have this opportunity today to express my deepest gratitude.

Wajed (Waj) Salam, Foresight International, 2202 West Azeele, Tampa, FL 33600; phone (813) 258-8744; fax (813) 726-8060.

THE POWER OF PERSONAL NOTES: 35 Ways To Say "Thank You" And Stay In Touch

Wajed Salam

"He who praises another enriches himself far
more than he does the one praised. To praise is an
investment in happiness."

—David Dunn, *Try Giving Yourself Away*

We sometimes tend to unnecessarily complicate the issue of building business relationships.

One of the greatest human needs is the need to feel appreciated. We implement elaborate customer appreciation programs, but often forget to write a simple thank you note.

This chapter is designed to make writing thank you and other notes as effortless as possible. Most people get bogged down in the process of how to write a short and appropriate message to convey their true feelings. Anytime you're stuck and need a little "magic," just refer to this chapter and reread the appropriate section.

WHO'S WRITING THANK YOU NOTES?

For the last five years, I have been training sales and management executives in all the major cities in the US, Canada, and the UK. No matter where I was speaking, I asked this question, "How many of you write thank you notes to your clients regularly?" Fewer than ten percent of the audience would respond affirmatively.

While I am surprised by the response, I find it to be true across companies, cities, and countries. To punctuate my point, I'd sometimes follow up my first question with a second one, "How many of you write thank you notes to non-clients or associates or anyone who goes 'above and beyond' to serve you?" To this question, even fewer people would respond. Why?

In general, people complain more than they praise. Want to make an impact? Just reverse the above trend, praise more than you complain...and do it in writing!

> "Help people reach their full potential—Catch them doing something right"
> —Ken Blanchard and Spencer Johnson, *The One Minute Manager*

WHY SHOULD I WRITE THANK YOU NOTES?

I've never had to convince anyone about the virtues of personal thank you notes. You probably know them too—all the "should" reasons.

- They're good for business.

- They're great for sales.

Use Time You'd Otherwise Waste

Jay Conrad Levinson, author of many *Guerrilla Marketing* books, says that you can convert dead time into profit-producing time. He says "Recognize the immense power of thank you notes to customers...For example, while waiting for almost anything... write a thank you note...or maybe write ten...You'll soon know that it was incredibly valuable time."

- They're invaluable for getting referrals.

- They create a favorable impression.

Reasons aren't enough, or everyone would already send thank you notes. People in general make decisions emotionally and then rationalize logically. Let me explain.

IT'S RELATIONSHIPS

The quality of life comes down to the quality of relationships. Acquiring anything of worth takes time and effort.

"Thank you" is an investment in your relationship with the person you are writing to. It promotes growth and development. It nurtures new friendship. It fosters teamwork. It expresses your commitment and caring that you have taken the time to write. Any relationship grows and develops better when given time, energy, and attention.

The mail is available to everyone, and correspondence is not an intrusion compared to a personal call on a stranger. There is no reason why, if you have something friendly to say, you shouldn't say it in a letter, even to an exalted personage whom you have never met. And the results can be momentous for you.

Why anyone should deprive himself of a po-

Written Magic

The difference in impact between verbally saying thank you and writing a personal thank you note is the difference between lightning and the lightning bug! Neil Simon in his famous play *Biloxi Blues* narrates through his lead role, "There is something magic about the written word. People seem to embrace it more if it is written. There is a sense of permanency with a message that has been put on paper."

tential friend, even at long range, is hard to understand, with the postal department delivering once a day in most communities.

THE PERSONAL TOUCH

Although the computer has made it easier to send form letters and respond to the masses, the handwritten note is still the most respected form of correspondence.

One survey showed that over 60 percent of the people surveyed preferred handwritten notes. With all the faster means of communications today, the personal note is still viewed as the most thoughtful and meaningful method of saying thanks.

Cards with pre-printed verses aren't enough. What you say in that note is not as important as the fact that you have made the effort to make your note a personal gesture of gratitude.

It's Proper Etiquette

Etiquette expert Miss Manners says the only proper thank you note is a handwritten one:

"Thank you letters should be written by hand. Miss Manners, who does not consider acts of kindness subject to fashion, grants exceptions only to people with specific physical disabilities that prevent them from writing."

The effect of a personal, handwritten note is much greater than most people realize. A note recognizes and reinforces others. It gives the sender the opportunity to express his or her appreciation. The writing of a note can make the full impact of what has been done come alive for both parties. It subtly expresses a desire for an ongoing relationship.

A Tiny Human Touch Goes A Long Way

by Tom Peters

Miss Manners I'm not. But I still say, "Send your thank you notes!"

I'm always surprised at how few thank you notes I get. I once interrupted a tense writing schedule to do a seminar for a CEO to whom I owed a favor. To top it off, I quickly sifted through a mountain of data to come to grips with his unique, competitive conundrum.

Hey, I was paid a ton for my efforts, so I'm hardly complaining. Well, actually I am. But all I really wanted was a thank you note, just a couple of lines scrawled on a card saying, "Tom, I know you busted your gut to do this. It worked out OK. Thanks. Harry." (And he needn't even include the modest "It worked out OK.")

BIG EFFECT FROM FEW WORDS

By contrast, a fellow who attended a speech I gave to several hundred folks about three weeks ago just dropped me a line: "Nice job! Thought you might enjoy the attached." The "attached" was a clipping from his local paper about a company that had dramatically speeded up delivery of its products—a topic I'd gotten worked up about during my speech.

You know what, I've re-read his scribble a couple of times, and I'll probably put it in my save box. "Nice job!" No big deal? Well, it is to me.

We wildly underestimate the power of the tiniest personal touch. And of all personal touches, I find the short, handwritten "nice job" note to have the highest impact.

WHICH CAME FIRST—THANK YOUS OR SUCCESS?

I think there's a strong correlation between the little thank you notes I get and the busyness, fortune, and fame of those who send them. That is, the more busy, rich, and famous they are, the more likely I am to get a note. There's one very renowned, very wealthy entrepreneur I've seen professionally several times a year for seven or eight years. I don't think he's ever failed to send a handwritten little (or not so little) note afterwards.

Incidentally, I understand that George Bush is a master of this art. Pithy personal notes (pecked out on a typewriter) have been his stock in trade—and key to network building—for years. (Typewritten is OK, as long as it's an old typewriter, not a computer. And if you're an expert typist, make a typo or two.)

There are other twists. One pen pal scrawls brief handwritten responses on the backs of letters I send him. I love it, and have copied his habit. Again: It's hard to overestimate the number of people who have commented favorably on the personalization of the message.

LETTERS YOU DON'T HAVE TO WRITE, BUT SHOULD!

One of the reasons personal notes have such impact is that you don't have to write them. They're an old fashioned courtesy that is now largely ignored.

Maxwell Cross, a well known sales promotion expert, listed fifteen ways letters and notes can be used to create good will—and eventually more business. "There's just one prerequisite," he said, "the person using them has to be a 'nice guy,' courteous, friendly, and above all, sincere."

Consider sending a friendly, personal note on some occasion when you would not be expected to send anything. Such letters create a tremendously favorable impression with clients, colleagues and other contacts.

35 REASONS TO STAY IN TOUCH

Not all the situations described here will apply to everyone. But take the appropriate ones and adapt the messages to suit your personal needs. The idea is to be different from others. This will give you an edge over competitors.

In many cases, there is more than one example per category. They range from earnest sentiments and genuine gratitude to one liners and humorous wisecracks.

Your relationship with the person, the occasion and your judgment will dictate which message will be appropriate. Adapt, edit, and combine these models to create your own personal messages. After a little practice, your own natural eloquence will follow.

BUSINESS LETTERS

1. Letter To Follow Up Your Salesperson's Call

Why not write a letter after your salesperson has made the initial call or proposal? As the president, head of the department, or the sales manager, you can write a wonderful letter of assurance to the prospective client.

Harvey Mackay, author and entrepreneur, is a class act in this regard. He will go as far as Guam or Sri Lanka just to tell the client in person, "As you may know, we're bidding on your contract. I just came here to tell you, as president of Mackay Envelope that we regard your business as significant. If we are fortunate enough to receive your business, I'll take personal interest in seeing to it that you will receive the service and craftsmanship you have every right to expect."

If you don't want to go that far, you could write something like this:

> John Davidson told me today of the pleasant visit he had with you about your insurance program. I know that John will do a fine job for you.

Then finish off in your own words.

2. Letters To Make Appointments

Yes, you can write, instead of calling, to get appointment. You start:

> It's about time for me to sit down with you, Jim, and go over your investment in the light of the new tax changes. I suggest that we get together late Friday afternoon. How would 4 o'clock be?

You don't need to say much more. Just call to confirm or fix a different time.

3. An Apology

It takes a big person to say I'm sorry. The only mistakes are those we never learn from. So take responsibility and correct the mistake.

> Ooops! Whoops! Oh-oh! Sorry! I goofed! Forgive me!

– or –

The devil made me do it. Be an angel and forgive me. Nobody likes to admit a mistake, but I was wrong when I said/did that to you.

4. Anniversary Thank You

Thank you—It is with warm regards that I send this note to say hello and again thanks for your patronage. We've now been doing business together since _____. We are continually changing and improving our products and services. If you would like an update on our latest advancements, please give me a call.

5. Letters On Holidays Other Than Xmas

If you only send holiday greeting cards to your clients during Christmas, it doesn't create as lasting an impression because they (your family, friends, and clients) were expecting it. Why not send letters and cards when they are least expecting it to make that lasting impression?

Everybody sends Christmas cards, and you should too. But to stand out in your client's mind, send a card for Thanksgiving (in the US) or any other special holiday of significance in your country.

In this season of giving thanks, we'd like to express our gratitude

Harvey Mackay, author of *Swim With the Sharks, Without Being Eaten Alive*, says that his company sends Thanksgiving cards rather than Christmas cards. They stand out and get a lot of response from clients.

for your continued support and for being our patron. We look forward to serving you for many years to come.

6. Thank You For Telephone Contact

I enjoyed talking with you on the telephone today. Thanks. In today's business world, time is precious. I want you to know that I'll always be respectful of the time you invest as we discuss the possibility of a mutually beneficial business relationship.

7. Thank You After In-Person Contact

It was a pleasure meeting you and hearing about your business. My "thank you" is for the time we shared. I hope we will be able to work together. If you have any questions, please don't hesitate to call.

8. Thank You After Demonstration Or Presentation

Thank you for giving me the opportunity to discuss our possible relationship for the mutual benefit of our firms. We believe that quality, combined with first-rate service, is the foundation for a successful business.

9. Thank You After Purchase

Thank you—for giving me the opportunity to serve you. I'm sure that you will be happy with this invest-ment towards future growth. My goal now is to give you great follow-up service so that you will have no reservation about referring others to me who have similar needs.

Thank You

10. Thank You For A Referral

Thank you for your kind referral. We value each one. You have my assurance that

*anyone you refer to me will receive the
highest level of service.*

11. Thank You After Final Refusal

*Thank you for taking your time to
meet with me. I'm sorry that your
immediate plans do not include our
working together at this time. However, if you need
further information or have any questions, please feel
free to call. I'll keep you posted on new developments
and changes that may benefit you.*

12. Thank You After They Buy From Someone Else

*Thank you—for taking your time to analyze my
services. I regret being unable at this time to prove to
you the benefit we have to offer. We keep constantly
informed of new developments and changes so I'll
keep in touch with the hope that in the years ahead,
we will be able to do business.*

These letters leave a classy impression. They suggest that you are
interested in building a relationship, rather than just a quick sale.

13. Thank You For Offering To Give You Referrals

*Thank you—for your gracious offer to give me refer-
rals. As we discussed, I'm enclosing three of my
business cards, and I thank you in advance for
placing them in the hands of three of your friends,
acquaintances or relatives who I might serve. I'll
keep in touch and be available to render my services
as needed.*

14. Welcome Aboard

When there's a new addition to your team, organization, or
business, make them feel welcome with a special note.

It's great to have you as part of the team.

– or –

Glad to have a new (potential, proven) superstar on our team.

15. We're Proud Of...

My good friend Mark Pester says to try to be the kind of person whom people put down as assets on a bank loan application! Do you know anyone like that? Why not let them know:

We're proud to have you as _____ (friend, colleague, representative).

– or –

The way you represented our organization (department, association, team) was great. You did us all proud. Thank you.

16. A Job Well Done

When a colleague or a friend or anyone has done an outstanding job, let them feel appreciated:

You are really a credit to your profession and the company with the service you provided to our association.

– or –

Thanks for making the rest of us look bad. Do it again anytime.

– or –

Anyone could have done what you did...if they had a whole year.

17. Enjoyed Working With You

When people are leaving or moving on to bigger and better things, let them know that they will be missed.

Though I'm sorry to see you go, I understand your

*need for a bigger challenge. If there's anything I can
do, I hope you'll call on me.*

COMBINED BUSINESS AND PERSONAL LETTERS

18. Letters To Congratulate Any Promotion Or Job Change
It's a nice gesture to send a letter like this:
*Congratulations on your appointment to District
Sales Manager. This is fine news, and I know you'll
do a great job.*

19. Saw-You-In-The-News Letters
When you read about a customer in the newspaper, send him
or her a letter. Clip the article, send it to him or her, and write:
*I don't know whether your children keep a scrap-
book of the nice things about the work you've done,
but just in case they do, here's an extra copy.*
— or —
*I really enjoyed reading about your success in the
paper the other day.*

20. Letters Congratulating Special Achievements
When a client is elected or honored in some way, perhaps you
could say:
*I've heard some nice things about the work you've
done for the Chamber of Commerce, so I was not
surprised to see that you have been elected vice-
president.*

21. Letters After A Favor
When someone has done you a
favor he/she will appreciate a note from
you.

*Thank you for those two extra tickets. I hope
I can repay the favor soon.*

22. Thanking Others For Great Service

I was riding in a bus one day when there was an accident. Women and children, bruised and cut with flying glass, became panicky. The driver took charge of everybody and everything at once, helping the injured, marshaling witnesses, sending someone to telephone for the ambulance, and keeping calm under the unjust abuse of the truck driver who had run into him.

After the ambulance had come, the driver got into his seat, wiped some blood off his eyebrow, and started to finish his run with his battered bus. Said a man next to him, "I'm going to report you!" Indignantly, I began to intervene, but he hastened on: "For efficiency and courtesy. If you'll tell me where to write, and give me your name, I'll tell your company you're the best man in a pinch I ever saw." "Gee, mister," said the driver, letting out a long breath, "I wish there were more in the world like you." How often someone performs unusual services for us that we allow to pass un-praised? Don't take courtesy and helpfulness for granted!

23. Letters Appreciating A Great Product

When some product pleases you, take time to write about it.

*I wanted you to know how pleased I am with our
new office system, and the courteous and efficient
way your men installed it.*

24. Thank You To Anyone Who Gives You Service

*Thank you—It is gratifying to meet someone dedi-
cated to doing a good job. Your efforts are sincerely
appreciated. If my company or I can serve you in
any way, please don't hesitate to call.*

GENERAL THANKS

25. Special Thank You

I feel doubly blessed; first I had the benefit of your help, and now I have the pleasurable duty of thanking you.

– or –

Just when I thought I had no debts, I find myself deeply in yours.

26. Thanks For Time

Time truly is the most precious commodity we have. So, when someone has given their time, be sure to thank them.

I know how valuable your time is, and I want you to know how much we appreciate the time you gave us the other day.

– or –

Now I know why your time is so valuable. Thanks a million!

27. Regrets

It is courteous and good manners to let people know if you can't make the engagement, especially when they sent you a written invitation.

I never wanted so much to be in two places at the same time. Sorry we cannot attend your function.

The Prince of Wales, Edward VII was known by his friends for his sense of humor. One intimate, relying on the prince's joviality, declined a dinner invitation with the following telegram: "Sorry cannot come. Lie follows."

Edward was immensely amused.

PERSONAL LETTERS

I Learn The Power Of Thanks

After I graduated from high school, my English teacher gave me a book as a present called *Write Better, Speak Better: How Words Can Work Wonders For You* by Readers' Digest. At 730 pages it almost buckled my knees. It was full of sample letters of personal correspondence. They were short, sweet, and of a nature we all love to receive.

28. Thanks For A Social Invitation

When I came to the United States in 1981, *Write Better, Speak Better* was one of the books I brought with me. An American lady hosted a party for all the new foreign students at her house. While we all enjoyed the festivities, I was the only one who took the time to write a personal thank you note.

Needless to say I immediately became her favorite. Within a very short period of time, the entire staff of the International Student Center knew about the letter. At the next party at her house, she showed me the letter beautifully kept in her scrapbook under cellophane to immortalize my action—a pretty impressive reaction to something that took me three minutes to write.

> Dear Mrs. Davidson:
>
> You are such a wonderful host! Everything you planned was wonderful, but the best of all was the talent show after dinner by the fireplace.
>
> Mrs. Davidson, I truly enjoyed every minute with your family, and thank you more than I can say for opening your home and more importantly your heart to a stranger.
>
> Very Sincerely,
>
> Wajed Salam

Up until then, I had no idea that words could work such wonders. I began to realize how many other such opportunities I missed to make someone happy.

I once wrote a personal thank you note to my friend's mother after spending a weekend at their house in Bangkok. The next time I saw her was in my place a decade later, and guess what?

She remembered me and thanked me for that simple gesture of appreciation. It made me realize the kind of *lasting impression* a personal note of thanks can create. I'm sure you can think of many such incidents where you were the receiver or the creator of such an experience.

Now I'm not saying all of your personal correspondence will have this kind of impact. But if you write personal thank you notes regularly, you will impress the recipient more often than not.

Do I write everyday, every time and to every person who deserves my thanks? No, I get lazy too. But I am never lazy when success is at stake.

28. Get Well Cards

When a customer is ill all you need to say is:

I'm certainly sorry to hear that you are laid up. I hope it won't be many days before you're back at your desk.

29. Letters Of Condolence

When there is a death in the family, a short message of sympathy, tactfully done, can mean a lot.

We are so very shocked to hear of the sorrow that has come to you. If there is anything we can do, I earnestly hope that you will call upon us.

30. Letters To Congratulate Newborn Or Any Marriage

These letters make no tangible effort to sell; they are simply goodwill builders—the kind that someday will bring something nice to you because you went out of your way to do something nice for somebody else.

31. Letters To Congratulate On New Home

When people buy a home, write to them. Your letter doesn't need to be long or fancy. Perhaps:

I hope you are enjoying getting
settled in your new home.

If you have something to sell, tell these folks you'd appreciate a chance to call when things are squared away. In some cases, an inexpensive gift like a rosebush or a young tree helps to create good will.

32. Birthday Greeting Card

Quite a few successful salespeople make a practice of keeping birthday lists and sending cards or letters. If you use a pre-printed card, write something in longhand on it.

33. Letters For Servicemen

When a serviceman comes home, write to him or to his parents. That's a small way to show your appreciation of all he or she has done for your country.

34. Letter Of Welcome

When people move to your town, a letter of welcome is an excellent source of new business. They don't know where to go for dry cleaning, laundry, or groceries. They don't know what service station to trade with, where to do their banking, or the nicer places to eat. So you write:

Welcome to Clearwater. We know you'll like it here.
If there's any way we can help you get settled,
please let us know.

As a nice gesture you could include a local restaurant guide or coupon book from local merchants.

35. Keeping In Touch

Go out and renew a friendship today.

It's been so long that I can't remember who owes
whom a letter. This puts the ball in your court, but a
phone call will do. I'd love to hear what you're up to.

– or –

We're still here and we'd love to hear from you.

36 And Counting

I've given examples of 35 different types of letters you can write. But there are many more. And there are many more reasons besides thanks.

In your business, there are specific times when it is logical to send people notes. For instance, if you were a car repair shop, a series of notes might include one to welcome them as a customer, one every quarter for an oil change, and two a year for other maintenance.

If you don't have a reason to contact people at least every quarter, create one. Have an open house or a sale. Invite them to a ball game. Fax them a cartoon. Send them interesting information by e-mail. There are no limits in showing you care about a relationship.

GOOD WRITING: A SKILL YOU CAN LEARN

"It took me fifteen years to discover I had no talent for writing, but I couldn't give it up—because by that time I was too famous."

—Robert Benchley

The ability to communicate clearly in writing is one of the most important skills we will ever master. It helps us to get our ideas across effectively and to get the results we want in our business and personal life. Fortunately, it is a skill anyone (even you and I) can learn.

Throughout my life I've always been amazed by people who could write. I've always considered myself a good speaker but never a good writer. I am still working at it. In the process, I've discovered a few simple things that help with the process of composing a personalized thank you note.

Today's good writing has less and less to do with punctuation, grammar, and style. I follow the same primary rule one wise traveler passed on for both speaking and writing:

"Do It To EXPRESS Not To IMPRESS!"

When you sincerely want to communicate, you are other-centered. When you try to impress people, you are ego-centered. Every time I got in trouble writing it was because of trying to impress, as opposed to expressing my sentiment simply and with sincerity. My ego got in the way.

Like anything else—how

The A-B-Cs Of Good Letter Writing

The ABC's of good letter writing stands for Accuracy, Brevity, and Clarity.

A **ccuracy:** Make sure you say what you mean. Make your point clearly and early.

B **revity.** Shorter is better in today's busy world. It was Ben Franklin or Mark Twain who wrote someone a long letter and apologized because he didn't have time to write a shorter one! Brevity supports the other two rules and helps your reader get your point.

C **larity.** The best rule for clear writing is to use short words, short sentences, and short paragraphs. Sometimes the attempt to write in a "fancy" way confuses our meaning—and the reader. If you try to impress others, your writing suffers. Clear writing makes sure your message gets through.

good a writer you will become depends on your desire, commitment, and how much time you're willing to devote. Most of us are not looking to become Shakespeare. We simply want to communicate effectively and easily in writing.

Express Your Personality

You can write the kind of personal notes and letters we all love to receive. This is the one that carries the writer's personality. He or she should seem to be sitting beside us and talking as if we were together instead of by proxy. And that's what your note is, a proxy for you in ink-made characters on paper.

The best thank you notes are those where the words make it sound both personal and appreciative. Make each note sound like you. Don't use words that make you feel uncomfortable, or use words you wouldn't usually say. You don't have to use formal stilted language. Just be yourself.

A note doesn't have to be long. A few lines that are brief but sincere are all that is necessary. Reading it should make the receiver feel as if you were writing to them personally. This isn't always easy, especially when you are writing a lot at a time. Just make each note sound like it is the only one you are writing.

Give Your Letters the Right Look

"Every job is a self-portrait of the person who did it. Autograph your work with excellence."

Yes, you took the time and

> True, we are not all of us as fluent as men of letters are. But no flowery style is required. Your friends want to hear from you in your own characteristic style. No rhetoric takes the place of sincerity.
> —*Donald Culross Peattie*

Writing Tip

When writing a note, try to picture the person you are writing to in your mind as you are composing the note. It will make it easier to speak directly to them in the same way that you would in person.

made the effort to write a personal thank you note, but what will make it stand out from the pile of mail? What will get the letter or the card opened?

A good part of the impression your letters make depends on their appearance.

The letter you write, whether you realize it or not, is a mirror that reflects your appearance, taste, and character. A sloppy letter—the writing running up and down, badly worded, poorly spelled, paper and envelope unmatched, smeared—proclaims a sloppy person. And it contradicts the caring of the letter.

Conversely, a neat, precise, evenly-written note portrays an organized person who cares. A messy letter is discourteous, clearly implying a lack of interest and care on the part of the writer—which invites a similar reaction by the reader.

Writing letters by hand is more difficult, but it is possible to make graceful notes, to space words evenly, and to put them on a page so that the appearance is pleasing. You can make yourself write neatly and legibly. You can, with the help of a dictionary if need be, spell correctly. If it is difficult for you to write in a straight line, use the lined guide that comes with some stationery, or make one yourself.

All business letters—from home as well as office—should be typed. However, some forms of correspondence must always be written by hand.

1. Never type personal letters of congratulations or thanks.
2. Never type letters or notes of condolence.

CREATING YOUR OWN PERSONAL NOTECARDS

In your personal and business life, you will have plenty of opportunity to send personal notes. Consider creating a personal card for your use.

Notecards designed specifically for you and your business with a personal photograph (or other professional images) give a very professional and successful image to your correspondence. Personalized cards are an easy, convenient, and quick way to communicate with others. Besides the obvious value of communication, these personalized notecards are a visual reminder of you and your business.

If you want to play in the big leagues, give yourself the stature, credence, and pizzazz that personalized notecards will add to your correspondence. This will give you an added motivation and you will find yourself more eager to send out notes to your clients, colleagues and other contacts.

Create A Special Card

There are several ways you can go about getting your personal notecards. With many of today's computer graphic programs, you can create your own and take it to the local print shop. I must warn you that unless you print a lot of cards (1000 or more), the economy of scale is not in your favor and it might be expensive. The cost is not so much in the paper but creating the templates and setting up the press for such a small run.

Unique Stamps Grab Attention

Jay Conrad Levinson, author of *Guerrilla Marketing*, suggests another way to make your cards interesting and unique: Buy unused older stamps at stamp shows. They are often available for about face value. When your card arrives covered with five 14-cent stamps, it gets noticed. Also, many people enjoy giving the stamps to their children.

My advice would be to find a specialty advertising company and let them take care of the design and printing. In the long run, the higher price of the cards may be negligible compared to the goodwill and additional business they will generate.

THE REAL REASONS PEOPLE DON'T WRITE THANK YOU NOTES

"What's easy to do is also easy not to do "

—Jim Rohn

Why do individuals who are intelligent, highly educated, and not particularly lazy not write? Perhaps they don't know and understand the true meaning and value of writing personal notes.

A few years ago, I began to study this phenomenon. I surveyed hundreds of people and asked why they didn't write personal thank you notes.

The most common answers were:

1. I'm too busy.
2. I don't have the time.
3. I'm too lazy.
4. I don't know how to write well.
5. It's too much trouble.
6. Do you know how much stamps cost these days?
7. I don't have the discipline.

These are what I call superficial answers. They're the first answers that came to mind and didn't require much thinking. So, I started digging deeper for the real reasons. The three core reasons follow.

1. They Just Don't Get Started

Many people don't have a strong reason. They like the idea, but a good idea doesn't move anyone into action, let alone form a habit. They haven't internalized the concept. It's a should, not a must.

The fact is, they aren't compelled enough to do what they know is right. I hope you will find enough inspiration throughout these pages to create some compelling reasons of your own.

2. They Get Distracted By Details

Another reason is task related. It is how people view what needs to be done. If you ask me about the task, I'll say—sit down, write the note, and post it when you go out next (period).

Let's take my wife as an example of how most people look at writing notes. She knows how I feel about the subject and she's absolutely sold on the idea. I often asked myself why she is hesitant. One morning she decided to answer my question and share all the things that go through her mind when she thinks about writing a note.

1. There are too many other things that are more urgent.
2. I can't find the time.
3. I'm not in the mood.
4. There are so many letters I haven't replied to.
5. I don't have the proper address.
6. Oh, it's been too long.
7. Why don't you write it from both of us.
8. I'm too tired now, I'll write it tomorrow.
9. I'll have to get dressed; carry my big heavy purse; get out of the house; walk to the car; get into the hot car and almost burn my fingers on the leather steering wheel; fight the traffic; stand in the crowded, slowest moving line; get my checkbook out, and buy the stamps; I hate licking stamps and envelopes, but I do it anyway; I get back in the car; fight the traffic again; and finally get back home.

(OK, OK, maybe I'm slightly exaggerating.)

Getting It Done. Are you still with me or have you gone into major "overwhelm" like she does? That long list of tasks will drive anyone crazy. And I want you to do this regularly and form a habit of sending notes? Am I nuts or what? Don't I have a life?

The fact is, not doing little tasks is a problem we all face. It isn't uncommon to make a mountain out of a mole hill. When we do, we've put ourselves in a position that makes the task appear more difficult than it actually is.

One thing you must understand is that most people do not consciously throw up barriers to accomplishment. The brain is the fastest computer and it processes information so quickly that we only feel the effect, which can be a feeling of being overwhelmed, fear, and some degree of pain.

We follow our body's built-in instinct which is to avoid pain and thus avoid the task and procrastinate. If we could slow down the computer and run our brain in slow motion we could see how our mind works to put us into inaction.

Just Do It. For any activity in our life that we dread and procrastinate about, it is because of the way we think about it. To stop the procrastination and do the task, we must change what we associate with doing the task (i.e., the way you think about it) and change the way the task is broken down.

The lesson is to watch how you break down a task in your mind. The goal is not to break anything into too many sub-tasks at the start. When you want to begin something, focus on the goal and the benefits of accomplishing it.

The marketing people at Nike understand this dilemma. That's why they created the slogan "JUST DO IT!"

Write Before It's Too Late

For years I intended to write my fifth grade teacher, who had started me, as I realized looking back much later, on my career as a scientist and writer. Finally, I wrote the letter. It came back, enclosed in a note from the school principal, saying that my old teacher had died two years before.

So I tried once more, this time to the professor of one of the stiffest science courses in college. He was regarded as an unapproachable old bear. Finding that his teaching had stuck as almost none other, I wrote him how much his course had meant to me. Here is the answer I received:

I found your letter last night just at a time when I was feeling particularly low. It seemed to make my whole lifework worthwhile. I may say that in thirty-five years of giving the best I know how to give, I have never before received one word of appreciation from a student. Thanks.

3. Set Up A System

The third reason is why most of the well-meaning people don't write personal thank you notes. It is because they don't have any system. They have the I-will-write-it-later syndrome.

We all intend to write letters, of condolence, of congratulation, of appreciation, and friendship—tomorrow, or next week.

Any System Will Work. Remember that a poor system is better than no system. What I mean by a system is a device, a step-by-step process or arrangement of units that function together to make the job of writing personal thank you notes easier. This is what Dr. Stephen R. Covey calls a quadrant II activity, that is, important but not urgent. Most people will not do it unless it is easy or doesn't require much effort. So, create a simple system by buying in advance all the things you need.

The easier you make it on yourself, the greater the probability that you will do what you know you should do. The quicker your letter flies out the door and into the hands of the recipient, the sooner you will have made an impact.

Yes, it does take some time and effort on my part to write the personal thank you and other notes, but the result it creates far outweighs the effort. *There are very few activities in life that take so little effort , but make such an impression*

SUMMARY

In conclusion, I can only tell you from personal and professional experience that sending notes is one of the most satisfying and rewarding habits you can form. I get a large number of referrals from my clients. I have the highest percentage of repeat sales. As a result, it also shows in the bottom line of my company.

Every day before going to sleep I ask myself is: Who can I write a thank you note today? Ask and you shall receive. I always find someone who has gone above and beyond the call of duty.

Personal Benefits

On a personal level, I always get better and personal service from the reference librarian. My car is always serviced with promptness even though my mechanic is busier than ever. I always get the best service from my personal clothier. My dry cleaner takes extra care of my clothes. Why? Because I'm one of the few who has taken the time and care to appreciate their extra efforts and express my gratitude through a personal thank you note. I let people know that I've not taken their business or their efforts for granted.

Be Sincere

I also want to point out that someone could very easily interpret my habit as manipulative behavior.

Just remember that the difference between manipulative and non-manipulative behavior is one thing—the intent! If your heart is in the right place, you'll never have to worry about that. I don't write (and I hope you don't either) to get anything in return. I do it because it is the right thing to do. If you do it for the right reason, you cannot help but get back many times in return.

Before you write one personal thank you note remember Maxwell Cross's one prerequisite, "the person using them has to be a "nice guy," courteous, friendly, and above all, sincere."

ACTION AGENDA

Start your engines and begin your journey by writing a personal note to someone now. It could be to:

- a customer
- a relative
- a supplier
- a past teacher or mentor
- a friend
- your boss

- Make your own list of people you could write to now.
- Buy stamps or any other material you'll need to write.
- Look for unusual note cards at the store.
- Write your three best customers a note today.

If you leave this chapter thinking that it was a good idea, but take no action, then you'll fall in with the vast majority of dreamers, not doers. I call them the "talkers." I know you are not in that category, otherwise you wouldn't have picked up this book.

Don't worry if you don't have your own personalized cards or stationery yet. Take out any piece of paper or a blank card and start writing.

A journey of thousand miles begins with a single step, as the Chinese proverb goes.

The first single step in this case is commitment. Nothing good happens in the long term if one is not committed.

Great minds with no action lead to nothing. The world is full of talkers and my challenge to you is—Be one of the few who does, versus the many who talks.

Enjoy the process!

CHAPTER 14

IMPLEMENTING MARKETING PROGRAMS:
A Sales Automation Example

Fran Berman

Fran Berman
has been in the computer industry since 1982. She gained much of her technical expertise at AST Computer, one of the world's largest personal computer companies. During her eleven years with the company, she was an award-winning salesperson, trainer, and manager.

Berman helps clients and audiences optimize personnel, technological, and information resources. She uses a step-by-step approach in assessing needs, choosing software, hardware, project team members, and vendors, designing and implementing the program, and measuring results. She helps people recognize and accept organizational and personal changes to increase productivity and job satisfaction.

Berman is an active member of the Sales Automation Association, National Speakers Association, the American Society for Training and Development, the Recycled Paper Coalition, and the California Resource Recovery Association. She is also on the faculty of CareerTrack, one of the leading public seminar companies.

Fran Berman, Future Focus, 26305 Yolanda Street, Laguna Hills, CA 92656-3114; Tel (714) 643-0803; Fax (714) 643-2741; e-mail FranBerman@aol.com.

IMPLEMENTING MARKETING PROGRAMS:
A Sales Automation Example

Fran Berman

Profitable marketing involves many skills, activities, and re-sources. But even the best marketing plan will be wasted if it is poorly executed. All too often, organizations lose valuable time, money, and effort on marketing projects that are not well planned.

This chapter will discuss how to implement a new marketing project. It will use a case study of sales force automation as an example to illustrate the process of implementation.

FAILING TO PLAN = PLANNING TO FAIL

Improperly planning the introduction of a new product or service not only wastes time and money, but also can be embarrassing. Are your best customers the last to hear about new products? Are salespeople and critical support staff told about the product at the last moment? Are salespeople acting on rumors that they pass along to customers and prospects?

Any one of these can hurt sales and customer relations, not to mention make customers feel misled.

Proper planning for effective implementation and meaningful follow-up can minimize the risk of failure and maximize the potential for success of a marketing program. The key here is a well developed process, whatever the project.

THE IMPLEMENTATION PROCESS

What is the best way to implement a new project? How do we move through the different stages? I'll answer these and other questions, first in general terms, then using an actual sales force automation (SFA) project as a case study to illustrate the practical applications of the concepts.

An Implementation Model

The figure shows a general implementation model. It portrays the set of steps from gathering input to measuring results (outputs). The model also shows that the process is continuous. Outputs create new needs for inputs and the cycle continues.

In their book *Management: A Book of Readings*, authors Koontz, O'Donnel, and Weirich define the communi-

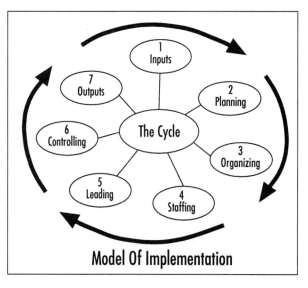

Model Of Implementation

cation system within an organization in seven phases: inputs, planning, organizing, staffing, leading, controlling, and outputs.

James A. F. Stoner and R. Edward Freeman, in *Management* (Fourth Edition), combine the same basic steps into a four-phase approach: *planning, organizing, leading, controlling.* Planning includes inputs, staffing is part of organizing, and controlling takes outputs into account. The marketing process suggested in this chapter is a blend of both the Stoner-Freeman approach and the Koontz-O'Donnel-Weirich model.

PHASE #1: INPUTS (GATHERING INFORMATION)

When deciding on a marketing program, it's important to first get the pulse of your market. What do your customers (or clients) and prospects think about your product (or services) or marketing strategies now? How can you find out?

Ask them.

The best salespeople in the world won't be able to work miracles if product availability is always poor, if the company is late to market, or if policies and procedures make it hard to do business. Find out what the problems are and how the customer wants those problems resolved. Look at the industry trends. Get a pulse on your customers' future needs and wish lists.

Trade Shows

Industry conferences and trade shows are great places for gathering input from your target market. The event can pay for itself not only in the sales leads generated, but in saving weeks of research. You can conduct a formal survey of customers and prospects or simply have booth staff turn up their sensors for certain types of information and feedback.

Don't Waste Your Trade Show

Unfortunately, many companies don't prepare their people to gather the wealth of information awaiting them. Have you ever gone into a trade show and seen booth after booth of sales or marketing people deep in conversation with each other, stopping to talk to prospects only when those prospects "interrupt" them? Or maybe you've finally reached the booth of that special vendor with the unique product that's going to turn your life around, only to have to wait in line while one of the vendor's staff spins his or her wheels on a "lookie-lou" with no intention of buying.

Train your trade show staff in a planning meeting before the event. Use people who enjoy the show setting and are good "on stage."

Brief them on how to conduct themselves in the booth, on the trade show floor, and in the hospitality suite. Have them review and practice asking qualifying questions to distinguish serious decision makers from "tire kickers." Consider implementing an automated survey of those who visit your booth. This may be the perfect opportunity to schedule a focus group or customer roundtable.

"Councils of Elders"

One of the most effective means of opening the lines of communication is to set up advisory

AFTER A SHOW
Conduct a post-show debriefing with all booth personnel. Share the results with the marketing team and sales management.

councils. A manufacturer may decide to establish several advisory councils:

- Distributors
- Resellers
- Major accounts (large end users)
- Sales force and customer service organization ("internal customers")
- Suppliers
- Engineering
- Field service staff
- Manufacturing

Involvement Leads To Commitment

A sometimes forgotten benefit of the group process is the buy-in it helps accrue over time. After all, the marketing plan really belongs to everyone, not just the marketing department.

Initially, you may need to "grease the skids" with these advisory councils. Resellers may not want to share valuable marketing strategies in the presence of competitors unless there's clearly something in it for them.

With "internal customers," build incentives into the compensation plan to generate creative and innovative thinking. Use contests and give out quarterly or yearly recognition awards.

The Internet

You can also get input when prospects, external customers, and internal customers are able to access you on line. For instance, you can put market positioning statements, press

---

Sales Force On-Line

Hewlett-Packard's internal Web site provides 13,000 documents to its worldwide sales force. Types of documents available include sales presentation materials. Sales reps say the system saves them about five hours a week. HP estimates that electronic delivery of documents saves $10,000 per mailing in printing and postage costs.

releases, project specifications, and pricing there. Some companies even allow customers to place orders through the Net.

Many companies use their Web sites to gather, as well as give, information. Online surveys can provide timely data from prospects and customers around the world. (See Chapter 11 for more about online marketing.)

Assessing Needs

Marketing programs must satisfy customers' as well as corporate needs. A sales contest or incentive for your own or your resellers' salespeople can encourage them to sell your products over competitors.

Maybe offering a rebate to end-users will be more effective than targeting the distribution channel. On the other hand, the secret to gaining market share or increasing sales of a strategic product may be right in your own backyard. Incentives, contests, and promotional dollars for your own salespeople may give you the best return on promotional dollars.

Assessing the Automation Needs

In our sales force automation project, we determined where we were and where we wanted to go.

We looked at information flow and work patterns, used written and telephone surveys, and monitored salespeople's behaviors on joint sales calls. We asked management what their expectations were, and asked the salespeople what they wanted.

Hear No Evil

Many companies go to their customers for input, yet they seem to just pay them lip service. Why aren't more companies open to criticism by customers who care enough to be the squeaky wheels?

For one thing, time puts pressure on everyone. In this era of downsizing, the remaining employees are working more for less, and there are still only twenty-four hours in a day. For another, sales or marketing management may be threatened, afraid that their mistakes or poor judgment will be revealed and jeopardize their positions.

Pressure At All Levels

Still another pressure is the ever-increasing rate of change in our society. By the time a survey's results are announced, market conditions may have changed. In the computer industry, no sooner does a new product start to ship than the next technological advancement is announced, making the new product obsolete. This is where a wish list becomes important as it gives insight into the future. A current problems list deals only with the past and present.

The traditional organization follows a top-down model with management at the top dictating direction. In fact, the entire organization exists because of the customer. Putting the customer on top with the front-line people on the second level will provide the right feedback on which to base long-term and interim goals and strategies.

The Sales Automation Example

Let's look at our sales force automation example with this inverted pyramid concept.

The customers are internal here—the sales force. But the problem involves external customers too.

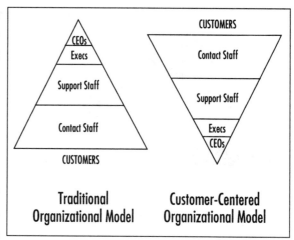

Traditional Organizational Model

Customer-Centered Organizational Model

What the Company Wanted. In 1990, sales management at AST Computer was dissatisfied with the quality of information it was receiving from the sales force, and the time involved in getting it. When territories changed or salespeople left the company, important account information had not been systematically entered into a database, thereby depriving management and the newly assigned salesperson the benefit of important account information.

What Salespeople Wanted. Salespeople complained of time-consuming reports and administrative duties. They felt deluged with the continual flood of information. There were announcements and updates of products and marketing programs, internal memos, trade journals, changes in competitors' strategies, price reductions, and customer issues. They seemed to always be ankle deep in paper and paperwork.

What Customers Wanted. Customers wanted quicker response to inquiries and faster resolution of problems. Resellers asked for better access to information that would eliminate or shorten many of their support calls. Major accounts (end user companies), too, felt that getting information for purchase decisions needed to be streamlined.

AST realized that it needed to use the same technology that it was selling to its customers, that it needed to "walk the talk." It computerized its salespeople in 1991 with the SMART (Sales Management and Resource Tracking) System. The sales automation project was so successful that AST expanded the scope and released a modified version of it to some of its resellers in 1992.

Get a Grass Roots Champion

In deciding to automate the sales force, one sales manager in particular championed the cause. He heard the many voices of dissatisfaction from salespeople, management, and resellers and took action.

He discussed the concept and benefits of sales force automation within sales management and at the executive level. Although not everyone agreed that the system was broken and warranted fixing, top management recognized the need for change and gave him approval to assemble a sales force automation team.

PHASE #2: PLANNING

You wouldn't think of getting in your car and driving down the highway without some idea of where you want to go and how you're going to get there.

In the same way, it's crucial to have a road map for your marketing programs, to set up a systematic, structured process. Whether you want to implement an outreach marketing program, conduct a direct mail campaign or market research, institute better customer service, or set up a sales force automation project, the processes are the same.

Put The Plan In Writing

A written plan will add cohesiveness to any sales or marketing effort. It may be as simple as a spreadsheet with a list of goals, benefits, tasks, and milestones needed to achieve those goals, the people assigned to execute them, due dates, and actual completion dates.

Transferring a marketing plan to a flow chart can help team members visualize the progression of events. It can serve as a road map for the project or sales objective. You may need to train marketing and sales personnel on the use of Pert and Gantt charts to track and manager projects. (See the example on the opposite page for a sample using the sales automation project.)

Why Don't Companies Create Formal Plans?

Why does it seem that many companies don't create written marketing plans?

Poor habits, perhaps. From the top down, writing marketing plans is a matter of habit, a good habit that the sales or marketing professional develops from the start, and that his or her manager exemplifies as a role model.

If a manager doesn't plan, then how can she or he expect subordinates to do so? If the manager is a good planner, then she or he is obliged to pass those techniques along to her or his people, pref-

MAKE MISTAKES ON PAPER
If you can't show specifically how your marketing program will succeed on paper, how will you do it in reality?

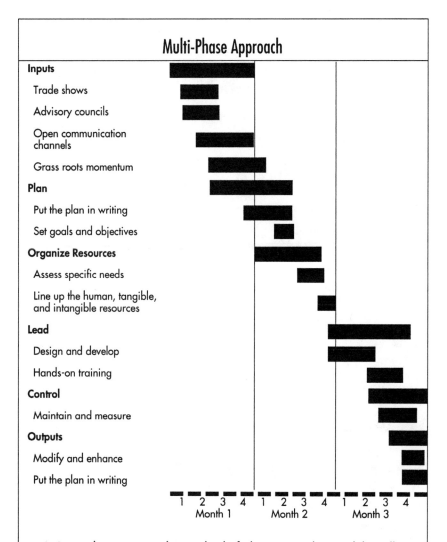

Multi-Phase Approach

Inputs
Trade shows
Advisory councils
Open communication channels
Grass roots momentum

Plan
Put the plan in writing
Set goals and objectives

Organize Resources
Assess specific needs
Line up the human, tangible, and intangible resources

Lead
Design and develop
Hands-on training

Control
Maintain and measure

Outputs
Modify and enhance
Put the plan in writing

1 2 3 4 1 2 3 4 1 2 3 4
Month 1   Month 2   Month 3

A Gantt chart is a graphic method of planning and control that allows a manager to view the starting and ending dates for various tasks. It is a popular tool for planning and scheduling simple projects. The Gantt chart enables a manager to initially schedule project activities and then monitor progress over time by comparing planned progress to actual progress.

erably in a formal training experience. It can start with the worker, but if upper management doesn't uphold and value the same good habits, the employee will meet with limited success and continual disappointment.

Set Goals and Objectives

When creating the plan for a marketing program, the first question to ask is, "What purpose will the marketing program serve?"

- Is the objective to increase market share? Perhaps the goal is to unseat a competitor.
- Maybe its purpose is to further penetrate existing accounts.
- Or it may simply be to introduce a new product or service.

Let's say that you want to increase market share with a particular product. Do you bundle it with an existing product that is selling well, or bombard the air waves with attention-getting ads? How will you decide on the strategy and approach?

First, have your staff set goals and objectives with time lines. Without them, it's too easy to get distracted or to lose a sense of priorities.

Sample Goals and Objectives

Obtain customer input in designing a new program, product, or service.

Increase sales by ____ % in ____ weeks/months/years.

Expand market share by ____ % in ____ weeks/months/years.

Expand the existing channel from ____ to ____ .

Expand sales in existing accounts ____ %.

Open up new channels (specify which ones).

Open new accounts or new geographic territories (specify which ones).

Obtain Buy-in

Next, secure buy-in from those who will be involved in achieving the goals and objectives, like the salespeople. Do this by making them part of the planning process. When people help make the decisions, those decisions become their own and are much more meaningful. There's a much greater level of commitment and communication. A good place to start involving your salespeple is your internal advisory councils.

Involve Customers

For a project with external customers, have salespeople sit down with these customers and get their input in the sales forecast.

Now the customers have become part of the process. As a result, you achieve a higher level of success and build customer loyalty. Customers feel as if they've helped set your company's direction. And, in fact, they have.

Salespeople also feel more in control of their own destinies and morale improves.

Input Creates Better Quotas

After the individual forecasts are rolled up to the regional, national, and company-wide level, they're adjusted by management and rolled back down in the form of quotas.

If those quotas reflect even some of the original input, salespeople and customers are more likely to accept and achieve them. They will also provide ongoing feedback. When marketing gets immediate feedback about a product's acceptance, it is able to adjust expectations to be realistic, and can take action to correct problems before they escalate.

Sales Automation Goals

In the case of sales force automation, the purpose typically is to increase productivity, and ultimately sales and profits. Further, the tool should fit the craftsperson's style, rather than try to change the salesperson to fit the tool.

What Salespeople Want

Specifically, the salespeople will be most interested in spending less time on administrative and non-selling activities and more time with customers. This may require changes in internal processes, providing the right tools, honing the salespeople's time and territory management skills (working smarter, not harder) or a combination of these.

Management's Goals

Management may be focused on increasing sales, streamlining communications, and maintaining control. The organization's goals may encompass maximizing return on investment and decreasing cost of sales, thereby increasing net profits.

While the hierarchical levels may have different goals and objectives, they all share the need for two-way communication, and complete and accurate information, promptly delivered.

Our Automation Goals

What were AST's goals? They were fairly simple.

- Give salespeople more selling time
- Improve the availability of customer data for sales and management
- Facilitate information flow between sales and management

What did the company achieve? Everything it set out to, and more.

- Increased efficiency and effectiveness
- Reduced duplication of efforts
- Enhanced customer satisfaction

PHASES #3 AND 4: ORGANIZING RESOURCES AND STAFFING

Salespeople, customer service, and even customers are important resources who are readily available for any marketing effort.

For example, if you're introducing a new product line with a series of seminars around the country, salespeople will know which cities, facilities, and times will draw the best audiences. Perhaps the seminars should be held not at the local office, but at a downtown hotel. Or maybe downtown is not the best place; maybe it's a location that's freeway-close outside the city.

It may be that the company has been visiting the same big cities, yet there are secondary cities that haven't been visited for a long time. These could be teeming with business just waiting for the asking.

If a product is not moving well, salespeople "in the trenches" are closest to the battles. They can tell management the lay of the land and recommend the best strategies.

Organizing for AST

In organizing resources for the sales force automation project, AST selected task force members from key stakeholders.

A three-way team representing Sales Training, Information Services, and Sales Management planned the process in a multi-phase approach. Sales Training was the liaison between the other two. With a total of twelve years in sales, six of them at AST, and newly transferred into Sales Training, I was chosen as project leader.

Reviewing Goals

After reviewing the goals, we lined up both internal and external resources.

We contacted prospective software vendors to evaluate their applications, assess their support capabilities, and discuss their level of participation in the roll out and training.

For the pilot program, we selected salespeople representative of the "customer base," from one who was very computer savvy to one who rarely went

6 Steps For Project Success

STEP 1: Define the job and any priorities within the job.
STEP 2: Plan how the job can be done.
STEP 3: Estimate costs and resources needed for the job.
STEP 4: Start to work out a schedule for the job, particularly the critical items which must be done on time or which must be done in a particular sequence for the job to be completed.
STEP 5: Set up systems for measuring the job in progress.
STEP 6: Monitor progress regularly and adapt as necessary to keep the job on schedule.

Include Salespeople

"We included our salespeople in the system design....Not only did this input create a feeling of ownership...it also resulted in a final design that best suited real-life selling needs"
—John Dvorske, Yellow Freight Systems, in *Sales and Marketing Executive Report*

beyond word processing.

We developed check lists and priorities that included consistency of screens and menus, software reliability, data accuracy, thorough documentation, fail-safe troubleshooting, time efficient training, measurement of success, and even spelling.

Periodic updates and field testing with sales and sales management were scheduled to keep us on track.

Through all phases, we consulted with various salespeople and the departments with which they interacted. After all, no one likes it when decisions are made for them. Making users part of the decision-making process improves the potential for acceptance.

PHASE #5: PROVIDING LEADERSHIP

How do you integrate the overall marketing program so that marketing, advertising, customer service, and sales work together to generate and follow up on leads, send a consistent message, and achieve "big picture" goals and objectives?

There must always be someone to champion the project, someone who believes in it, who will promote it, fight for it, nurture it, and advertise its successes. It may be the project leader, someone in management, one of the internal "customers" (users), or a few people in different areas of the company. The champions are leaders, and they may or may not have management titles.

Hands-On Training

Training the sales force and support staff is particularly important when launching a new product. Effective product training typically covers features, functions, benefits, objections and how to overcome them, and competitive comparisons.

Multiple Ways To Train

Today many innovative and cost-effective training technologies are available. These include classroom experience, role modeling, audio and video tapes, video conferencing, and computer-based training on CD-ROM, the local area network, and the Internet.

But product knowledge isn't the only kind of training for the sales force that is necessary in a successful marketing effort. Traditional schooling teaches us reading, writing, and 'rithmetic. All too often, it doesn't formally teach us how to learn (e.g., see Chapter 3), how to communicate clearly or how to resolve conflicts. It's surprising how much money many companies spend on the tools and how little they spend on training their people to use the tools.

A good product, a good marketing plan, and a good experience by the customer are a winning combination. Marketing can get a lot of mileage from simply training customer service staff on interpersonal and communication skills. Oh, yes, some product training for these support personnel would be a big plus, too!

Sales Automation Training

Back at the AST ranch, the pilot program helped us determine the training objectives, the skills necessary to meet them, and the minimum acceptable levels of competency.

The contact management software vendor agreed to help us customize the software and conduct the training on its product. Before the actual roll out,

Information Systems installed the programs and shipped the new notebook computers to each training site.

During our 60-day training schedule, we involved every domestic sales office.

We scheduled the training in a way that would not require the salespeople to be out of the field for more than a day. In the first hour of training, we introduced the goals and objectives, registered users, assigned systems, and had everyone sign for the systems, accepting responsibility for security of the hardware and data.

We familiarized them with the dos and don'ts of using the hardware, the "care and feeding of your portable computer," and new policies and procedures.

Use Real Examples

To make the training meaningful to the salespeople, we created a sample database with real data (and names changed to protect the guilty), and simulated real life situations. To make it easy, we gave each person a detailed user's manual, quick reference card, and keyboard template.

Build Teams

The training team consisted of one person from Sales Training and someone from the Information Services development team. The sales trainer conducted the hands-on training. The programmer gave the overview of the behind-the-scenes mechanics and was available to fix any unexpected technical problems, which turned out to be a wise move.

TEAM SELLING

On many technical sales, a team approach, using technical and sales people together can cut the sales cycle time in half.

— *VAR Reseller*

The team approach can also be valuable on sales calls. Using a team of sales and technical people can sometimes speed up the decision process of your customers.

PHASE #6: CONTROLLING

We tested for mastery of software skills and their application to day-to-day situations using exercises and a competitive learning environment. After all, salespeople thrive on competition, so why not use it to our advantage?

During the initial roll-out, we announced at the beginning of each training session that the day would end with a contest. It was a hands-on quiz on the ten software functions they would need to use most often. The first one to finish would then be asked to stand in front of the group and demonstrate the technique. If she or he was right, the prize was $5 cash, on the spot. If not, there was no shortage of eager volunteers to try for the brass ring. This worked like magic! It held their attention and enhanced retention.

An Ongoing Process

Every three months we rolled out another module. We used the same hands-on approach, usually as part of a regular sales staff meeting. The salespeople were going to be there anyway; we just took advantage of the centralized meetings.

We should have reviewed the previous quarter's module to reinforce learning and addressed the salespeople's issues and dislikes. But time constraints and internal issues prevented us from doing so. Instead, we trained for a half day strictly on the new module.

Our later analyses showed that everyone used all the programs to varying degrees. When graphed, they created a skewed bell curve with more users at the low usage end and a few "technoids" at the high end. We remedied this later in the evolution of the process.

Feedback On Performance

True goal setting presupposes regular reviews and updates. Although a simple process, it isn't always followed by many organizations.

Some measures are clearly quantitative. Salespeople can compare business closed against forecast to see how they're doing.

For the marketing team, all too often performance reviews are done annually. Although goals and milestones may be set, they're often not measured until the next year. Meanwhile, marketing team members go from quarter to quarter without updates, not knowing whether they have been doing well. This can create unnecessary surprises at the next performance review.

Qualitative Feedback

But the numbers don't tell the whole story. Customer satisfaction and teamwork are qualitative performance measures. For example, the training department may be able to report how many people it trained during a certain period of time, but it takes some strategic work to translate those numbers into how many sales were closed as a result of the training.

Marketing may be able to report how many units salespeople sold during a spif, contest, or rebate. But measuring how many customers it truly won over can be elusive or disappointing.

Salespeople Overestimate Customer Relationships

Salespeople greatly overestimate the quality of the relationships they have with customers. That is the conclusion drawn from a study in which 173 business people purchased from 193 sales reps, and both groups also rated the quality of the salesperson-customer relationship.

—Hawes et al., *Psychological Reports*, Vol. 72, 607-614.

Both marketing and customer service personnel have fewer quantitative measures available to them than sales. They rely more on their managers to give them feedback and guidance.

Team goals and rewards can nurture interpersonal skills and foster better communication. Having co-workers vote for their MVP will foster teamwork. Another feedback technique is surveying customers about their experiences.

There are other areas where improvement may be quantifiable:

- Faster telephone response
- Fewer and shorter incoming support or information request calls
- Reduced telephone transfers or disconnects
- Fewer complaints
- Higher response rates or revenues from direct mail campaigns
- Lower cost of sales or manufacturing.

How To Measure Product Training Effectiveness

The effectiveness of product training can be assessed by a mystery shopper, either on the phone or in the store. Design key questions about the new product, service, or program. Winners accrue points and cash them in for merchandise. A variation of this for outside salespeople and resellers is to coach each other a few days or weeks after training. Using checklists, they can critique each other on what works and what doesn't work, and can uncover shortcomings in the products, processes, or infrastructure. Skills and insight improve for everyone.

Rewarding Participation

Once your marketing plan is in place, what must you do to keep it going? How will you know its level of success?

To keep it going, use rewards and special offers to customers and resellers. These will catch their attention and usually spike sales. Incentives for the marketing team can help fuel diligence, enthusiasm, and teamwork alongside the salespeople.

Compare Results To Objectives

To measure the level of success, look back to the original objectives. A program whose purpose is to improve customer service can be measured with a customer survey. Ideally, the survey is done as a baseline before the program is put in place and again once the program is deployed. More and more companies involve suppliers and employees in this future-seeking information-gathering process.

The Sales Automation Example

To maintain momentum and support, we made automation training part of the quarterly orientation for new sales hires.

A quarterly newsletter updated our customers on changes and enhancements, and reminded them of ways to use the system to increase productivity. We included technical tips to either solve or avoid a problem, and reported success stories of how someone closed a sale using these new tools.

To measure and report our progress, we conducted written surveys before automation, six months after the initial roll-out, and once a year thereafter. The surveys told us what the salespeople were using and how often, how much productivity they saved or lost, and what else we

---

Computers Impress Customers

"Carrying computers allows sales reps to provide instant information to prospects and customers. Computers also allow reps to display information inexpensively. For instance, laptop computers can run video or slide presentations."
—James J. Rafferty,
Price Waterhouse

could do to satisfy the needs of our customers, the salespeople. Management received the survey results with return on investment stated in quantitative and qualitative terms.

PHASE #7: OUTPUTS BECOME INPUTS

If you're caught in a traffic jam, you can either sit amidst the exhaust fumes and contribute to the pollution, or you can find an alternate route. If you're lost in an unknown neighborhood, odds are that you'll pull out the map and navigate your way back on course.

Successful marketing is no different.

Modify and Enhance

In the computer industry, technology seems to move at such a rapid pace that by the time you get the product out the door, it's obsolete. Your competitors have leap-frogged you, one-upped you, or done something unexpected. Intel, the long-time leader in semiconductors, is keenly aware of this and never drops its guard. It's not afraid to cannibalize its own product line, even when it's way ahead of its competitors.

Don't Be Lulled To Sleep

In less volatile industries, the slower pace may give you a false sense of stability and security. People may not see change coming because of its slow progress. If they do see it coming, they may fight the need for them to change, saying, "This is how we've always done it." They may refuse to accept the possibility that a better way may exist.

Slower-paced industries can use companies in high tech as models for learning how to streamline processes and pick up the pace in their own industries. For instance, the solid waste industry is undergoing transformation as recycling technologies advance. Waste disposal companies with smaller hauls to landfills and higher costs have found new sources of incremental revenues by adding recycling to their list of services.

The worker who doesn't retool and retrain may find himself or herself in the unemployment line asking "Why me?" and blaming his or her former employer instead of "Number 1." In the same way, the marketing team must always rethink and re-tool to stay ahead of the competition.

Sales Force Automation

In our sales force automation example, we achieved several direct results from conducting surveys after each stage. We replaced the cumbersome, cryptic electronic mail system with one that was Windows-based and much more user-friendly. We enhanced print functions where they did exist and added them where they didn't. Salespeople complained that the mechanism for delivering their data to them was unreliable and very slow. Although we could not remedy the situation right away, we did eventually address and resolve the problem.

Automation Saves Money and Time

"Tandem Computers put 1000 pages of sales support material on one CD-ROM disk. Reps now have instant access to material they often couldn't find. Five times more information is available to sellers. And costs have been cut 56%!"
—Linda Heidemann, Tandem Marketing Department

Ongoing Changes

As sales force automation evolved, we replaced the contact management software with Lotus Notes, the widely-touted "groupware" product from Lotus Development, Inc. This became the basis for our worldwide customer database.

Then the salespeople complained about the inconvenience of having to dial in three times: once for electronic mail, a second time for Lotus Notes, and yet a third time for their custom application with customer shipment and order backlog information. Three separate phone calls also cost the company extra money in telephone time. We consolidated the last two phone calls into one by sending each salesperson's files to him or her via electronic mail using high speed modems.

The praise we heard from the sales force for this simple change was deafening. Our users' satisfaction and utilization went up. Our costs went down, too.

This brings us right back to the beginning of the process, using the input to plan, organize, and continue to provide products that benefit our customers. As one mar-  keting program ends, another one begins. The programs may be different, but the process remains essentially the same.

SUMMARY

If experience is the best teacher, then we learned very well. If you follow our example, then any program will have a better chance of success.

Make sure management is behind you. More specifically, actions speak louder than words, and that applies to management. If management demands participation by the sales force and excludes itself, the salespeople will not take the project seriously. Building management tools into the project raised our level of success.

Formally announce the project to customers. Create antici- pation by marketing the benefits the sales force and management will reap. This worked particularly well with new modules and upgrades.

As stated earlier, we achieved everything we set out to, and

more.
- Increased efficiency and effectiveness
- Reduced duplication of efforts
- Enhanced customer satisfaction

Keep Salespeople Happy

The first post-implementation survey was conducted after the system was in place six months. Salespeople reported saving up to 11 phone calls and three hours each week in administrative tasks, retrieving information, and resolving problems.

They spent an hour and a half more per week with customers, and the other hour and a half each week researching competitors and learning more about their own products.

In their first year using the system, resellers reported saving six phone calls and three hours each week doing business with AST.

---

4 Tips

Remember your customers. Keep in touch with them and with those who are closest to the customers, the customer service and salespeople.

Look and listen. Be aware of what the competition is doing and has done, both right and wrong.

Benchmark across industries. Look outside your own backyard and see what works for other industries.

Retool. Retool your marketing plan, your team, and yourself. Be on the lookout for change and use it to your advantage.

IMPLEMENTING ANY MARKETING PROGRAM

This basic process applies to areas beyond sales and marketing. Whether it's setting up a systematic marketing process, launching a new product, changing the company's image, automating a sales force, or training the general work force on soft skills, the fundamentals remain the same: Plan the process with a multi-phase approach to ensure long-term change and a positive impact on the bottom line.

One project may be completed, but the process is evolutionary. It is ongoing.

The way you make the next marketing program more successful than the last is by having a process with which to work. Then you can use the experience gained from the last marketing program in planning the next one.

ACTION AGENDA

Think about what you can do to improve the implementation of your next marketing project.

- Can you create a simple Gantt chart to start outlining the necessary steps?
- What measurement tools can you implement to report on the degree of success?

Look at your responsibilities and involvement within and outside of your immediate area. When implementing these concepts for the first time, start small.

- Try a simple project to be accomplished in a short period of time affecting few people. Limited visibility will provide a relatively low risk opportunity to experiment.
- Promote an existing product or service that is already doing well.
- Perhaps try a new advertising approach with a product or service that does not have a major impact on the company's bottom line or market position.

After testing the process and securing one or two successes, it's easier to undertake a larger scale project than to do so with no prior experience with the process.

Most importantly, define and utilize an effective, fluid process that can evolve with the needs of the organization. This will allow you to learn the most, will minimize your risk of failure, and will give you maximum marketing success.

INDEX

A

Accountability chart
 for customer service 98
Act! software 319
Action orientation 161
Activity-based selling 117
Address book
 for fax machine 319
Advertising 6, 286-288
 customer service 87
 revenues on the Internet 287
Advisory councils 376
America Online 279, 286
American Society for Quality Control
 (ASQC) 54
Apologies, written 349
Apple Computer 256, 277, 289, 307
Apple® Pippin 307
Appointments
 made by writing 349
 setting 197-198
Artificial intelligence 308
AST Computer 380, 381, 387, 388,
 390
AT&T 92
Attitude
 positive 229
 in sales process 178-180
 for success 228
Automation needs assessment 378
Awards 377

B

Bailey, Bob 317
Banjo and Bus 39-41
Banks 76-77
Baseball 24
Bed and breakfasts 19
Benchley, Robert 360
Benefits
 communication to customer 258
 and features 7
Berman, Fran 373
Berns, Fred 5
Biloxi Blues (Simon) 345
Binary file transfer 332
Biscotti Mio 265
Blanchard, Ken 90, 148, 344
Bookmarking Web sites 297
Books
 how to read 62-70
 marking key phrases 64

Borrolo's Pizza 257
Bowen, D.E. 46
Brachman, Robert 25
Brainstorming 93
Brangus Steakhouse 89
Broadcast faxing 319, 321, 332-333
Brochure via Web site 285
Buddha 268
Buddhism, sales philosophy 249
Bulletin boards (computer) 277
Business cards 140, 218
Business thank yous 348-354
Buyer
 needs 205, 206
 social styles 204
 types of 279

C

Canter, Laurence 302
Career development 189, 190
Carlson, Jan 82
Catalogs
 online 290
 supplements via fax on demand
  335
Chimney sweeps 42-44
Client(s)
 analyzing 216
 contact via newsletters 110-111
 development 189-190, 192
 retention 117
Clipping services (online) 293
Code system, for reading books 64–
 65
Coggins, Bud 225
Cole, Larry 75
Commitment 190
 establishing in sales process 177
 questions 179
Community involvement 259
Company image (see also Image) 244,
 255
Competition on price 33-58
Competitive analysis (see also Market
 Research)
 online research 293
Competitors, unfavorable impressions
  created by 12
CompuServe 279, 280, 286, 331
Computer bulletin boards 277
Contests 377
Corky's Barbecue 88
Costco 35

Cover pages (fax) 320, 326
Covey, Stephen R. 53, 147, 214, 243, 244, 252, 267
Crandall, Rick 273
Creativity 93-94
  rewards for 377
Credibility 30
Cross, Maxwell 348
Custom newsletter (online) 293
Customer(s)
  anniversary thank you notes 350
  comment cards 99
  decision process 392
  focus 229
  holiday notes 350
  input
    into marketing plans 385
    value of negative input 378
  keeping in touch with 170-171
  loyalty 77-78
  recovery WoW 89-91
  satisfaction 264, 393
    sales growth 257
  telephone contact thank yous 351
  thank you after purchase 351
  thank you notes to 344
Customer service 75-100, 267, 290-291
  accountability chart 98
  advertising 77, 87
    creating the "WoW" factor 88-89
  questions used to improve 88
  recovery WoW 89-91
  decisions made close to the customer 87-88
  e-mail 290
  empowered workers 90
  expectations 86
  legendary service 90
  measurement 82
  meetings 94-99
  moments of truth 82-83, 84-85
  product knowledge 85-86
  receptionists 84
  recovery 89-91
  setting up a system 91-92
  telephone contacts 83-84
  training 78-79
Customers for Life (Sewell) 89
CYMaK Technologies 262

D

Daly, Jack 189
Dare-to-be-different checklist 32
Death of a Salesman (Miller) 226
Decision process of customers 392
Decision makers, getting through to 164-165
Decision making 260
  close to the customer 87-88
  irrational component 260
  purchase 260
Denny's 38
Desire to serve 228
Determination 229
Diasonics 256
Differentiation 5-34
  by name 25
  on trust 208
Dissatisfaction, helping prospects recognize 173
Domino's pizza 16
Dunn, David 343

E

E-mail
  computer fax as e-mail 330-331
  customer service 290
  gateways 331
e-Marketing (Godin) 291
The E Myth (Gerber) 38
Ecco software 319
Electronic data interchange (EDI) 277
Edward VII 356
Effectiveness 153
Ego-strength 228
Einstein, Albert 6
Electronic data interchange 277
Elevator speech 149-150
Emerson, Ralph Waldo 37
Empathy 228
Empowered workers
  customer service 90
Energy, networking 152
Entelechy 241
Enthusiasm 152, 230
Etiquette, online 302
Excel (telephone) 93
Expectations, customer 86

F

Fax
  address book 319
  attention-getter 323
  broadcast 321, 332-333
  catalogs via fax on demand 335
  conciseness 326
  cost effectiveness 322
  cover pages 320, 326
  delivery speed 323-324
  fax on demand 333-335
  features 319
  junk 325

mailbox services 329-330
marketing 317-338
newsletters 335-336
remote retrieval 328, 328-329
selling seminars 327
software 318-319
surveys 326-328
use of graphics 326
Features 239-240
and benefits 7
Feedback, sales 393
Fine, Marc 249
Fishing industry 20
The Fishing Tackle Trade News 21
Floyd, Elaine 108
Focus groups (online) 292
Follow-up calls, laying the ground-
work for 170-186
Ford, Henry 244
Forum Corp. 84
Frankfurter, Felix 10
Freeman, R. Edward 375

G

Gandhi 268
Gantt charts 382
Gatekeepers 162, 163
Gates, Bill 300
Gerber, Michael 38
Getting your price 22
Goals
marketing program 154, 202, 389
setting 149, 161
Godin, Seth, 291
Graphics
in faxes 326
Web pages 298
Greenberg, J. & H. 228
Gretzky, Wayne 29, 221
Gross, Scott 88
Guerrilla Marketing (Levinson) 77,
344, 364
Gutscher, Mary Lou 103

H

Haberstroh, Richard 35
Haskell, John S. 135
Hayes, Rutherford B. 273
Highest value needs
determination of 205
prospect's 203
Hill, Napolean 61, 171
Holiday notes to customers 350
Holmes, Oliver Wendell 245
How to Swim With the Sharks...
(Mackay) 120, 350

HTML (hyper text machine language)
311, 312
basic commands 312
Hughes, Mary 259
Hum-Drum to Hot-Diggity (Schuster)
97
Huthwaite, Inc. 230, 231, 233, 242

I

Identifying influencers 144-148
Image 52, 193, 255, 363
pre-marketing campaign 194
via telephone 254
Imgarten, Victor 42
Implementation
marketing programs 375-400
model 374-375
Implication questions 237-238
Impressions, unfavorable 12
In-person contact follow-ups 351
Incentives 394
sales 378
Influencer relationships 146, 147
Information gathering (see also *Market
Research*) 375-381
Information superhighway 273
definition 275
Innovative thinking, rewards for 377
Integrity 229
Interior decorators 22
*International Journal of Bank Market-
ing* 41
Internet 139, 273, 306
advertising revenues 287
"boxes" 307
connections 306
cultural differences of users 282
definition 276
history 281-282
map 275
marketing 377
etiquette 282
number of users 278
searching for information 308
security 309, 309-311
shell accounts 306
Interview
prospects 202
sales 200-206
Intranet 277
Introductions, highlighting your
uniqueness 14-15, 149

J

Java 313
Jesus 268

Jobs, Steve 256, 289
Johnson, Spencer 344
Journal of Services Marketing 41, 43
Junk faxes 325
Justification statements 163-165

K

Kmart 20, 38
Karasic, Paul 47
King, Martin Luther 268
Klaybor, David 61
Knowledge
   industry 220
   "installation" 61-70
   product 85-86, 257
Koontz, H. 374
KPMG Peat Marwick 136

L

Lawyers 135
Leadership, marketing program 389
Learning 242-243
   messages to yourself 67
   repetition 66–67
   teaching others 70
LeBoeuf, Michael 212
Legendary service 90
Letters, and your image 363
Levinson, Jay Conrad 77, 344, 364
Lexis-Nexis 277
Listening 203, 229, 258
   to customers 259
   importance to selling 258
   skillful listening 258
   skills 258
Los Angeles Business Journal 140
Lotus Notes 397
Low-cost promotion techniques 9
Loyalty, customer 77

M

Mackay, Harvey 120, 216, 349, 350
Mailbox services, fax 330
Management (Stoner & Freeman) 375
Management: A Book of Readings
   (Koontz et al.) 374
Managers magazine 47
Managing Management Time (Oncken)
   88
Market research 281, 375-381
   competitive analysis 293
Marketing
   definition 148, 285
   fax 317-338
   feedback 393
   finding a need 7

planning, rate of change 379
   online 273-314
   plans 225
      customer input 385
      obtain buy-in 385
      value of 382
   product knowledge 257
   programs
      feedback 393
      leadership of
      management support for 399
      need assessment 378
      planning 381-387
   quantifiable feedback 393
   qualitative vs. quantitative people
      251
   role of 226
   team incentives 394
   vs. selling 225
Marketing With Newsletters (Floyd)
   108
Mary's Futons 259
MacArthur, Douglas 144
McDonald's 83
MCI 92, 331
McKenna, Regis 193
Meetings, customer service 94-99
Mental attitude 229
Merchandising (online) 294
MicroBiz 278
Microsoft Corp. 277, 300
Miller, Arthur 226
The Milwaukee Journal 26
Miss Manners 346
Moments of truth 82-83, 84-85
Moments of Truth (Carlson) 82
Montgomery, Jim 264
Moore's law of computer technology
   306
Motivation 196
   document your success 69
Motley, Red 215

N

Name differentiation 25
National Association of Chimney
   Sweeps 42
Nebraska Furniture Mart 22
Need
   development questions 172
   finding and filling 51
   payoff questions 239-240
Nelson, Lindsey 24
Netiquette (online) 296
Netscape browser 299, 301
Networking 135-155
   goals 154

measuring progress 149
online 296
personal interests as benefits 153
power networking steps 141
Networking With the Affluent (Stanley)
    44
Newsletters 103-132
    action plan 107
    benefits 106
    client contact 110-111
    client retention 117
    company-sponsored 128-129
    distribution 121, 123
    editorial material 124
    expense vs. investment 111
    fax 335-336
    generic 114-115, 129
    goals 107
    identification of market 107
    internal production 126-127
    investment 113
    mistakes 111-113
    personalization 120, 125
    prospects 105-106, 108-109
    publicity 119
    recruitment tool 122-123
    referrals 114
    relationship builders 109-111, 119
    for sales staff 129-131
    writing 124-126
NeXT software 289, 312-313
Niche development 48
Nightingale, Earl 28
Norman's clothing store 77-78
Notarius, Barbara 19, 20

O

Objections 203
    anticipating 206-207
    how to counter 182
    how to overcome 212-214
    identifying underlying reasons 183
    projection 174
Objectives, in telephone selling 161
O'Donnel, C.O. 374
Olive Garden restaurant 86
Oncken, William Jr. 88
The One Minute Manager
    (Blanchard & Johnson) 344
"One sheets" 151-152
Online marketing 273-314
    24-hour availability 284
    advantages 282-285
    commercial services 277
    customized 283
    diversity of audience 284
    etiquette 302

focus groups 292
giving away information 301
interactive nature 283
international audience 284
measuring effectiveness 288
merchandising 294
multi-step approach 304
research 291
shopping 280
your "signature" 295
speed 283
Web sites 300
Open Your Own Bed and Breakfast
    (Notarius) 19
Opening statements
    examples of bad ones 165-166
    interest creating 165-171
    model 166
    model statements 166
    preparation tips 168
    Word and Phrase Menu 169
Organizational structures 379
Oxenham, John 55

P

Passion 190
Patience, in selling 240-241
Paul and Paula's Pancake Palace 17
Payne, Linda 265
Peattie, Donald Culross 2362
Personal interests, as networking
    benefits 153
Personal notes 218, 356, 357-360
    birthday greetings 359
    condolence letters 358
    congratulations 358, 359
    expressing your personality 362
    get well messages 358
    keeping in touch 360
    note cards 363-368
    regrets 356
    servicemen's return home 359
    setting up a system 368
    sincerity 369
    social invitations 357
    welcome to neighborhood 359
Personality style, of buyer 233
Pert charts 382
Pester, Mark 353
Peters, Tom 16, 84, 105, 139, 154,
    220, 347
Pink sheets 141-143
Pizza Hut 16
Planning
    marketing programs 381-387
    new product or service 373-374

Positioning 5-34
  name 25
  "one sheets" 151
  price 35-58
  through "elevator speech" 149-150
  trust 208
Positive mental attitude 229
Positively Outrageous Customer Service
  (Gross) 88
Power networking 135-156
Power of "only" 6-7, 13-15
Pratt, Jim 189
Pre-marketing campaigns 194
Presentations 210-211, 220
  preparation 208
  tips 176
Press conferences, online 289
Press releases, via e-mail 289
Price 22, 35-58, 205
Principle-Centered Leadership
  (Covey) 244
Problem questions 236-237
Product knowledge 85-86, 257
Promotions 378
  low-cost 9
Prospects
  call sheet 199
  interviews 219-220
  target list 191
Prospecting 191
  benefits of "no" 160
  target list 192
Public relations, online 288
Public speaking 8
Publicity 8
  newsletters 119
  online 288

Q

Quaker Lane Bait & Tackle Ltd 21
Quality 206
  emphasis on 37-39
Questions 171, 219
  commitment 179
  customer service 88
  implication 237-238
  need development 172
  payoff 239-240
  preparation 173, 173-174
  problem 236-237
  situation 235
  SPIN® 225-245

R

Rackham, Neil 177, 227, 230, 231,
  232, 234, 236, 238, 241
Rebates, customer 378

Receptionists (see also *Screeners*)
  customer service 84
  help in getting to prospects
    200-202
Recognition awards 377
Recruitment, via newsletters 122
Referrals 44
  from newsleters 114
  source development 197
  thank you for 351-352
  thank you notes for offer 352
Reilly, Tom 48-50
Rejection 196, 263
Relationship building 189-221
  online 296-298, 304
Relationship selling 189-221
Relationship Selling (McKenna) 193
Relationships 231
  influencer 146, 147
  strenthened by newsletters
    109-111, 119
Remote retrieval of faxes 328-329
Repeat business 44
Repetition, method of learning 66–67
Reputation 265
Resilience 229
Resistance, how to address 182
Restaurants 15, 76
Retailers 136
Ries, Al 12, 13
Right action 268
Risk taking 28
Rockefeller, John D. 218
Rohn, Jim 25

S

Salam, Wajed 343
Sales (see also *Selling*)
  advances vs. continuations 233
  asking for the order 262-263
  calls 215
    analyzing 216
    four stages 232
  critical path model 201
  demonstrating capability 232
  documenting successful techniques
    214, 219
  expanding client list 193
  fuel of company 262
  growth, and customer satisfaction
    257
  implication questions 237-238
  importance to career 257
  investigation stage 232
  need-payoff questions 239-240
  obtaining commitment 232-233
  online 293-294

patience 240-241
preliminaries 232
problem questions 236-237
presentations 174-176
questions 2023, 219
rejection 263
setting appointments 198-200
    call reluctance 196
situation questions 235
solutions 243
teamwork between qualitative and
    quantitative types 252
training 227, 390
understanding your prospect 207-
    208, 217
why everyone is in sales 250-251,
    253-254
Sales automation, case study 373-
    400
Sales presentations 174-176
Salespeople
    professional 191
    qualitative vs. quantitative types
    251
Salmon Stop 20
Sample Web page 276
SBT Internet Systems 293
Schneider 46
Schuster, John 97
Screeners162, 163
Security, online 309
Self-appreciation 29-30
Self-esteem 196, 228
Self-image 229
Self-motivation 229
Self-promotion 10
    credibility 30
    differences 11
    increased visibility 30
    self-appreciation 29
Selling (see also Sales)
    activity based 117
    attitude 228
    Buddhist middle way 264
    by questions 171
    goal 226
    "heartful" selling 249-269
    image 52-53
        negative image 226, 230
    new rules 189-222
    president should make first sale
        255
    relationship 189-221
    setting up the next call 180-182
    team approach 391
    telephone 159-186
    ten characteristics for 229

upscale market 35, 37, 43-44
value added 48, 51, 171
vs. marketing 225
yourself 10
Seminars
    by retailers 21
    selling via fax 327
Service, emphasis on 37-39
Sewell, Carl 89
Siegel, Martha 302
Simon, Neil 345
Situation questions 235
Sobczak, Art 159
Social styles, buyers' 204
Software
    fax 319
    personal information managers
        (PIM) 319
Spamming 301
Speaking 257, 258
Specialization 55
Speed 206
SPIN® Selling 225-246
SPIN Selling (Rackham) 177, 227,
    236, 238
Sprint 92
SRI International 279
St. Louis Business Journal 52
Stanley, Thomas J. 44
Stengel, Casey 24
Stock brokers 46
Stoner, James F. 375
Success, documenting 69
Surveys, fax 326-328

T

Target groups 8
Teaching, as learning method 70
Team approach to selling 391
Telephone contacts with customers
    83-84
Telephone selling 158-186
    call endings 181-182
    call reluctance 195
Text file transmission, binary file
    transfer 332
Thank you notes 341-372
    after demonstration or presentation
        351
    after prospect buys from someone
        else 352
    after purchase 351
    appreciating a product or service
        355
    customer anniversaries 350
    customer telephone contact 351
    differentiation from competitors

enjoyed working with you 353
final refusal 352
follow up to salesperson's call 238
for offering referrals 352
for time 356
getting it done 366-368
job well done 353
others for service 355
personal 356
personal benefits 369
prospects 351, 352
proud 353
referrals 351-352
service providers 355
setting up a system 368
sincerity 369
social invitations 357
welcome to team 352
Think and Grow Rich (Hill) 61
Time management 229
Toastmasters 324
Trade shows 375-376
  market research 376-377
Training
  customer service 78-79
  methods 390
  product 390
Travel, tours 39-41
Trout, Jack 12, 13
Trust, point of differentiation 208
Trustworthiness 231
Try Giving Yourself Away (Dunn) 343

U

Unfavorable impresions
  created by competitors 12
Unique sales proposition 13
Uniqueness, position in market 9-10
Upscale market 35, 37, 43-44
USA Today 46

V

VALS 2 psychographic system 279
Value added selling 51
Value-added selling 48
Value-added service 192

Values
  importance in marketing 259
Van Dyke, Henry 52
Ventures 38
Vickers, Bob 21
Voice mail 161

W

The Wall Street Journal 19
Wal-Mart 20, 35, 38, 46, 55
Waxman, Al 256
Web page
  design 298, 311
  key words 300
  master marketing file 285
Web sites 276
  as billboard 287
  bookmarking 297
  custom pages 299-300
  drawing people to your site 299
  linking to other pages 288, 297
  updating sites 299
Weirich, H. 374
Welch, Jack 86
What It Takes to Succeed in Sales
  (J. & H. Greenberg) 228
Window washers 50-51
WinFax PRO fax software 319, 327,
  328, 331, 332
Winning the Service Game (Schneider
  and Bowen) 46
Word-of-mouth sales 265
World Wide Web (see also *Web sites)*
  139, 276
  Sample Web page 276
WoW factor in customer service 88-89
Wozniak, Steve 256
Write Better, Speak Better (Reader's
  Digest) 357
Writing techniques 360, 361
Wylie, Ken 43

Z

Ziglar, Zig 117
Zimbardo, Phil, 62

A Note About The Disk Inside The Back Cover

The attached disk contains more marketing material for your use. The files are text files that can be opened by any word processor. If you have a Macintosh® computer that won't read a DOS-formatted disk, return this disk with a self-addressed stamped envelope (55¢) to Select Press, P.O. Box 37, Corte Madera, CA 94976, and we'll send you a Mac-formatted disk.